Rovshan Ibrahimov

Small State Foreign Policy
in Contemporary World

The Azerbaijani Studies Series

The Azerbaijani Studies Book Series presents scholarly works dedicated to exploring and understanding the history, culture, and society of Azerbaijan. By offering a multidisciplinary approach, the Azerbaijani Studies Book Series aims to foster a deeper appreciation of the countries' past and present while providing a solid foundation for future research and dialogue in Azerbaijani studies.

Editors of the Azerbaijani Studies Book Series

M. Hakan Yavuz - Professor of Political Science at the University of Utah, USA.

Ceyhun Mahmudlu - President of the Caspian Research Institute (CASPRI), Dallas, Texas, USA.

Shamkhal Abilov - Historian affiliated with Berlin Humboldt University and a researcher affiliated with the TLM (Initiatives and Projects Center), Baku, Azerbaijan.

Caspian Research Institute (CASPRI)

The Caspian Research Institute (CASPRI), established as a non-profit think tank and formally registered in Dallas, Texas, is committed to the pursuit of rigorous academic inquiry and the dissemination of comprehensive analyses concerning the Caspian Region. This geostrategically pivotal area, encompassing the littoral states of Russia, Azerbaijan, Iran, Turkmenistan, and Kazakhstan, represents a nexus of significant geopolitical, economic, and environmenta interests. Recognizing the region's critical importance, CASPRI endeavors to facilitate scholarly collaboration and intellectual synergy among researchers originating from these five states, thereby fostering a multifaceted and nuanced understanding of the Caspian Basin's complex dynamics.

Rovshan Ibrahimov

Small State Foreign Policy in Contemporary World

The South Caucasus States
(Azerbaijan, Georgia, and Armenia)
and Beyond

LIT

Bibliographic information published by the Deutsche Nationalbibliothek
The Deutsche Nationalbibliothek lists this publication in the Deutsche
Nationalbibliografie; detailed bibliographic data are available on the Internet at
https://dnb.dnb.de.

ISBN 978-3-643-91444-6 (pb)
ISBN 978-3-643-96444-1 (PDF)

A catalogue record for this book is available from the British Library.

© LIT VERLAG Dr. W. Hopf Berlin 2024
  Contact:
  Fresnostr. 2   D-48159 Münster
  Tel. +49 (0) 2 51-62 03 20   Fax +49 (0) 2 51-23 19 72
  e-Mail: lit@lit-verlag.de   https://www.lit-verlag.de
  Distribution:
  In the UK: Global Book Marketing, e-mail: mo@centralbooks.com

Contents

ACKNOWLEDGEMENTS III

INTRODUCTION 1

THE EXISTENCE OF SMALL (STATES) POWERS IN THE INTERNATIONAL
SYSTEM: FEATURES AND THEIR PRIORITIES 5

The Definition of Small Powers... 5
Historical Context: Small Powers Attitudes after Westphalia Peace........... 8
The French Revolution and the Napoleonic Wars 14
Consequences of Chaumont Treaty for Small Powers and Formation
of the New World Order at the Vienna Congress 18
Europe after the Vienna Congress... 21

THE NEW WORLD ORDER AFTER WWI AND WWII: GUARANTEE FOR
THE EXISTENCE OF SMALL STATES 25

The First World War and Small Powers 25
Results of the First World War and the New World Order...................... 28
The Second World War and Small Powers.. 32
New World Order and the Cold War 35

THE FOREIGN POLICY OF THE SMALL POWERS AFTER THE COLLAPSE
OF THE EASTERN BLOCK AND FORMATION OF THE UNIPOLAR WORLD:
HOW TO ACT? 43

New Developments after the Cold War 43
Relations of NATO and the EU with the Central and Eastern Europe 45
Relations with the Former Yugoslavia... 48
EU relations with Newly Independent States (NIS) 55

THE EMERGENCE OF NEW SMALL POWERS AFTER THE COLLAPSE OF
THE SOVIET UNION AND INTERNATIONAL POLICY 61

Russian Dominance in NIS 61
Formation of New Regional Organizations in NIS.................................. 67

"Color Revolution" in the NIS 69
Geopolitical Rivalry in the Post-Soviet Region 71
Selection of Foreign Policy by NIS Small Powers Stationed in Europe ... 76

THREE SMALL POWERS OF THE SOUTH CAUCASUS REGION: AZERBAIJAN, GEORGIA, AND ARMENIA AND FACTORS THAT AFFECTED THEIR FOREIGN POLICY 79

The Main Features of the South Caucasus Region 79
Factors Influencing the Formation of Foreign Policy of the South Caucasus Countries 81
Regional Conflicts and Their Impact on the Foreign Policy of Regional States 84
The Energy Factor in the Foreign Policy of the South Caucasus States 87
Relations with Russia 89

AZERBAIJAN: FOREIGN POLICY IS DESIGNED TO MAINTAIN THE BALANCE 95

Formation of Foreign Policy during the First Years of Independence 95
Foreign Policy During Heydar Aliyev 99
Continuation of Balanced Policy 105

THE FOREIGN POLICY OF GEORGIA: TOWARDS EURO-ATLANTIC AREA INTEGRATION 113

The Formation of Foreign Policy at an Early Stage 113
Foreign Policy during Saakashvili 119
Georgia after Saakashvili 123

ARMENIA AND POLITICAL AND ECONOMIC DEPENDENCY ON RUSSIA 131

Armenia Foreign Policy during Levon Ter-Petrosyan 131
Foreign Policy in the Time of Robert Kocharyan 137
Foreign Policy of Serzh Sargsyan 142
Foreign Policy of Nikol Pashinyan 147

ENDNOTES 149

REFERENCES 171

Acknowledgements

Working on this book started a few years ago. It was a good time for such type of research, as the statehood of the countries that appeared after the collapse of the Soviet Union was formed (that is true, even though 30 years have passed since these countries gained independence, we still refer to this event to designate and explain this group of states. A new definition may form over time. However, now that the current wording is still relevant), there was a need for both a theoretical review and a generalization of explanation of their foreign policy behavior.

It is worth noting that post-Soviet countries belong to the group of *Small Powers*. It took this definition as a basis for interpreting their actions internationally. At the same time, it was necessary to analyze the foreign policy of the *Small Powers* from a historical perspective, considering the evolutionary changes in the international system.

An important aspect was also to clearly define the international environment and order in which the former countries of the Soviet Union found themselves. For models based on the formed theoretical concept and for the analysis of the foreign policy of the *Small Powers*, three countries of the South Caucasus region were selected: Azerbaijan, Georgia, and Armenia. It was not done by chance: even though geographically the South Caucasus occupies small geography, the three countries in this region have opposed approaches to the perception of the international system and its behavior. Thus, an explanation is given on why these three countries have different foreign policy approaches.

I would also like to thank the Caspian Research Center (Caspi), which kindly agreed to publish my manuscript. It is precious to me that this is the first publication of this kind by this center, and the number of research will only grow.

In addition, I want to thank my former students Farid Naghizade (Azerbaijan) and Nurlyaiym Zhaksybayeva (Kazakhstan), who became the first readers of my study and shared their opinions. I also want to thank my other students Dr. Mehmet Fatih Oztarsu (South Korea) and Dr. Namig Abbasov (USA), who kindly shared their opinions on my research and Ph.D. Candidate Shamkhal Abilov (Germany) contributed his efforts during the publication of this book.

With his critical perception of the information and knowledge provided in the text, the reader will assess this study.

Prof. Dr. Rovshan Ibrahimov

Introduction

The discipline of International Relations (IR) has historically concentrated on examining the behavior of Great Powers and their role in shaping the international system, and the study of small-state foreign policy behavior needs to be addressed. Given the anarchic nature of the international system, such a situation is inevitable because power plays a dominant role in IR. It is no coincidence that IR as a discipline and its grand theories developed principally in the research centers of the Great Powers, mainly the United States. The rest of the world, especially developing countries, had a peripheral contribution to the development of the IR discipline. Consequently, IR, as social science, aims to resolve the problems related to the actions and expectations of Great Powers in the international system.

While the IR discipline has conventionally focused on studying Great Powers' politics, many Small Powers emerged during the twentieth century, and their study also bears particular importance. These powers have limited resources and cannot influence international events, and for the most part, are a product of the system formed by the interaction of the Great Powers. However, small states are not just passive objects of the international system but, like Great Powers, have their national interests and carry out their policies. Great Powers determine the system's features and guarantee its maintenance and changes. At the same time, Small Powers, due to various circumstances, also can become constituents and actors shaping the international system.

By conducting an effective foreign policy and increasing their capabilities, several Small Powers have eventually turned into Great Powers and gained a new power status, which has allowed them to influence global events in the international arena. Developing a long-term policy based on a correct assessment of their capabilities, current situation, and future actions is the primary factor that allows powers to implement optimal foreign policy and reach their potential success.

At the same time, there is an evolutionary approach to change, in which the Great Powers of the system try to find ways to prevent major international conflicts that could threaten the balance of the proposed system of relations. Such changes like the international system and relations between states in the time domain positively impact Small Powers. In short, it reduced the threat to their existence and security while increasing the role and importance of Small Powers, even though they still are not decisive actors in the international system. Over time, the number of Small Powers began to grow, and these countries are also trying to participate in shaping the agenda of international politics more actively to develop independent instruments that allow them to influence international events. In the meantime, Great Powers were forced to reckon with the opinions and expectations of Small Powers.

It became essential in the 20th century with the outbreak of international organizations that aim to ensure the collective security system to protect the actors: all national states. The increase in the effectiveness of international law enabled Small Powers to minimize their national security challenges and strengthen their role in the international system. However, the impact on Small Powers is still of secondary importance to the international system. They do not play an essential role in it but are the only components of policies pursued by the Great Powers. At the same time, opportunities for Small Powers operating under their interests are somewhat limited.

Nevertheless, studying Small Power foreign policy behavior is essential to explain their actions under various situations and predict the best course. Thus, these studies provide an opportunity to optimize possible courses of action for Small Powers to achieve these countries' most excellent possible targets. As events unfold, and the factors that influence the formation of the international system, the changes can be traced foreign policy of Small Powers. Thus, the diagnosis of trends in the international arena, as well as the correct evaluation of their capacities and capabilities, allow Small Powers to determine the right course of action in their foreign policy. It increases the probability of realization of right-formed goals and avoiding undesired results that might threaten their security. Whereas Small Powers are mainly passive actors in the international system, optimizing all available factors under favorable conditions may allow them to play an active role.

The simulation of Small Powers' behavioral actions is also essential from the point of view of the foreign policy of Great Powers and general international politics. Because as the number of Small Powers in the system increase, their value to the system is also expanded, it is essential to avoid undesired miscalculation in the potential and expectations of these Small Powers. Despite this, in conjunction with Great Power- Small Powers, Great Power is a responder, while Small Powers, in the main, is reflective of the actions of the main actor.

This study covers the period from the signing of the Peace of Westphalia in 1648 and forming a new international system based on the actors of legally equal states. It seeks to examine the dynamism of the international system and the influence of this factor on the foreign policy of Small Powers. This study is limited to Small Powers in Europe. After analyzing changes in the behavior of Europe's Small Powers in the historical context, the study will determine the factors that have influenced these changes in different periods. By identifying these factors, it will be possible to analyze the foreign policies of newly independent states that emerged on the world map in the late 20th century.

In 1991, the Soviet Union collapsed, and then on the world map appeared fifteen newly independent states, except Russia, which fell under the qualification of Small Powers. Former Soviet republics began to be formed as independent states in the realities of the international system. A new unipolar international system based on Western values such as democracy, the market economy, and human rights began to form. For newly independent countries, the priorities of the only surviving Superpower - the United States and other Western Great Powers and organizations - became the basis for developing the course they have taken. For these New Independent States (NIS) and all the countries of the former Eastern Bloc, it was necessary to go through a transition period, which is the transformation of the socialist political system into a liberal. In this case, the successful transition of these countries depended not only on their own will and desire but also on the active support of the West.

Among the new countries that gained independence are three states of the South Caucasus, Azerbaijan, Georgia, and Armenia, which are also experiencing problems common to all countries of the former Soviet Union. It was necessary to form a state, to allow political and economic problems, and to transform the entire system. In addition, these three countries have experienced military conflicts. They inherited a legacy from the Soviet Union.

This study aims to determine the behavioral actions of Small Powers in general and their application in relation to the three South Caucasus countries, Azerbaijan, Georgia, and Armenia. Based on determining factors that influence the formation of the foreign policy of these countries, to identify the best possible form of action of these countries, as well as a comparative analysis between the optimal formula and the actual foreign policy of these countries.

CHAPTER 1
The Existence of Small (States) Powers in the International System: Features and Their Priorities

The Definition of Small Powers

The modern world is the order of more than the *Small Powers* of hundred states, which differ in size, population, opportunities, and potential. Along with the *Great Powers*, which determine the specificity of the international order, there are countries with limited influence (*Middle Powers*) or lacking (*Small Powers*). As a result, the behavior of these states in the international arena and the formation of their foreign policy depends on their capacity and properly selected potential strategy.

The basic concept in the classification of these countries is *power*. Consequently, *Small Powers* in the international system are the countries with the lowest potential and limited resources, which do not allow them to act independently in the international system to realize their interests.

"*Power*" is a crucial concept for the realism paradigm in International Relations. The anarchic nature of the international system results from the Westphalia Treaty signed in 1648. According to this Treaty, all actors of the international system, national states, were recognized as equal.

However, legal equality did not provide it in absolute terms. At a time when fundamental state interests in the international arena were resolved with a position of strength, the critical components of this power are the country's geographical position, the availability of natural resources, a strong economy, a large population, and the armed forces. In this case, the theory of classical realism leads to the main action of nation-states in the international arena, namely an increase in their capacity and strength. The availability of necessary resources and capacity allows realizing their interests in the international arena.

Thus, *Small Powers* are ranked as the states that cannot provide for their safety due to the lack of capacity and resources and do not have or have limited opportunities to realize their interests based on their wishes and expectations.

However, it is also wrong to completely ignore the existence of these states in terms of International Relations in the formation of the world order. Separately, a few such countries have no influence, but their number has risen with time, besides the possibility of their collective action. As a result, *Small Powers* also must seek ways for joint action in the international arena.

The primary objective of these states is to survive and protect their existence. Therefore, these states try to form their foreign policy based on limited resources. In this case, if the geographical position of *a Small Power* is favorable, then this state can choose the policy of non-intervention in international politics and maintain neutrality. In other cases, *Small Powers* will seek the protection of *the Great Powers* by creating coalitions and alliances with them. As history shows, only a few countries (*Small Powers*) could pursue policies that allow them to survive for quite a long time.

Small Powers are also interested in developing international law because its presence increases the probability of their existence. The development of inter-state law and the formation of institutions eventually changed the concept of threat and its perception on the part of these states.

A significant influence on the behavior of *Small Powers* plays a concrete international order formed in a particular historical period. It should be noted that the very *Small Powers* have no ability of their form. However, in turn, these countries are very interested in establishing a legal basis for the behavior of international relations actors, in which these countries feel relatively safe and have the potential to realize national interests.

Nowadays, a general universal definition can be applied to the *Small Powers*. Several definitions have been drawn up under the different perceptions of the concept of *power*. Among the definitions, there are those directly related to the size of the territory, population, and economic opportunities of the country.

One of the definitions of *Small Powers* is provided by *Tom Crowards*, who made an interesting study on it. He quantitatively analyzed 190 countries by controlling for their size, population, and GDP. It should be noted that an essential factor in determining a *Small State* in the *Crowards* analysis is the size of GDP. Therefore, some states with low-income but large populations, such as Burundi, Eritrea, and Haiti, are called *Small States*. At the same time, countries with a small population but a significant income, such as Kuwait and Slovenia, in this category are not included. As a result of his research, 79 countries in the world can be classified as "*small*," 75 as "*middle*," and 34 as "*large*".[1] However, *Tom Crowards*' definition does not reveal these factors' role in shaping the Small States' foreign policy and their possibilities. As a result, the analysis revealed a group of states that, compared to the others, has a shortage of resources.

One of the first researchers who studied the foreign policy of *Small Powers* was *Annette Baker Fox*. In her book, *The Power of Small States:*

Diplomacy in World War II, she conducted a study of the *Small States'* foreign policy in the conditions of the Second World War on the example of the five European countries (Türkiye, Spain, Norway, Sweden, and Finland). The study aimed to determine how *Small States* can resist the *Great Powers* in crises.

As a result of her research, *Annette Baker Fox* concludes that the great importance of the possibility to pursue a neutral policy and avoid being drawn into a war plays the geographical remoteness of the *Small States* from the central action region. The further the state of the main area of conflict, the greater the likelihood that a country will be able to avoid involvement. Furthermore, *Small States* are advantageous if the two conflicting sides are equally interested in it. It enables them to maneuver. As a result, considering the likelihood that the *Small States* may act in a bloc with the enemy, the main parties to the conflict prefer that those countries remain neutral.[2]

Regarding how limited resources can influence the formation of the foreign policy of the country, another researcher *David Vital* gives the following description: the *Small Power*, compared to the *Great Powers*, is more vulnerable to possible pressure on it in the international arena, more compliant with the tense atmosphere, has fewer options for a political solution and correlation between internal and external policies is visible. Vital believes that the *Small Powers*, due to their limited human and material resources, are unable to be fully independent members of the international community.[3]

Robert Rothstein defines *Small Powers* as the ability to ensure their safety. According to *Rothstein*, *Small Powers* are the states that recognize having no ability to provide their security independently. They depend on the help of other states, institutions, processes, and developments. In addition, the *Small Powers* join the alliance to increase their security only in exceptional cases.[4] In the context of international security, *Small Powers* are very passive, reactive, configured, and their contribution to global security is negligible and even, on the contrary, can cause destabilization.

Robert O. Keohane gives his definition of *Small Powers*. According to him, during the Cold War (in the period when he conducted his research), countries such as the US and the USSR were the "system-determining," countries such as Britain, France, and West Germany were "system-influencing," Canada, Argentina Pakistan, Sweden are classified as "system-affecting." At the same time, *Small Powers* are "system-ineffectual." At the same time, *Keohane* concerns the behavior of *Small Powers*, in the period after the Second World War, towards the policies of international organizations or the balance of power system. Keohane argues that *Small Powers* rationally realize that under particular conditions or actions of *Great Powers*, international organizations can or will not ensure their safety. Although *Small Powers* understand that together they are capable of small things, individually, they cannot do anything.[5]

Dutch researcher *Jaquet* offered another definition for Small Powers. According to him: "*Small Power* is a country that is neither global nor at the regional scale cannot realize its political will or protect their national interests through power politics.".[6]

According to *Maurice A. East* and some previous researchers, a definition of *Small Powers* is based on four assumptions: a *Small State* has a small area, a small total population, small GDP, and low military capabilities. As a result, based on these factors, *Small Powers* can demonstrate the following behaviors:

    a) low level of participation in world affairs;

    b) high level of activity in intergovernmental organizations;

    c) high level of support for international legal norms;

    d) avoidance of the use of force as a technique of statecraft;

    e) avoidance of behavior and policies which tend to alienate the more powerful states in the system;

    f) a narrow functional and geographic range of concern in foreign policy activities;

    g) frequent utilization of moral and normative positions in international issues.[7]

As can be seen from the proposed models, the *Small Powers* in the rational management of foreign policy prefer to minimize the use of their already limited resources. It is important to note that for *Small Powers*, calculating the maximum of their forces and the possible behavior in particular circumstances is critical. Because any mistake in the strategic planning of medium and long-term foreign policy can cost a great price, which is sometimes impossible to repay, in this case, the *Small Power's* foreign policy should be maximum rational and preventive to avoid undesired effects. It is essential to calculate the possible actions of the main actors- *Great Powers* in the international system, the consequences of which impact these *Small Powers*. It is also essential for *Small Powers* to create a model of behavior in foreign policy which is predictable from the main actors to avoid misunderstanding and miscalculation. In this way, it has been able to avoid the undesired actions of *Great Powers* actors due to misunderstanding.

Historical Context: Small Powers Attitudes after Westphalia Peace

Before forming a new Westphalia international system, founded on the legal equality of bare actors- States, the central policy of survival of *Small States* was based on delegating its sovereignty to the suzerain. This vassal relationship allowed their governors to retain their authority. The modern system of international relations was formed after the signing of the *Westphalia Treaty* in 1648. To be more exact, *the Treaty of Westphalia* is not one, but two agreements, *Osnabrück* and *Münster* (talks were held in the Protestant and Catholic bishopric Osnabrück and Bishopric Münster), and signed, respectively, on May 15 and on October 24, 1648.[8] This Treaty resulted in a new kind of diplomatic relations, which ended the *Thirty Years War* in the Holy Roman Empire and inspired the creation of a new order in Europe, formed on the co-existence of sovereign states.

The signing of the *Westphalia Treaty* marked the victory of German states, recognized as sovereign power with the right to self-government and conduct their foreign policy. The role of the Holy Roman Empire went by the wayside. The *Westphalian Peace* ended the aspirations of the Habsburgs to conquer Germany and their dominance in Europe. On the map of Europe, about 350 new countries were formed, many of which were *Small Powers*. At the same time, the head of the independent states in Europe, who had the title of king, had equal rights with the emperor.[9]

After forming the Westphalian international system in Europe, a central factor in international relations becomes a state. The most important result of the *Westphalian Peace* became the basis for forming relations between sovereign states, which have been recognized as equal. It was made possible thanks to the crush of the two Great Powers of the time: the Papacy and the Holy Roman Empire. The national interests of the state began to prevail over the interests of religious purposes.[10] For the first time in history, the borders of the states were clearly defined. The concept of equal and sovereign states has also led to the anarchic nature of the existing international system, in which the actors of this system, with the aim of self-preservation in the first place, must rely on their strength and potential. Thus, a solid will to search for ways to dominate, while as weak- resistance to this, achieving this through the formation of coalitions or increasing individual power.[11]

In this sense, the *Small Powers* have become more vulnerable and must find methods to realize their interests. Relatively safely may feel the states which are geographically located in the inaccessibility of *the Great Powers*. It could be a geographical feature of this state (to be surrounded by mountains, located on the island) or a location at a sufficient distance from the main *Great Powers*. The rest of the *Small Powers* were forced to resort to political maneuvers in the international arena, which would enable these countries to neutralize the challenges posed by *Great Powers*. Such the opportunity for this kind of foreign policy of *Small Powers* provided the international system formed after the *Westphalian Peace*. It became the basis for international policies that allow *Small Powers* to a certain extent to prevent aggression and to ensure non-interference in domestic affairs.

The ability to maneuver for *Small Powers* was possible due to the presence of several *Great Powers*, which presaged the formation of a multipolar system of European states in which each country acted per its national interests.[12]

The system allows this kind of *Small States* participation in *balancing power* between the main actors or maintaining a position of neutrality. With the spread of Europe's influence in the world, the concept of Westphalian principles of sovereign states has become central globally.[13] Based on this system, international law began to develop. Based on the obligation to execute the signed agreement, international law passed the formation stage, further strengthening its position. At the same time, diplomacy is becoming an essential element of practice in state relations. The extraordinary distribution of diplomacy gains in those days, when thanks to the *balance of power*, the country was unable to fight wars, achieve their interests, and look for alternative solutions, the main of which was diplomacy. Due to forming a *balance of power* in Europe, the *Small Powers* were able to participate in this system, taking the side of one or another block, due to which it became possible to reduce the threat of conflict, and therefore calls for their existence.

The central European *Great Powers* formed between the XVI-XVIII centuries, which increased their potential and wealth by expanding their core areas and colonial possessions. There is a constant struggle between the *Great Powers* for the expansion of their possessions.[14] As a consequence, there is a struggle for universal domination. As a result, to prevent the emergence of hegemony, other forces unite to try to balance its power.

Since the second half of the XVII century, many European monarchical states proclaimed as the basis of their foreign policy *balance of power* on the continent. From then on, if a European state aggressively attempted to upset the balance of power in their favor against him, they immediately formed blocs and coalitions, aiming to restore the *status quo*. In this case, if the coalition of forces were strong enough to control the aggressor, then formed the *balance of power*; if not, the country achieved hegemony.[15]

However, *Small Powers* were appendages of the system rather than active participants. Despite the legal equality of states, at that time, their existence was guaranteed in the event of a multipolar *balance of power* between the main actors. The superpowers' imbalance and appearance became the reason for the threat of the existence of *Small Powers* and limited their field of action. In the period of instability, the probability of extinction of some *Small Powers* increased. In such cases, *Small Powers* may be sacrificed to win a particular time by the weaker Great Power.

On the contrary, the unequal distribution of *the balance of power* made it possible for *Small Powers* to participate more actively to achieve their goals. In such cases, even a *Small Power* was of great importance. The presence of *Small Powers* becomes significant in shaping a balance of power. However, if there is a significant difference in balance, the weight of *Small Powers* has no importance.[16]

At the same time, the existence of the balance of power has yet to give the *Small Powers* the guarantee for the continuation of their existence and the possibility to realize their interests. However, even in this situation, if they did not achieve their interests, then at least reduce the possible risks and challenges. Participation of *Small Powers* in alliances ensures the *balance of power* locally, while *Great Powers* have to balance the entire system. If the local threat could affect the overall *balance of power*, in this case, the interests of *Small Powers* can be donated, or it may lose much of its ability to influence the situation. At the same time, if the local conflict has no impact on the *balance of power*, it can be ignored entirely until the situation changes.[17]

The existence of a *balance of power* and participation in the alliance allowed some *Small States* to build up their strength, which is paramount to survival. Over time, due to the successful maneuvering between the *Great Powers*, these countries could turn themselves into a group of big states by increasing their capacity. The foreign policy of small European powers of that time can be seen in their behavior in significant conflicts.

So, in the XVII century, a country that appeared as a troublemaker in Europe was France, which during the reign of Louis XIV, began to grow, becoming a superpower and threatening its neighbors. Released after the *Thirty Years War*, on the first role in international relations, France has managed to expand their ownership through several cities of the Spanish Netherlands (Belgium), the province of Franche-Comté, which was a part of the Holy Roman Empire, as a result of the war with Holland. Then in 1681, France suddenly seized Strasbourg.

Growing France's ambitions troubled Europe. The threat was beginning to loom over Holland. As a result, this country began forming a coalition against France, which included Austria, Spain, England, Sweden, Denmark, and such *Small States* of Europe, as the German states Brandenburg and Savoy. Many countries had only a tiny army and acted in a limited area. However, it was a coalition of countries that had enough force to quell the growing influence of France.[18]

Despite forming a coalition, France, believing in the previous successes, was launching a new *Nine Years' War*, which took place in Europe, the West Indies, and North America. On the side of France, the Ottoman Empire has joined in a war. The protracted war led to the signing of the *Treaty of Ryswick* in 1697.

Two years later, the war with the Ottoman Empire was also ended. The war resulted in France being unable to expand its holdings, while the Ottoman Empire was defeated and no longer threatened Europe. According to the *Treaty of Ryswick,* former borders of states were restored. It has been restored to the pre-war status quo. Only the acquisition of France was to be able to maintain dominance over Strasbourg. In turn, after many years of confinement in France, the Duchy of Lorraine has become independent. At the same time, France's ambitions were thwarted, the country lost power, and its navy was destroyed.[19]

The positive results of the war had Brandenburg, which strengthened its position in Europe and gradually transformed into a *Middle Power*. Over time, Brandenburg expanded her territory and power; appeared as a new player in Europe, like the Kingdom of Prussia. Regarding the Savoy, the war began badly for her. France defeated Savoy and then had to change the block and enter into an agreement with France to maintain its existence.

In the XVIII century, the main confrontation occurred between major European states: Austria, France, England, Spain, and Prussia. At this time, there was a constant *stately quadrille* to create a *balance of power* that would allow preventing a possible hegemony of one of the states or the alliance. The early XVIII century was marked by the War of *the Spanish Succession*, which began in 1702. As before, the conflict has dragged the whole of Europe, as well as overseas colonies.[20] *Small Powers* near the conflict zone joined one of the alliances. In short, most German states, including Prussia, Hanover, and Savoy, entered the war on the side of the Union of Austria and England. In turn, such *Small Powers* as Bayern, Cologne, and Portugal supported France and Spain. As for Venice, she announced her neutrality. At the same time, these *Small Powers* could not withstand another country in the case of violation of its sovereignty.

As a result of this war, *the Treaty of Utrecht* in 1713, the *Treaty of Rastatt*, and the *Treaty of Baden* in 1714 were signed. An essential outcome of the war was that a result of the hegemony of France ended in continental Europe, and the idea of a *balance of power*, as reflected in the *Treaty of Utrecht*, became part of the international order. As a result of the redistribution of Europe, three *Small Powers*: Brandenburg-Prussia, Hanover, and Savoy, began to strengthen their position on the continent and became a significant power, which began to be considered. The Elector of Brandenburg was recognized as King of Prussia and the Elector of Hanover as King of Britain.[21] Thus, one of the results of the European war and the signing of the agreement was to strengthen several *Small Powers* and move them into the category of *Middle Powers*. Through participation in the formation of alliances and a permanent *balance of power* concerning the *Great Powers*, these countries were able to strengthen their positions and participate more actively in European affairs. Spain was the main loser, seriously affecting her status as *Great Power*.

The next major conflict, another challenge for *the Small States,* was the War of the *Austrian Succession*, which began in 1740 and lasted eight years. The conflict was the attempt of the European powers to challenge the Austrian Emperor Charles VI. The newly formed two opposing alliances were joined on the side of France, Spain, and Prussia, such as *the Small States* Sicily, Genoa, Bavaria, and Saxony. In turn, there were Hanover and Sardinia in the opposite camp, along with the Holy Roman Empire (Austria), England, and Russia. The Treaty of Aix-la-Chapelle was signed at the end of the war in 1748. As a result of the agreement, the warring parties have returned to pre-war borders, formed even in the time of war of the *Spanish Succession*. A significant change was the shift of Silesia from Austria to Prussia. At the same time, Austria was ready to concede the Austrian Netherlands, which France had occupied, to regain Silesia. However, England and Dutch demanded that she keeps these areas in the interests of the *balance of power*. Due to the annexation of Silesia, Prussia doubled its population and strengthened economically. On the map of Europe, a new *Great Power* has emerged to compete in the issue of domination in Germany with Austria. [22]

Prussia took part in several other wars that defined the *balance of power* to approve of the status of a new power in Europe. Thus, Prussia was involved on the side of various coalitions, changing allies per her interests. However, it is worth noting that, unlike England, which transitionally shifted from one block to another in order to maintain the status quo in the international system, Prussia acted from purely individual interests.[23] Ultimately, it led to its success and becoming a system-forming actor.

An essential result of the War of *the Austrian Succession*, in addition to the strengthening of Prussia, was the drop-in value of the Electorate of Bavaria and Saxony, where the army suffered a crushing defeat. These states have ceased to play an independent role in European politics. Consequently, although *Small Powers* were able to take an active part in shaping European policy, their disappearance as independent actors did not affect the formation and restoration of the *balance of power*.

Peace of Aix-la-Chapelle made the next war inevitable in Central Europe: neither side was satisfied with the results. The only thing it has determined on which side the *Great Powers* will participate in the next war. The next European war began eight years later, in 1755, and became the *Seven Years' War*. Austria, England, Prussia, and France were already on opposite sides in this war. Only contradictions between Prussia and Austria remained stable because of Silesia. The *Seven Years' War* was both in Europe and overseas in North America, the Caribbean, India, and the Philippines. The war was attended by all the great

European powers and the majority of the *Middle* and the *Small States*. Brunswick-Lüneburg, Portugal, the Principality of Hesse-Kassel participated on Prussia and England's sides. While, on the opposing side, together with France, Austria, and Russia, such *Small Powers* as Saxony and the Neapolitan kingdom were joined.

At the end of the war *Treaty of Paris* was signed. At that time, France lost almost all colonial possessions. England became the dominant colonial power, although later, she would lose dominion over territories in America. It affirmed the right of Prussia over Silesia and the Country of Kladsko. Prussia finally entered the circle of the leading European powers by dividing Poland together with Austria and Russia.[24] In parallel with this, the process began, culminating at the end of the XIX century with the German states' union. In 1807, Prussia officially became a kingdom,[25] and would continue to play a central role in the association of German lands.

The reason for the participation of Small Powers in the balance of power in this period was conditioned according to which side they supported. If the Small Power took the side of balancing block, the primary purpose of this was to prevent further enhancing the potential hegemon because it posed a risk to the existence of this state. Nevertheless, if the Small Power joined a coalition with a potential hegemon, its goal was to curry favor with this power in the future balance of power. The great importance here was the ability of the rulers of Small Powers to assess the situation of events. If the Small Power could manouver and select the party of its choice, it could strengthen its position sufficiently. In addition, at a low effort, it was possible to increase its capacity and move into the Middle and Great Powers category.

A balance of power system has allowed several Small Powers to actively participate in the continent's policy to create favorable conditions for themselves. The theme of balance of power would continue to be a significant factor in European politics until the time of the French Revolution, which once again resurfaced in the XIX century.

The French Revolution and the Napoleonic Wars

In 1789 there was a revolution in France. As a result, the most significant transformation of the social and political system in France led to the destruction of the old order in the country- the absolute monarchy and the proclamation of the First French Republic. The consequences of this historical event had an impact not only within the country but also far beyond its borders. In Europe, there were only a few states which were republics. The Dutch Republic was far from its times of dawn, and the Swiss Confederation was in stagnation. Independent republic in North America has only begun to emerge.[26]

In the initial stage in France, it was established a constitutional monarchy. The king was forced to accept the new order. On August 26th, 1789, the Constituent Assembly adopted the *"Declaration of the Rights of Man and of the Citizen,"* a significant event for Europe at that time, the formation of nationalism against the background of absolutism. It impeded the process of the irrevocable spread of democratic ideas, which was a real threat to the absolutism of monarchies. For them, it was necessary to prevent the process until it had spread to their state.[27]

1791 French King Louis XIV tried to escape but was found on the border in Varennes-en-Argonne. The royal family returned to Paris. The king tried to escape accelerated the establishment of the republic in France, as well as hastened the military conflict with monarchical Europe.[28] On August 27, 1791, Austria and Prussia signed the *Declaration of Pillnitz*; revolutionary France threatened armed intervention. Thus, Austria came to this position with great caution: This state stated she would go to war only if all the other major European powers also went to war with France. The agreement was signed in connection with the demand of the French nobility, who was in exile. However, this did not affect expected action, causing a stimulation of the revolutionary forces that only complicated the position of the king. On April 20, 1792, the Legislative Assembly of France declared war on Austria. It was done to show the impossibility of monarchical Europe restoration. Followed in June, Prussia entered the war against France. On August 10, by the decision of the Legislative Assembly, King Louis XVI was deposed from the throne. On September 22, in France, a republic was declared. On January 21, 1793, Louis XVI was beheaded in Revolution Square. In this way, the French Revolution rejected the legitimacy of the monarchy, offering an alternative to the power of the people, which was a severe threat to the European *Great Powers*.[29]

In the war against Prussia and Austria, the young republic achieved some success, forcing the army's retreat from these countries. Along with this, the young republic declared war on England and Spain. The war took place with varying success. Initially, France was losing the war on all fronts; a successful offensive was led by Prussia, while Austria invaded northern France. Spanish troops launched an offensive against Perpignan. England invaded Alsace.

However, then the situation changed radically: the French managed to repel the attack, and she had invaded Spain, the Kingdom of Sardinia, and the western German states. Soon after, in 1793, there was a *battle of Toulon*, where for the first time, a young and talented military leader Napoleon Bonaparte showed himself.[30] Then the army led by Napoleon, defeated the Austrian army. On 17 October 1797, *the Treaty of Campo Formio* between Austria and France was signed. In this way, the war of the First Coalition was finished.[31] Its recent enemies have recognized France. Only Britain continued the war in France.

In turn, France continued its expansion policy. She conducted a campaign in Egypt. In Europe, France began to promote the emergence of satellite republics: the Batavian Republic in the Netherlands, the Helvetic Republic in Switzerland, the Cisalpine Republic, the Roman Republic, and the Parthenopean Republic in Italy. The New Republic and other conquered territories were politically dependent and economically exploited by France. In all republics, the French garrisons were settled. In foreign policy, these states were dependent on France. Over time, the dependence on the satellites only intensified: The Cisalpine Republic was transformed into the Italian Republic, whose president became Napoleon.[32] France needed new subordinated Small Powers to create a new *balance of power* on the continent where authoritarian regimes were dominated. These states had no absolute independence; even legal equality has been questioned since France quickly interfered in the internal affairs of the satellites and even assigned them to the rulers.

This development could not arrange a multinational empire in monarchical Europe. The successful promotion of France on the continent directly threatens the existence of their regime. Its main goal of Napoleon was the creation of a new empire, like the Roman Empire, which was a threat to the existence of some states.[33] In this case, the *Small Powers* were the most wounded because they were the primary building material for creating a new order.

In the spring of 1799, after Switzerland replaced on France side, on the England side, Russia, Austria, Türkiye, Sweden, Naples, and several German states joined. The Second Coalition created it. The coalition was created to limit the influence of revolutionary France during the revolutionary wars and restore the monarchy.

On November 9, 1799, in a coup, Napoleon seized power in France, and declared himself the first consul of the country, dictatorial regime in France was established.[34] In June 1800, at *the Battle of Marengo*, French troops under the command of Napoleon defeated Austrian troops. After the defeats of the Austrian army on December 3, 1800, at the *Battle of Hohenlinden*, on February 9, 1801, the *Peace of Luneville* was signed,[35] and Austria committed to transferring the lands on the left bank of the Rhine to France. Austria officially recognized the independence of the Batavian Republic and the Helvetic Republic, the existence of the Ligurian Republic, and the Cisalpine Republic.[36] The exit of Austria from the war meant the actual disintegration of the Second Coalition. As in the case of the First Coalition in the war with France, only England remained. Nevertheless, having lost all its allies on the continent, she was forced to sign the *Peace of Amiens* in 1802. France became the leading power on the continent. Austria finally lost its importance as a great European power. On May 18, 1804, Napoleon was proclaimed emperor.

In April 1805, a *Treaty of Saint Petersburg* was signed between Russia and England that laid the foundation of the Third Coalition, which formed England, Austria, Russia, Sweden, and the Kingdom of Naples in the same year. French diplomacy managed to achieve the temporary neutrality of Prussia in the impending war. However, this time the coalition also failed to break France. The victorious Napoleonic wars continued and were successfully carried out in the Austrian campaign of 1805, the Prussian and Polish campaigns in 1806-1807, and the Austrian campaign in 1809. The military victory helped transform France into a *Great Power* on the continent.

In July 1806, an agreement between France and eighteen western and southern German states had signed, under which the Confederation of the Rhine was created under the protectorate of France and with the responsibility of forming an army of sixty thousand troops. At the same time, Bavaria and Württemberg became kingdoms.[37] Furthermore, Prussia had taken away all her possessions between the Rhine and the Elbe, where the kingdom of Westphalia was formed, the head of which was Napoleon's brother Jerome Bonaparte.[38]

As a result, on August 6, 1806, Austrian Emperor Francis II announced the resignation from the title and authority of the Holy Roman Emperor, and thus, this centuries-old institution ceased to exist. The Grand Duchy of Warsaw was formed from the Prussian possessions in Poland.

The expansion of France in Europe was based not on national interests but on preserving the achievements of the revolution and the spread of republican ideals in Europe. The universal principles of freedom, equality, and fraternity founded the fight against monarchic regimes. France hoped to create a Commonwealth in Europe, where she played a key role. Since 1807, satellite states supported by France were established in Italy, Spain, and Germany. The rulers of some were relatives of Napoleon. France managed to transform Prussia into second-rank power and significantly weaken Austria.[39]

However, the unfortunate rivalry between France and England on the sea did not allow the country to declare total European hegemony. There was also the continent's *Great Power*- Russia, against which France marched in 1812. Even though Napoleon managed to get the Russian capital Moscow, eventually, France was defeated and had to leave the territory of this country.[40]

The defeat of the French army in the 1812 war against Russia was the beginning of the collapse of the Napoleon Empire. After *"the battle of the Peoples"* in Leipzig, Napoleon could not resist the united army of the anti-French coalition.[41] The entry of the coalition troops in Paris in 1814 forced Napoleon I to abdicate. He was exiled to the island of Elba. However, soon, he escaped and again took the throne of France in March 1815. After the defeat at *the Battle of*

Waterloo again abdicated and spent the last years of his life on Saint Helena as a British prisoner.[42]

Monarchy prevented the spread of the Napoleonic ideas, threatening to preserve the *balance of power* in Europe and the states and their regimes. Ideas of universal freedom and the right to self-determination were destructive to the monarchical order in Europe. It was necessary to create a new structure to prevent such developments in the future and maintain the *status quo*.

Consequences of Chaumont Treaty for Small Powers and Formation of the New World Order at the Vienna Congress

The outcome of the Napoleonic Wars was that Europe was ready to establish an international legal order based on the principles of the *balance of power* for the first time in its history. It was the first attempt to establish peace in Europe based on a collective agreement, the principles of legitimacy, and balance. It was necessary to conclude an agreement based on shared values, which would prevent any desire to overthrow the system.[43] The winners in the last war have begun to create a legal basis for balancing power and preserving international order. The formation of such an order directly affected the ability of *Small Powers* in Europe, much of the potential for modifying the action.

In 1814, a *Treaty of Chaumont* was signed between Austria, Prussia, Russia, and Britain, which determined the action of the Sixth Coalition (it included Austria, Prussia, Russia, England, Portugal, Sweden, Spain, and several German states), suggesting the formation of a closer alliance, if France rejected conditions offered to her by the conditions for peace. Each party undertook to put 150,000 soldiers in the field against France and to guarantee European peace (once obtained) against French aggression for twenty years. The Treaty, in exchange for a cease-fire, demanded France's return to the country's borders in 1791, that was, to the pre-war situation. If Napoleon rejected the Treaty, the Allies pledged to continue the war.[44]

According to *Robert Rothstein,* this Treaty revealed a formal separation between *Great* and *Small Powers*. *Small Powers* obtain the benefits related to their security in the conflict between the *Great Powers* when they constantly have to change sides from weak to strong once they determine the eventual winner. It makes the system less stable. So, *the Treaty of Chaumont* converted *Small Powers* into only objects in the new forming system.

The need for separation between the *Great* and *Small Powers* was connected to the Napoleonic Wars. *Treaty of Chaumont* to dissociate them as *Small Powers* are unable to fulfill the obligations specified in the document. The decisions were again ratified and put into effect by the *Congress of Vienna* of

1814-1815. The difference between the *Great Powers* and *Small Powers* has been institutionalized at the Congress. It was to define the criteria according to which *Great Powers* are the countries with the *"general,"* *Small Powers* – *"limited interests."*[45]

Thus, *the Great Powers* were given the right to speak on behalf of Europe. Theoretically, this means *Great Powers* would decide while *Small Powers* had to obey. The main definition of *Great Power* was the ability to conduct a successful war against a recognized *Great Power*.[46] Congress intended to allow *the Small States* to discuss only those issues that concern them directly. The ability of the *Small Powers* to influence was reduced to zero. In addition, the *Small Power* had no right to make mistakes that could affect the formed system. In this case, the punishment for her would be inevitable.[47]

The most optimal form of foreign policy for *the Small States* was not participating in the alliance but the proclamation of neutrality. At the same time, in many cases, the significance of this status was a demand of the *Great Powers*. Concurrently, the neutrality of the *Small States* was provided by the *Great Powers*. These *Powers* were interested in the demilitarization of the sphere of conflict. In different periods *Great Powers* guaranteed the neutrality of Switzerland, Belgium, Luxembourg, and Krakow. However, these guarantees were not a panacea for the security of *Small Powers*. Despite the neutral status of these countries, they were occupied at different times. Krakow has disappeared from the map as a free city, and the neutrality of Belgium was violated by Germany in 1914.[48]

At worst, these *Small Powers* may be the subject of partition between the *Great Powers*, as was the case with Poland. Since *Small Powers* became an object of the system and were not equal partners, their policy of alliances became ineffective and non-existent. In such circumstances, *Small Powers* were also deprived of their capacity to increase and become stronger. This situation would continue until the Franco-Prussian War in 1871.[49]

Despite dissatisfaction with this development, *Small Powers* decided to take advantage of France. Its representative at Congress - Talleyrand, managed to win over the *Small States*, promising them to provide the right to participate in negotiations on an equal basis with four allies. The *Small States* feared the absorption of their lands by the *Great Powers*, and their collaboration would seriously improve the situation of France. The desire to use the potential of *Small Powers* from France only strengthened the belief in the rightness of *Great Powers* and the desire to determine the further destiny of the international system.

The reign of the Bourbons was restored in France; the country again became a monarchy. Even though it lost the war, this country, to preserve the *balance of power,* has been recognized as a *Great Power.*

The Treaty at the end of the Congress of Vienna marked the beginning of the "*European concert*" era - the *balance of power*, which was based on the general agreement of Great European States: Russia, Austria, Prussia, France, and England. The system of international relations, which was based on the absolute monarchies that existed before the Napoleonic Wars, was revived. It restored the legitimacy of the state and the monarchist rule. The difference was that the former *balance of powers* had no place for *the Small States*; the Great Powers provided all the responsibility for peace. These states were responsible for maintaining and preserving *the balance of power* and were obliged to prevent any problems threatening the world. For the first time to preserve the *balance of power* in Europe, the system did not rely only on power but was supported by the legal framework. Several agreements were signed, which obliged the parties to act under the formulated rules. In other words, the Congress of Vienna was guided by the principles of legitimacy and political balance.

Representatives of Russia, France, Prussia, Austria, England, Spain, Sweden, and Portugal signed the final Act of the Vienna Treaty. In order to neutralize France in the future, it was decided to create barriers from the several *Small States*. In short, at the end of the congress, it was decided to unite Belgium and Holland as part of the Kingdom of the Netherlands, which was to eliminate the possibility of French dominion in Belgium.[50] Also, the Rhine Province of Prussia played a barrier for France. The same task played to Switzerland, the boundaries of which have been expanded and included mountain passes, and it was also reinforced by the Kingdom of Sardinia, which returned Savoy and Nice. Thus, *the Great Powers* decided the fate of *Small States*, reshaping their borders following the form of the new *balance of powers* and to their interests. The fate of Poland is significant in this sense, Duchy of Warsaw, established by Napoleon, was divided between Russia, Prussia, and Austria. In addition, 39 German states under the hegemony of Austria created the German Confederation. The union has also been created to balance France in the case of another desire to become hegemony. At the same time, the fragmentation of the German Länder itself has also been retained to prevent the emergence of a new hegemony.

Another outcome of the Congress was the creation by Austria, Prussia, and Russia, a *Holy Alliance* to suppress the national liberation and revolutionary movement in Europe. Even though France was unable to destroy the social and economic basis of the old order, the germs of a democratic society have already begun to grow up to become an integral part of the French political tradition and have a significant influence on the rest of Europe.

The new Vienna order strengthened the relatively long-term peace on the European continent, preventing quite a big war between the *Great Powers*. In this sense, the *Congress of Vienna* proved that it was more successful than its predecessors, which signed *Westphalia* and *Utrecht Treaties*.[51]

Europe after the Vienna Congress

In the first years after the formation of the Vienna order, the *Great Powers* were acting in concert. *Holy Alliance* representatives have met several times in congresses to discuss actual issues. Under their decisions in the early 20s of the XIX century, Austrian troops crushed the uprising against absolutism in Italian states - the Kingdom of Naples and Piedmont, and the French army opposed the revolution in Spain. In Italy and Spain, absolutist order was restored and reinforced measures against supporters of constitutional government.[52] In 1820 the monarchs of Russia, Austria, and Prussia signed a joint declaration on the right of rulers to armed intervention in other countries' internal affairs without their governments' consent to fight against the revolutionary movement. The *Small Powers* were the object of the action of *the Great Powers* to support the Congress of Vienna that established international order.

In 1821, the national liberation revolutionary uprising of the Greeks against the Ottoman Empire began. The rules of the Vienna order demanded that the Holy Alliance of European monarchs consider the uprising a revolt against the legitimate sovereign. However, each of the *Great Powers* sought to take advantage of developments in Greece, primarily to strengthen its position and weaken the influence of other countries in the region. Eventually, among them, an agreement was reached on the recognition of the independence of Greece. In 1823, England withdrew from the *Holy Alliance*. This country has adhered to the principle of non-interference in the internal affairs of other states.

In the early 30s, there was a new aggravation of the international situation in Europe in connection with the revolutions in France and Belgium, then part of the Kingdom of the Netherlands. The differences between European states were not allowed to organize joint action and keep the former regime and borders. The *Holy Alliance* has disintegrated; to convene a new congress was impossible. As a result of the revolution, Belgium became an independent kingdom.[53] The emergence of new *Small Powers* on the map of Europe meant that the system boundaries established by the Congress of Vienna began to break down.

The next blow to the Vienna System has suffered by revolutions from 1848-1849. The peoples of Germany and Italy - the only ones in Europe who lived in political fragmentation, sought to unite and create national states. It was one of the main tasks of the revolution in these countries. On the other hand, the struggle for national equality and independence woke up in the Austrian

Empire, which was a multinational state. It is primarily manifested in the desire in Hungary.

Although the liberal revolution in Austria, Germany, Italy, and France was defeated, they staggered Vienna System, which was established immediately to prevent any threat to the monarchy in Europe.[54] The established collective system of mutual assistance between the *Great Powers* needed to be revised. Only at the final stage could Russia provide military aid to Austria against the rebels in Hungary and France, and Austria took part in defeating the revolution in Italy.

In the 50s, Russia intended to achieve separation of the Turkish Balkan possessions inhabited by Orthodox peoples. To put pressure on Türkiye, she occupied Moldavia and Wallachia, which previously were under the protectorate of Russia under the terms of the *Treaty of Adrianople*. As a result, this led to the declaration of war by Türkiye to Russia in 1853, followed by England and France. This war lasted three years and ended with the defeat of Russia and the signing of the *Paris Peace Treaty*. Russia was forced to return to the Ottoman Empire all occupied territories in southern Bessarabia, at the mouth of the Danube River and the Caucasus; it was forbidden to have a military fleet in the Black Sea, which waters proclaimed neutral.[55] The Vienna System completely collapsed, marked by a series of events that preceded the war. Significant events after this were the unification of Germany and Italy. The equally important fact was also the Russian dissatisfaction with the term, which it had imposed after the Crimean War.[56]

In 1860, significant events took place in Italy. Giuseppe Garibaldi and his volunteers sailed from Genoa and landed in Sicily; it eliminated the influence of the King of Naples. The Kingdom of Naples wound up and joined Piedmont. The Italian kingdom appeared on the map. Then the Venice region joined Italy, and the complete reunification of the country lacked only Papal Rome. It was reunited with the kingdom in 1870, and Rome became its capital. Thus, the unification of Italy was completed.[57]

Three victorious wars were carried out in the unification of Germany. The position of Prussia was expanded and strengthened. In 1864, the war waged: Prussia with Austria against Denmark and another in 1866 against Austria. In 1870-1871, wars broke out against France, which sought to preserve its hegemony in Europe and prevent the unification of Germany and Prussia. During the Franco-Prussian War, the Second Empire fell in France. Prussian troops occupied a considerable part of the French territory and annexed the province of Alsace-Lorraine.[58] An important event in warfare's history was applying the principle of compulsory military service in 1866. After that, the entire state, its economy, and its population were coordinated for war.[59]

The Franco-Prussian war has changed the *balance of power* in Europe. France was weakened and lost its leading role. Nevertheless, this state possessed the idea of revenge, restoring national honor, and the return of land taken away by pushing the ruling circles to look for allies.

In January 1871, an agreement was signed on forming the German Empire in Versailles. 22 German states joined Prussia. Wilhelm became Emperor of the German Empire. Hailed, the German Empire aspired to be a European leader and secure itself from France by isolating her with a complex system of alliances. German Empire became the new *Great Power*, and international relations developed a new principle. Parallel to this, Austria, the Ottoman Empire, and Russia have intensified the struggle of national movements for their independence from multinational dynastic empires.[60] Although the world maintained over the next 40 years, the contradictions between France and Germany constituted a constant source of tension in Europe, becoming one of the causes of the First World War.

In 1879, Germany established a military alliance with Austria, in which, in 1882, Italy was also joined. Thus, between these countries, a *Triple Alliance* was formed. The emergence of a strong Germany on a map of Europe and the formation of the *Triple Alliance* was the cause of the rapprochement between France and Russia, which felt threatened by this new *Great Power*. As a result, the reaction of these countries was the creation 1891 of the *Franco-Russian Alliance*. In 1907, this union joined England. The formation of two rival unions initiated the division of Europe into hostile camps and played an essential role in the preparation and unleashing of the First World War.[61]

Once the configuration changed in Europe, the *balance of power* was saved by a formed bipolar international system consisting of two units of Great Powers. While the main rising power in Europe, Germany, supported conserving the former *status quo*.

With the change of the system, the *Small Powers*, albeit limited, re-acquire the agility to act. At a time when the *Great Powers* were in confrontation with each other, they were less closely monitored adjacent to the *Small Powers*. However, this does not mean that the immunity of *Small Powers* increased in proportion to the involvement of *Great Powers* in conflict. The *Great Powers* still retained sufficient unity to cooperate against possible peripheral threats, which may come from the *Small Powers*.[62] According to *Rotshtein*, the optimal policy of *Small Powers* for this period was to participate in multilateral alliances with *Great Powers*. At the same time, they should avoid bilateral alliances, where a *Great Power* will initially dominate and will be able to require *Small Power* to act per her wishes. Concerning the existence of the alliances might give a probability to the *Small Power* to maneuver between the *Great Powers*.

However, it was difficult to reach because, at that time, *Small Powers* still played a minor role.[63]

According to *Rotshtein*, another possibility for *Small Powers* in the implementation of foreign policy to achieve their objectives was the creation of alliances among *Small Powers*. However, it is also necessary to clarify that the nuances in the bipolar political world of such alliances are useless when attempting to prevent the military intervention of *Great Powers*. A possible positive effect of alliances on *Small Powers* may be a desire to gain time. Consistency between the *Small Powers* can allow them to operate in a situation where the attention of the *Great Powers* concentrates on other issues. In this case, the alliance of the *Small Powers* has an opportunity to change the local status quo successfully. In short 1860, the *Balkan League* could not succeed, as the Union of *Great Powers* was still very effective. However, already in 1912, in the war against the Ottoman Empire, the *League* had reached the desired results. The reason for this was the division of Europe into two blocs and the inability to consult. In addition, if both blocks intervened, the war could grow. However, after the victory over Türkiye, the alliance of *Small Powers* broke up because there was nothing left that could coordinate them.[64] The *Second Balkan War* has already been held between the former members of this alliance.

CHAPTER 2
The New World Order After WWI and WWII: Guarantee for the Existence of Small States

The First World War and Small Powers

Long before the outbreak of World War II in Europe, the growing contradictions between the *Great Powers* already increased. The main reason for this was Germany, which in the mid-1880s began to change its status quo policy and strive to achieve hegemony in Europe. Germany later embarked on colonial expansion. They were already divided among the other *Great Powers*, but Germany was deprived of them. The rapidly growing industry of the country needed raw materials and markets, besides the rapidly growing population in need of new space and the timely provision of food. To solve these problems, it needed a new division of the world in favor of Germany and the German capital. In this way, Germany had to become a hegemon in Europe, which required her to defeat the opposing block of the *Great Powers*, which included Russia, France, and England.

Before the war, there were twenty-six fully functioning countries in Europe. The number of states in Europe fell due to the unification of Germany and Italy. In the period between the second half of the XIX century and early XX century, the new *Small Powers*, Romania (1881), Serbia (1882), Bulgaria (1908), Montenegro (1910), Albania (1912), appeared in the Balkans. These countries gained their independence from the weakening of the Ottoman Empire during the First Balkan War and expanded their territory by winning over this country.[65] Moreover, all formed new states were monarchies, as was required by the status quo formed after the Napoleonic Wars. None of these countries was satisfied with those boundaries formed after the First Balkan War. Additionally, Bulgaria also suffered severe losses during the Second Balkan War. So, this country wanted revenge.[66]

As mentioned earlier, before the beginning of the First World War in 1914, two blocs were formed in Europe: Block Entente, which included Russia, Britain, and France, and the Triple Alliance, initially composed of Germany, Austria, and Italy. However, Italy entered the war in 1915 on the side of the Entente.[67] Virtually all *Great Powers* in Europe were in one of these blocks. Türkiye and Bulgaria joined the German and Austrian block during the war, forming the Quadruple Alliance (or Central Powers unit). All *Small* and *Medium* European powers chose to remain neutral in a possible war without going into any of the blocks. On the other hand, the *Great Powers* did not seek to attract a *Small Power* in their blocks. One of the reasons for this was preserved since the time of the Vienna system about the perception of the world order and the role of *Small Powers* in it. However, with time, some *Small Powers* entered the war, hoping to achieve their national interests.

The formal reason for the war was the murder of the Austrian Archduke Franz Ferdinand on June 28, 1914, in Sarajevo, Bosnia-Herzegovina, annexed by Austria in 1908. Austria accused Serbia, saying that she was behind the assassination of the Archduke, and on July 28, declared war on this state. Serbia wanted to unite all Slavic peoples in the Balkans and create a Greater Serbia. So, she was tolerant of anti-Austrian propaganda. Austria knew a confrontation with Serbia would lead to a war with Russia. However, it was believed that this war would not be soon. Moreover, it was not perceived as a severe risk because Austria had the unconditional support of Germany.[68]

So far, diplomacy failed to prevent a war between Austria and Russia. In response to the announcement of war by Austria to Serbia, Russia began mobilization to support the Serbs. The *Great Powers* have been involved in the Balkan crisis. As a result, Germany declared war on Russia, started military operations against France, and occupied Belgium,[69] despite its neutral status and without a declaration of war. Belgium had a strategic location through the territory of which Germany intended to invade France. Thus, at the time of the war, the neutral status of the *Small Powers* did not become a guarantor of her security. Germany's invasion of Belgium was the cause of her coming against England.[70]

Over time and on the other side, there were new allies, and the theater of war was highly expanded. As mentioned earlier, Türkiye and Bulgaria joined the war on the side of Germany and Austria. In contrast, on the side of the Entente, Italy, Japan, Portugal, Romania, Greece, Montenegro, and even tiny San Marino have joined. On the side of the Entente, 34 states have fought. Mainly being *Small Powers,* these states could not maintain their neutrality and stay away from the war, as one of the main theaters took place near their borders. Albania was the only state that tried to maintain neutrality due to internal instability. However, in 1914 it was occupied by Greece and later divided between Italy, Austria, Bulgaria, and France. The territory of Albania has been proclaimed an autonomous entity obeying the occupiers.

In this case, a *Small Power* in the Balkans had to choose one of the parties to the conflict and take her side. The neutrality of these countries was not possible. As the region was the main center of the fighting, more power tried to bring Greece, Bulgaria, and Romania on their side, promising territorial gains for them. All countries, except Bulgaria, entered the war on the side of the Entente.

Bulgaria was initially declared neutral, but shortly after that, in 1915, it performed on the side of the *Great Powers* of the Central Block. The decision of Bulgaria influenced the successful promotion of Germany in Russia.[71]. Romania declared war in 1916 at the insistence of Russia, but within six months, was occupied by the Central Powers.[72] In the case of Greece, despite the neutral status, France and Britain landed troops in Salonika, which eventually forced this country to declare war against the Central Powers in 1917.[73] Allying with the Entente was a rational choice of small countries, which suggests that they enter the war on the side of the future winners. It was especially true of the Balkan countries, which were expected to expand their territories at the expense of the Ottoman Empire, believing in its division.

Unlike the Balkans, the Nordic countries of Europe have been able to preserve their neutrality in times of war. Again, the main reason for this was that the main theater of the war action was happening in other places in Europe. However, in 1915, it was a critical moment in which these countries could not guarantee their non-participation in the war or could have been occupied by the *Great Powers*. At that time, the plan of creating a connection with Russia was discussed among the Entente states. There were two options: via the Baltic Sea or through the Dardanelles towards Istanbul and the Black Sea. As a result, the second variant was selected, and Scandinavian states could stay neutral.

In turn, Germany, several times, tried to persuade Sweden to join an alliance against Russia, but the Swedish government has expressly waived.[74] Given the close trade relations between Sweden and England, Germany decided that the presence of a neutral Sweden met its interests if this country decided to join the Entente. Moreover, the small countries, which already joined to war, preferred to do it on the side of the Entente.

An important turning point in the war was the entry of the United States into it on the side of the Entente. On April 6, 1917, the United States declared war on Germany, thereby stopping the isolation policy and non-interference in the affairs of Europe, which it followed within the Monroe Doctrine, proclaimed as early as 1823. The reason for breaking the neutrality of the United States was the sinking of American ships by German submarines.[75] Since the United States joined Entente, the preponderance of power has become even more significant.

Closed to the war, in January 1918, the President of the United States, *Woodrow Wilson*, presented to Congress his famous "*14 Points*", a joint declaration of the US goals in the war. The declaration presented the recovery of the international stability program and called for creating the League of Nations as a collective security measure. This declaration formed the basis for forming a new world order in which the US played a vital role for the first time in history.[76]

The First World War ended in 1918, resulting in an enormous loss of human resources. Soon after, the truce was signed with all the countries on the losing side. On September 29, an armistice was signed with Bulgaria; a month later, on October 30, with Türkiye; on November 3, with Austria; and on November 11, the *Treaty of Armistice of Compiègne* was signed with Germany.

Results of the First World War and the New World Order

The First World War radically changed the balance of power in foreign policy, not only in Europe but worldwide. As a result, the war ceased the existence of four empires: Russian, Austro-Hungarian, Ottoman, and German. It began another division of the world in which such Great Powers received the leading award as the US, Britain, and France.

After the signing of the armistice, the winning *Great Powers* began to develop plans for post-war settlement. The start of this process was given with the *Treaty of Versailles*, signed with Germany. Separate peace treaties were signed with Austria (*Treaty of Saint-Germain-en-Laye*), Bulgaria (*Treaty of Neuilly-sur-Seine*), Hungary (*Treaty of Trianon*), and Türkiye (*Treaty of Sevres*). Later, *the Treaty of Sevres* was replaced by the *Treaty of Lausanne*, signed in 1923.

The peaceful post-war settlement in the interests of the victorious powers completed the Washington Conference in 1921-1922. Agreements with Germany and its allies were signed at the Washington Conference, making up the so-called Versailles-Washington system of world order. As a result of compromises and deals, not only did not eliminate the contradictions between the imperialist powers, but they significantly strengthened them.

As mentioned earlier, the basis of the system is laid down on the "*14 points*". One of the main points was to provide the right to self-determination of peoples, members of the former empires. The war resulted in the loss of considerable territories and colonies from defeated countries. Besides, Austria, Germany, Russia, and Türkiye became a republic. In addition, the first socialist republic in the world- the Soviet Union, was set up in Russia in 1922 after the Bolshevik Revolution was held in 1917.

After the war, Austria and Türkiye have become *Small Powers*. Severe losses were Germany and Russia. At the same time, the new *Small Power*s appeared on the map of Europe. After the unification of some territories of the former Austrian Empire and Bulgaria, the Kingdom of Serbs, Croats, and Slovenes (from 1929, referred to as Yugoslavia) emerged. Poland was established in the territory ceded to it by Russia, Germany, and Austria. Belgium was restored, Serbia and Romania expanded their territories.[77] Germany lost 13% of its previous territory. Part of this territory was given to Poland, some lands to

Belgium, and Alsace-Lorraine again transferred to France.[78] Czechoslovakia and Hungary emerged on the territory of the former Austrian Empire. Finland, Latvia, Lithuania, Estonia, Belarus, Ukraine, Azerbaijan, Georgia, and Armenia separated from Russia.[79] The last five republics in 1922 were annexed and became a part of the Soviet Union. Azerbaijan, Georgia, and Armenia joined the Soviet Union as the Transcaucasian Soviet Federative Socialist Republic.[80] *Small Powers* like Belgium, Greece, Romania, and Denmark expanded their territories. In general, at the beginning of the 30s, by implementing the principle of self-determination, the number of states in Europe reached thirty-five.[81]

At that time, there was active cooperation between *Small Powers* to create alliances based on shared objectives, mainly to ensure their safety. Newly appeared on the map of Yugoslavia, Czechoslovakia, and Romania to preserve their acquisitions created the "Little Entente" alliance. Members of this union pledged to support each other to prevent attempts to restore Austria or if Hungary decided to recover their territories. Another form of alliance became the "Baltic Entente," created between Latvia, Estonia, and Poland. This alliance was created to protect against Russia.[82]

Apart from territorial changes, the outcome of the First World War was creating a new world order. In his testimony before the US Congress, President *Wilson* declared his vision of ending the war that would bring a "just and secure peace," not merely "a new balance of power." Wilson's critical statement was also "adjustment of colonial claims based on the principles of self-determination."[83] This principle allowed the emergence of new *Small Powers* and increased their number on the map.

An essential point for *Small Powers* was the issue of their security in the theses. *Wilson* became last among the "*14 points*". According to this point: "A general association of nations must be formed under specific covenants to afford mutual guarantees of political independence and territorial integrity to great and small states alike." This item was provided for the establishment of an international organization for collective security and the prevention of further wars. For the first time in history, an attempt was made to establish an international mechanism for protecting the state, primarily the *Small Powers*. Thus, the League of Nations was established in 1919 - an organization that was aimed at maintaining the existing world order to prevent the destabilization of the international system at the behest of one of its actors by maintaining peace in Europe.[84] *Wilson* suggested that maintaining stability through collective security differs from the traditional European approach based on forming alliances and balancing power between the *Great Powers*. The system was established again, but this time institutionally.[85]

The difference of the new system was that it had to be done considering the interests of others (which means not only the *Great Powers*). *Kissinger* believes that throughout the XIX century, England and Austria tried to prevent the collapse of the Ottoman Empire because they believed that if the number of the *Small Powers* increased, the ethnic rivalry would rise. In addition, the weak states would be the reason for the assault on the part of the *Great Powers*. According to England and Austria, the *Small Powers* had to subordinate their national desires. In this connection, to maintain balance, France was not allowed the occupancy of the French-speaking Wallon part of Belgium, and Germany did not complete the union with Austria.[86]

After the establishment of the League of Nations, all countries and members of this organization have had their representatives in the Assembly, where each country had one vote. Thus, it established legal parity and equality between all the world's independent countries. The Assembly has broad authority that covers the entire scope of activities of the League. Paragraph 3 of this organization's Charter states that: the Assembly may consider "any matter within the scope of authority of the League or affecting the issues of peace around the world."

At the time of the League of Nations, the number of founder states was 44 members. In general, during the period of existence of this organization, the total number of members of the League of Nations came up to 60 states. All members of the League of Nations agreed to "respect and preserve" the territorial integrity of all members within the principles that had been formed after the First World War.[87]

Although President *Wilson* was the author of the idea of creating this organization, and the United States was its founder, this country has not ratified the statute of the League and returned to its traditional isolationism in foreign relations policy.[88]

The main body of the organization was the Council of the League, which consisted of four permanent (Britain, France, Italy, and Japan, and after joining the League, Germany, and the Soviet Union) and four temporary members, whom the Assembly elected. Availability of temporary seats in the Council of the League allowed by *Small Powers* involved in the work of this organ.[89] The number of members of the Council was constantly fluctuating. By 1940, the number of countries in its membership has reached 14.

This condition also radically differed from the system of Vienna, where *Small Powers* participated fully ruled out. The League of Nations guaranteed them equal status, as well as an arena where they could discuss their problems.[90]

Although the participation of *Small Powers* was limited in time, and the value of their participation was not decisive but somewhat conciliatory, it is a fact that the international system of relations formed since the Peace of Westphalia has continued to evolve.

The main measures of the collective security organization statute were set out in the 16th paragraph of the Covenant of the League of Nations. The new system, with a view to the preservation of peace, involves the use of some measures, such as measures to reduce and limitation of arms, the application of economic and military sanctions, the League's members' collective appearances against the aggressor.[91]

However, the League of Nations did not have its military forces and could not act without the unanimous consent of the Council. The League of Nations generally failed to resolve several critical international problems during its activity. Most of the League of Nations activities addressed the issue of general disarmament.

However, the use of these measures for political reasons has yet to be fully realized. Several processes taking place in the international arena prevented the League of Nations from realizing the objectives for which it was created entirely. Without a doubt, one of the most critical factors impacting the success of the Nation League, as mentioned above, is a return to the United States policy of isolationism. This *Great Power* again departed from participation in world politics as it was after the declaration of the Monroe Doctrine. Congress did not support the intentions of their president; *Wilson's* principles were implemented without US participation. As a result, the League of Nations became a platform that did not ensure collective security, and more tried to *balance powers* in Europe. In 1925, out of 55 members of this organization - 26 were in Europe, and 48 were the nations with predominantly Western heritage.[92]

At the same time, Europe's brewing revisionism: countries unsatisfied with the outcome of the *Treaty of Versailles* wanted to change the existing status quo. Thus, radical forces have emerged in Germany, Italy, and Japan. The Bolshevik Soviet Union was also looking to change the status quo. On the other hand, the other two *Great Powers*, Britain, and France, the main supporters of the preservation of formed after the First World War status quo, needed more time to be ready to take decisive action on the interests of *Small Powers*. Both countries have preferred appeasement, a policy of avoiding a direct conflict, through concessions to the aggressor, in minor to their national interests and issues.

As a result, the corridors of the League of Nations were not the primary site of action of world politics formation. Its main actors- were supporters of changing the status quo, or it was passively defended, as the small states' diligence needed more to achieve the desired and guaranteed the new organization's objectives.

Despite the legal possibility of cooperation with *Great Powers*, *Small Powers* were once again targeting the developing processes in the international arena. In this case, England and France hoped that the revisionist ambitions would be limited due to the small states. The situation was different; concessions only fueled the aggressors.

Meanwhile, the position of the League of Nations increasingly weakened. 1932 Germany was excluded from the organization; in 1939, the same happened with the USSR because of the war against Finland. As a result, Germany and the Soviet Union began to actively cooperate and help each other to overcome economic and somehow political isolation. Also, militarist Japan (1933) and fascist Italy (1937) withdrew from the League of Nations. The League of Nations failed to prevent Japan's occupation of Manchuria in 1931, and in 1935, Italy of Abyssinia.[93] League of Nations' actions could have been more effective. After the invasion of Japan in Manchuria, the League of Nations Council voted on a resolution that was proposed to the country in three weeks to withdraw its forces. As a Council of the League member with the right of veto, Japan voted against it, so the resolution was not adopted.[94] Regarding Italy, the Assembly of the League of Nations recognized the aggressor, and its 50 votes to four, on October 7, 1935, decided to apply economic sanctions to Italy. However, even they had their limitations: the sanctions were not fallen oil, iron ore, and England refused to close the Suez Canal.[95]

The Second World War and Small Powers

Soon, Germany has been actively violating the *Versailles Treaty*. She sent troops into the demilitarized Rhineland. Further 1936, in conjunction with Italy, it started aggression against the Spanish Republic and, in 1938, held the Anschluss of Austria. In 1938 it annexed the Sudetenland belonging to Czechoslovakia.[96] It occurred with the consent of England and France: Czechoslovakia`s opinion did not consider by the *Great Powers*. In 1939, Germany, in violation of the agreement, seized other parts. Over the annexed territories German Protectorate of Bohemia and Moravia was declared. The rest of the Czech Republic was divided between Hungary and Poland. Only Slovakia remained on the map, which also was under the protectorate of Germany.[97] The process of redistribution of the map of Europe has intensively started.

Then Germany filed a claim against Poland. At the initial stage, it was a requirement for the extraterritorial overland road to East Prussia and then to hold a referendum on the accessories "Polish Corridor." After Britain and France promised military support and guarantees for the protection of independence to Poland, it became clear that the war between these two *Great Powers* with Germany and these countries was inevitable. After September 1,

Germany invaded Poland, Britain and France declared war on her, and the Second World War began. In just six weeks, Germany occupied France. [98] With the German occupation of Poland, the eastern part of this country was annexed by the Soviet Union. The line of demarcation between German and Soviet troops was established.

The Second World War again turned *Small Powers* into objects of the international system. The collective security system completely collapsed: even security guarantees to Poland by Britain and France were not granted in the framework of this organization. Romania, Greece, and Türkiye received the same type of direct guarantees. However, even these guarantees have not prevented the occupation of the first two countries. Only Türkiye has been able to maintain the integrity of its borders while retaining neutrality. The country has avoided involvement in the war thanks to the skillful maneuvering between the *Great Powers*: The Soviet Union, Germany, England, and France. As a result, each stakeholder failed to attract Türkiye to their side. As a result, every *Great Power* satisfied with Türkiye`s carried out policy of neutrality.[99]

Later, Germany captured Denmark and Norway, despite their neutral status. These countries did not have the opportunity to manipulate Türkiye. Norway was in the interests of Germany and the Allies. However, England's interests concerning that country were negligible compared to Germany's. As a result of an incorrect assessment of its capability, Norway was occupied by Germany.[100]

In turn, the British and French troops occupied the Danish overseas possessions: Iceland, Greenland, and the Faroe Islands. Next, Germany invades Belgium, the Netherlands, and Luxembourg.[101] In 1940, between Germany, Italy, and Japan, the Tripartite Pact was created, the Axis, which included delineating zones of influence in establishing a new world order and military mutual aid. By occupation and coercion, these countries have been able to win over several countries in different regions of the world. [102] Some *Small Powers*, such as Hungary, Romania, and Slovakia by that same year, Bulgaria, and Yugoslavia 1941 joined this Pact. However, after the revolution in Yugoslavia, the new government refused to join the Pact and concluded a treaty of friendship with the Soviet Union. As a result, Germany invaded Yugoslavia. Further, together with Italy, she occupied Greece.

In turn, in 1939, the Soviet Union invaded Finland. The primary purpose was to create a buffer zone for Leningrad. During this operation, the Soviet Union was expelled from the League of Nations,[103] while not all countries voted in favor of the exception, Sweden, Denmark, and Norway were among them. As a result of the war, the border of the USSR was moved to the northeast within the Finnish territory. Like many other *Small Powers*, Finland could not prevent participation in the war based solely on its neutral status. Finland needed more strategic value to offer in the context of its neutrality. At the same time, Finland was forced to fight with the Soviet Union and Germany. At the same time, Finland couldn't benefit from threatening the Soviet Union and Germany in that it could act on the side of one of them against the other.[104]

After Finland, the Soviet Union occupied the Baltic countries of Latvia, Lithuania, and Estonia. After entering Soviet troops there, these countries became a part of the USSR, on the rights of the union republics. In 1940, the Soviet Union demanded the return of Bessarabia from Romania, which was not counting on the assistance of the League of Nations. So, Romania accepted this demand. After the transfer of Bessarabia to the Soviet Union, the Moldavian Soviet Socialist Republic was established on its territory.

In 1941 Germany and the Soviet Union faced a war with each other directly. This year, German troops invaded the Soviet Union, taking in the short-term large areas.[105] In the same year, the United States entered the war after its naval base at Pearl Harbor was attacked by the air forces of Japan. The theater of war has taken the whole world.[106]

Immediately after the German invasion of the USSR, representatives of Great Britain and the United States expressed their support for the Soviet Union and began to provide economic assistance.[107] Important events took 1 January 1942, when the Washington representatives of the USSR, the US, Britain, and China signed the Declaration of the United Nations, marking the beginning of the antifascist coalition. Later, it was joined by 22 other countries.[108]

After *the Battle of Stalingrad* on November 19, 1942, the Soviet Army went to the offensive, inflicting a heavy defeat on the German troops. It was a turning point in the war between the USSR and Germany in 1943; the Soviet Army had already launched a counter-offensive on all fronts. In the first half of 1944, military operations were taking place on the border of the Soviet Union, after which the Soviet army entered the territory of Romania. Meanwhile 1943, Britain possessed all of the Mediterranean Sea, and on July 10, 1943, the US and British armies landed in Sicily.

In November 1943, in Tehran, the Allies: leaders of the United States, Great Britain, and the Soviet Union, held a conference to agree on the further conduct of the war plans. The main topic was the opening of a second front in Western Europe.[109] In addition, the parties talked about the new order that had developed in Europe after the war. In particular, it was agreed that in exchange for the Polish territories ceded to the Soviet Union, German territories would be transferred to the East and included in Poland. Also, US President Roosevelt presented the American point of view at the conference concerning the future establishment of an international security organization on the United Nations principles.

In June 1944, a second front opened in Normandy, freed France and Belgium, and began the invasion of Germany. Meanwhile, with the advent of the Soviet Army, in turn, surrendered Romania, Bulgaria, and Hungary. As a result, German troops had to leave Yugoslavia and Greece. In April 1945, an offensive began in Berlin. On the night of 8 to 9 May, the German High Command signed the act of unconditional surrender of all Nazi Germany. The war in Europe was over. Germany was divided into four occupation zones: The Soviet, American, British, and French.[110]

In February 1945, a regular meeting of allies was hosted in Yalta. There was no doubt about victory in the war. The meeting was devoted to the establishment of the post-war world order. It discussed the future of European borders. Again, it was agreed on the future fate of Poland.[111] In addition, realizing the idea became incarnate in establishing the United Nations. It was agreed that the framework of UN activities in dealing with critical issues of peace and international security would be based on the principle of unanimity of the Great Powers - the permanent members of the Security Council with veto power. It was also decided to start work on the Charter of the Organization, which was supposed to happen at the San Francisco Conference in April 1945.

New World Order and the Cold War

One of the primary outcomes of the Second World War was the establishment of the United Nations based on the anti-fascist coalition formed during the war to prevent future world wars. With the development of the new organization's Charter, on 26 June 1945 in San Francisco, fifty states put their signatures under the document and became its founders. The United Nations replaced the League of Nations, which ceased to exist. In general, as well as the League of Nations, a new organization was also founded on the principle of collective security, which was to ensure the preservation of international peace and prevent any possible aggressive actions of any of the states.[112]

As in the case of the League of Nations, all countries become a member of the General Assembly, and the Security Council has taken the role of the Council.[113] This body has fifteen members, five of whom are permanent (the United States, the Soviet Union, China, Britain, and France) and have the right to veto decisions. The remaining members are elected for a term of two years, which makes it possible for *Small Powers* to participate in the work of this body. Theoretically, these countries can also influence the decision since its adoption requires nine votes (including all the permanent members) of the fifteen.

The UN has become the symbol and guarantor of the formal post-war world order, authoritative and sometimes quite compelling organization in resolving inter-state problems. At the same time, the winners prefer to solve challenging questions of their relationship through bilateral negotiations outside the framework of the UN. The UN has also failed to prevent the war that the US and the Soviet Union were in the following decades.

Although England and France are permanent members of the UN Security Council, which indirectly confirms their status of *Great Power*, according to the war results, Europe is relegated to the role in global politics for the first time. Britain and France, despite the victory, were significantly weakened. European countries were now unable to contain the vast colonial empire. The process of anti-colonial movements in Africa and Asia led to a process of decolonization. The Soviet Union and the US have become the main powers in the world. In the following years, world politics would be defined by these two *Super Powers*.

After the war, in 1946, the ideological confrontation between these two countries, known as the Cold War, began. This confrontation strengthens that both countries have become owners of weapons of mass destruction: nuclear weapons, and formed a new bipolar international system with two main actors.

The confrontation between these two countries also affected the UN collective security system. As permanent Security Council members with veto power, these countries could sabotage the decisions of the body and, throughout the Cold War, constantly voted against each other. As a result, for the entire period of confrontation in the Cold War, the collective security mechanism was used only twice, during the conflicts in Korea (1950) and Kuwait (1990). Moreover, both times, the decision was possible under exceptional conditions. So, during the vote on the Korean problem, the Soviet Union did not participate in the Security Council meeting due to her boycotting the replacement of China with Taiwan. However, the absence of the Soviet Union did not mean using the right of veto, so the decision on Korea was made. Realizing this, the Soviet Union representative returned, took its place in the Security Council, and never again left it. About Iraq's invasion of Kuwait in 1990, as a result of a thaw in relations between the US and the USSR, as well as the deterioration of the situation in the country, the Soviet Union was not able to resist the development of events in the international arena and supported the operation against Iraq.[114]

Even though the work of the UN Security Council has been limited due to the confrontation during the Cold War, in contrast to the system formed in the period between the two world wars, the new one was able to achieve important objectives, namely, to ensure the existence of actors in the international system – states. Since the creation of the United Nations, neither country in the world has disappeared from the world map because of the armed attack of another country. The termination of states occurred only at the expense of voluntary separation and the emergence of newly independent states or by voluntary unification. By the way, the formation process of new states has also been limited. Thus, according to the UN Charter, the right to self-determination and independence was recognized only for colonial territories, the list of which has been clearly defined. Any other form of self-determination, but the two, voiced above, are not legal.

The first attempt at preserving the state's existence was made when the League of Nations was created, and collective security was formed to fight the aggressor. However, as shown by events, many recognized *that Small Powers* could not maintain their independence and, throughout history, were absorbed by the more powerful states. Among the countries that lost their independence in 1920-21, there were countries such as Azerbaijan, Georgia, and Armenia. These countries, in turn, were occupied by the Red Army and became part of the Soviet Union.

Even though the new world order ensured the continuation of the existence of every existing state, the new system did not guarantee another central tenet: territorial integrity of the state. Thus, even though the threat to the state's existence disappeared after 1945, primarily for *Small Powers,* their territorial integrity is still a challenge. Priorities have changed in the national interests and foreign policy of *Small States*. If *Small Power* faces a threat to its territory, its entire resource is used to prevent this threat or restore its territorial integrity.

The redistribution of territories was carried out immediately after the Second World War. Romania passed Transylvania, which had previously been part of Hungary. In turn, the transfer of such Romanian territories as Bessarabia and Northern Bukovina to the Soviet Union and Southern Dobrudja to Bulgaria was approved. Some small territorial gains had Czechoslovakia. Lithuania, Latvia, and Estonia disappeared from the world map which, as has been said before, became part of the Soviet Union.[115] A significant development of that time was the creation of socialist regimes in several countries, which after the war, were under the control of the Soviet army. Communist regimes came to power in Czechoslovakia, Hungary, Poland, Romania, East Germany, and Bulgaria. In addition to these countries, communist leaders, who led a guerrilla war against Nazi Germany, came to power in Albania and Yugoslavia.[116] In order to prevent the spread of communism in Europe, the United States pursued an active policy. She gave Western European countries economic aid under *the Marshall Plan* and Greece and Türkiye using *Trumann Pact*. These programs have contributed to the fact that some countries averted the threat of communist regimes coming to power. Also, it began to finalize form the division of Europe.[117]

During this period, Europe was divided into two opposing camps. In Eastern Europe, occupied by Soviet troops, there were established socialist regimes; the capitalist countries represented another camp. Both units were expected to achieve economic and political domination and military superiority and take a leading position in the world.[118] Relations between the two blocs had deteriorated sharply. Both units were represented by military alliances, the North Atlantic Treaty Organization (NATO) and the Warsaw Pact, the members of which were primarily European countries. Western military alliance was established in 1949, which became a collective institution of containment against the Soviet Union and its allies. At the initial stage, the members of NATO were the United States, Canada, England, and France, as well as small European countries such as Denmark, Iceland, Norway, Italy, Portugal, and the countries of Benelux. 1951 Türkiye and Greece joined the alliance, and in 1945, West Germany.[119] In turn, the East European Mutual Assistance Treaty, or the Warsaw Pact that, was established in 1955, was included the Soviet Union, Poland, Romania, Czechoslovakia, Hungary, Bulgaria, Albania, and the German Democratic Republic, an occasion then was the entry of West Germany in NATO.[120]

In 1951, Europe began a phased economic integration process based on the steel and coal resources of the opposing two World War countries - France and Germany. Given the painful experience, these two countries concluded that the confrontation was a threat of mutual destruction, and so instead of this made the first steps towards European integration. At an early stage, in addition to these two states, Italy, as well as three small states: the Netherlands, Belgium, and Luxembourg (which were established in 1947 by a customs union, Benelux), joined in this process. Over time, the number of participants in this integration process has increased, and the degree of deepening cooperation- expanded. Parallel with all of these developments, a Council of Europe was created.[121]

In turn, the socialist countries established the Council for Mutual Economic Assistance (COMECON), which included such Eastern European countries as Bulgaria, Hungary, East Germany, Poland, Romania, the USSR, and Czechoslovakia.[122]

The *Small Powers* were part of the confrontation between the *Super Powers*. The United States and the Soviet Union dictated policies that were to follow the Western and Eastern blocs, the leaders of which were.[123] The struggle of contradictions between the two models of the state system continued until the collapse of the Soviet Union and the *Eastern Bloc*. At the same time, the Cold War was not a direct conflict between the two *Super Powers* but a proxy war in which confrontations took place on the territory of third countries. The European countries were no exception. Thus, the United States has placed nuclear weapons on the Allies' territory within the containment policy. In this case, the first blows (including nuclear) from a possible outbreak of war with the Soviet Union were to receive NATO European allies. At the same time, the territory of the US itself would remain untouched. It was not a desired situation continued until 1957 when the Soviet Union produced the first artificial satellite into orbit.[124] In this way, the Soviet Union received the intercontinental ballistic missiles (ICBM) carrying nuclear warheads that could reach US territory. Thus, the US strategy toward the Soviet Union has been changed.[125] Over time, England (in 1952) and France (1960) also became the owners of nuclear weapons, which seriously altered the balance of power in Europe and in deterrence strategy.[126]

In turn, the Warsaw Pact protected members in the event of aggression against one of them and was based on the principle of non-interference in internal affairs. However, as subsequent events showed, the Soviet Union maintained the right to interfere in the internal affairs of the countries that made up the Socialist Bloc, if they became a threat to the state regime.[127] Thus, the first time the troops of the Soviet Union invaded Hungary in 1956 after there were mass protests against the socialist leadership.[128] Although Hungary has addressed a protest to the UN, the international community's response has been sluggish. Apart from the fact that the Soviet Union could prevent any not desired for themselves development using the veto in the UN Security Council, the international community's attention was directed to the conflict in the Suez Canal. At that time, Britain, France, and Israel invaded Egypt, and the United States' attention focused on the following developments. Thus, the revolt in Hungary was crushed by Soviet troops.[129]

In 1968, the Soviet Union announced a new foreign policy strategy concerning the Socialist Bloc countries: *the Brezhnev Doctrine* or Doctrine of limited sovereignty, according to which the Soviet Union retained the right to intervene in the internal affairs of these countries to ensure the stability of their political course based on the principles of socialism. Thus, the sovereignty of the Socialist *Small Powers* was limited in favor of the guarantee of conservation in these countries, the current regime. It was within this doctrine in August 1968 when Soviet troops invaded Czechoslovakia after the suspension of the reforms that started with the Prague Spring.[130]

It is worth noting that the existence of two conflicting *Super Powers* and formed blocks did not mean that the policy of *Small Powers* only limited the opportunity to participate in Europe in one of the camps and to follow the rules that its leaders determined: the US and the Soviet Union. During the Cold War in Europe, there were also *Small Powers* that were not included in any of the blocks and carried out a policy of neutrality: these were Switzerland, Sweden, Finland, Austria, and Norway. In addition, in 1961, Non-Alignment Movement was created, caused by a policy of non-participation of *Small Powers* in military blocs, particularly NATO and the Warsaw Pact. The difference between neutral countries and movement members was that, unlike the first, they carried out an active foreign policy to consolidate their capacity to achieve the desired results. They have learned to use their *Super Powers* against each other in order to obtain the desired dividends.[131] Formation of the Non-Alignment Movement became possible in the 1960s after accelerating the process of decolonization, and as a result of it on the world map, in Africa and Asia, many newly independent states established.[132] These countries have yet to seek to be part of any of the blocks and to be able to use the dividends from maneuvering between them. According to *Kaplan*, such a system is referred to as the loose bipolar system, in which, along with the existence of the two *Great Powers* and their dependent blocks, several states can carry out a relatively independent policy and not be included in any of the presented these *Super Powers* blocks.

One of the active participants and the leader of the movement was Yugoslavia. As a socialist country, Yugoslavia was not a member of the Warsaw Pact or COMECON and preferred to pursue its independent policy. It is symbolic that the movement itself was created at the Belgrade Conference. The members of this unit became known as the Third World, distinguishing them from the West, referred to as the First World and the Second World, representing the Socialist Block. Overall Non-Alignment Movement tried to act as a single block in the UN General Assembly meetings, expected to achieve the developed countries facilitate the raising of the economies of former colonies. However, in general, these steps could have had the desired effect.

An interesting development happened in 1973, when the Organization of the Petroleum Exporting Countries (OPEC), where the major oil producers united and achieved consolidation, dramatically increased the price of oil, using this resource for the political and economic purposes of member states. Partly, they have achieved their goals concerning the Western countries.[133]

The confrontation between the two blocs led to a severe depletion of resources on both sides. A particularly negative impact was on the Soviet Union. The arms race demanded a significant investment, but the primary income of the Soviet Union was based on the sale of oil. However, in the 80s, the price of oil fell sharply, which also led to a reduction in the income of the Soviet Union. In addition to 1983, US President Ronald Reagan declared a Strategic Defense Initiative. The main objective of this initiative was to develop a missile defense system that excludes or limits the possibility of loss of land and sea targets from space. In other words, it was assumed that a missile "shield" to cover the United States from the Soviet ballistic missiles reliably. In turn, the Soviet Union could not respond to new challenges proposed by the United States; it was necessary to look for new ways to break the deadlock.

Attempts to change the situation and to carry out structural reforms have been made since 1985 by the coming to power in the Soviet Union, a new leader Mikhail Gorbachev. His adjustment policies and the acceleration assumed political and economic reforms in the country. Despite the reformation attempts, it failed to keep the system in general and the country in particular. The Socialist Bloc gradually began to fade.

At the same time, Gorbachev sought rapprochement with the opponents in the international arena, making unprecedented steps in this direction. In December 1989, at the summit on the island of Malta, Presidents of the USSR and the United States, Gorbachev, and Bush, officially announced the end of the Cold War. It has also been given to start the unification of Germany and the change of regimes in Eastern Europe.

The communist governments in Eastern Europe lost the support of the Soviet Union and began to give way to democratic regimes. The Warsaw Pact formally ceased to be effective on July 1, 1991. Soon, in December 1991, the Soviet Union collapsed, burdened by political and economic crises and social and international problems.

CHAPTER 3
The Foreign Policy of the Small Powers after the Collapse of the Eastern Block and Formation of the Unipolar World: How to Act?

New Developments after the Cold War

The collapse of the Eastern Bloc and the Soviet Union marked the beginning of a new era in the international arena. The *Western Block*, which possessed liberal values, such as multi-party democracy and a market economy, has announced the unconditional victory over the *Socialist Bloc*. The world is rapidly begun to turn from a bipolar into a unipolar: only one *Super Power*- the US, remained on the planet.

In turn, all the institutions of the *Eastern Bloc* ceased to exist: Warsaw Treaty Organization was collapsed, COMECON was also ceased to exist. Western institutions such as NATO and the European Communities began to form new formats per the new realities that emerged after the demise of the Eastern Bloc. The main mission of NATO again began to take a new shape as its main opponent was gone.[134]. European integration reached a new level after the European Union (EU) was established in 1992. This year, member countries have completed creating a common market by ensuring the free movement of people, goods, services, and capital. At that time, the Union was represented by twelve states. In 1995, the EU enlarged when the three neutral *Small Powers* in Europe: Austria, Finland, and Sweden, joined the organization, and the number of members reached fifteen.[135] It should be noted that the reason for the attractiveness of membership in the EU is related to the voluntary wish of the candidates who want to enter into this structure. Since this structure has a supranational character and demands the delegation of sovereign rights of member states, the candidates need to determine whether the EU is the structure that will allow realizing their national interests. In short, not all countries feel that the EU is such a structure. For example, Norway, which applied together with Austria, Finland, and Sweden for membership, lately, because of the referendum results, refused to join this organization.[136] However, such action in Norway is still the exception to the rule.

These changes severely impacted the further development of the situation in Europe. It is worth noting that NATO and the EU will play a key role in varying degrees of promoting and supporting the *Socialist Bloc* countries in transition.

The collapse of the *Eastern Bloc* was marked by economic collapse, political instability, and, in some places, territorial and ethnic conflicts. All the countries of the former *Eastern Bloc* and the new states that emerged after the collapse of Yugoslavia and the Soviet Union were faced with the task as soon as possible to transition to new political, economic, and social relations. It would not be effortless to achieve the desired objectives independently. It was especially true for the countries that gained independence after the collapse of the *Socialist Bloc*.

The EU was the most attractive development model and possible integration for countries in transition, which offers ample opportunities for both countries and their citizens. At the same time, the EU has provided the opportunity for the *Small Powers*, who become members of the Union and use this platform to realize their interests. It is worth noting that the differences between the *Great Powers* and *Small Powers* within the EU declined. It was achieved through the mechanisms created by the founding Treaties: namely, by the system which set weighted votes in the Council, equal representation in the Commission, and the presidency, which provides via the rotation system, where each state, for six months, became the head of this organization.[137] The *Small Powers* in the *EU* after the Cold War have gotten more opportunities to maneuver in determining their foreign policy. An important cause of greater freedom for maneuvering was the regulation of interstate relations utilizing laws and the *EU* institutions, which radically changed the traditional issues of the security of *Small States*. After joining the *EU*, the *Small Powers* gain positions, which resolve the dilemma between the delegation of sovereign rights and opportunities for more effective implementation of national interests.

Therefore, for all the countries of the former *Eastern Bloc*, the priority was the integration into *NATO* and the *EU*. This desire also had a symbolic meaning: breaking all ties with the past. That is why all countries of the former *Socialist Bloc* have become members of the *North Atlantic Cooperation Council* (*NACC*), created on 20 December 1991, as a forum for dialogue and cooperation with *NATO*'s former Warsaw Pact adversaries. The primary purpose of this structure was to eliminate mistrust between *NATO* and the former Warsaw Pact member states. In 1997 the name of the structure was changed to the *Euro-Atlantic Partnership Council*.[138] In 1994, *NATO* proposed a new *Partnership for Peace* (*PfP*) program. This initiative was proposed in January 1994, with the main objective of providing stability and security in Europe. The *PfP* program acknowledged principles of self-defense cooperation, development of dialogue, and cooperation between *NATO* and partner countries.[139] As in the case of cooperation under the *NACC*, all the countries of the former *Soviet Bloc* were also involved in the PfP program. All these partner countries were seen this initiative as a step for further integration into the organization. However, things were somewhat different.

Despite the landslide victory of Western values and the formation of a unipolar world, the West's influence and effect of the reform process were not uniform for all countries of the former *Eastern Bloc*. So, while some countries provided various assistance in implementing political and economic reforms, others have received limited support. To this end, they had both objective and subjective reasons. However, this approach has had different results and consequences for those countries. It is worth noting that the most successful reforms were those countries that, besides assistance, promised full membership in *NATO* and the *EU*. *NATO* and the *EU* were not prepared to carry out large-scale integration processes for all countries that appeared on the map after the collapse of the *Eastern Bloc*. The approach to these countries was different, with the result that seriously affected the further fate of these states and the formation of their foreign policy. In short, the support by the US and the Western institutions to the former *Eastern Bloc* countries during the transition period was divided into three groups.

Relations of NATO and the EU with the Central and Eastern Europe

The *Small Powers* of Central and Eastern Europe, which were independent states at the time of the existence of the *Eastern Bloc*, received full and unconditional support from the *West*. So, NATO and the EU provided a complete program during the transition period for the former Eastern Bloc countries, also known as the Central and Eastern European Countries (*CEEC*). In short, both organizations offered the *CEEC* full membership based on the success of political and economic reforms. This group included such states as Poland, the Czech Republic, Slovakia, Hungary, Romania, and Bulgaria. In addition to them, the former Yugoslav Republic of Slovenia and the former Soviet Baltic republics - Lithuania, Latvia, and Estonia were included in this group.

It is worth noting that the relationship between the *West* and the *Small States* of the *Eastern Bloc* began to develop only in the late 80s when the Soviet Union began to improve relations with the West. Before this, the Soviet Union did not recognize the European Communities and had no relationship with them. Consequently, the opportunity for forming relations has also been deprived for the satellite countries of this *Great Power*. At that time, these countries were members of *COMECON*. When the situation started to change, Hungary was the first country from the Eastern Block with which the European Communities signed *Trade and Cooperation Treaty*. Later, a similar agreement was also signed by Poland, in December 1989, by the Soviet Union, in April 1990, Czechoslovakia and Bulgaria, in November 1990, and Romania in March 1991.[140] To facilitate the development of reforms in these countries, the *EU* has designed a *PHARE* program (*Poland and Hungary: Assistance for Restructuring their Economies Program*), which aimed to provide economic assistance to Poland and Hungary, and later, other *CEEC* countries have also joined. At the initial stage of the development, the *PHARE* Program was proposed as financial and technical assistance to the transformation process to democracy and the market economy of the participating states. Over time, this mechanism gained significant importance in encouraging the states to apply for full membership in the *EU*. In other words, it became a significant subject in exercising incentive reforms.

The *PHARE* Program was a primarily economic mechanism. However, the *EU* considered that more than economic measures would be needed to support reforms in these *Small States* of the former *Eastern Bloc*. In addition, in the case of the failure of reforms in these countries, political and economic instability could also threaten the *EU* countries. The situation could become complicated if the instability covers several countries.[141] In addition, governments of these countries declared that their foreign policy priorities included integration with *NATO* and the *EU*, and if these countries had no prospect of membership in the medium term, this could lead to a destabilization of the situation.[142] Therefore, the *EU* was interested in the successful completion of the reforms. In this connection, due to the successful completion of the transition period, these countries were invited to membership in the *EU*.

Fidelity to this assumption and to achieve stability in the region by the chosen strategy can consider the example of the dissolution of Czechoslovakia into two new states: the Czech Republic and Slovakia, which passed without consequences and did not lead to any significant conflict. Two of these new countries hoped that they would be provided with all opportunities afforded by integration with the *EU*, but the West would only approve this if the collapse would not lead to conflict.[143]

It should be noted that for these countries, one of the conditions for membership in the *EU* was the entry into *NATO*. Thus, for these countries, joining *NATO* and the *EU* occurred in parallel. For the first time in the enlargement process, the *EU* developed a mechanism by which the countries of the former *Socialist Bloc* before the *EU* accession, as a prerequisite, shall receive *NATO* membership. In other words, before the accession to the *EU*, the former *Eastern Bloc* countries were to meet all the requirements of *NATO* and join the organization. For example, in 1997, the European Commission published a report titled *Agenda 2000,* which examined the level of implementation of the requirements from the candidate countries in the accession period. According to the document, the states that achieved the most tremendous success in implementing reforms among the candidate countries were Poland, Hungary, the Czech Republic, Estonia, and Slovenia. Curiously, the report was published two weeks after Poland, Hungary, and the Czech Republic were officially invited for full membership in *NATO*.[144] It can also explain why at that time, *NATO* invited Slovenia and Estonia for full membership. Slovenia was a former Yugoslav republic where a major conflict broke out. As for Estonia, it was a former Soviet republic, and the process of integration was carried out gradually so as not to irritate Russia. In addition, these countries were supported by some *EU* member states. For example, their support for Slovenia's membership in the *EU* provided Italy and Austria, at the time, as the Nordic countries supported Estonia.

At the same time, *NATO* and the *EU* considered the integration with these countries, as the policy of their return to Europe, after nearly half a century of being in a separate block. It was considered that these countries wanted to exert their rights to "*Return to Europe*," becoming once more part of Western institutions. The new elites of these countries were also supporters of the new "modernization" of these countries, based on the Western model, which would replace the failed communist model of development.[145]

Membership for these countries to *NATO* was important also because its members preserved the only *Super Power* in the world- the United States. Thus, these countries were also allowed closer cooperation in the framework of collective security with this country and confirmed the final out of the orbit of influence of Russia. Overall, Russia was still viewed as a threat to countries in the region, and the *EU* alone would not be able to ensure their security and thus, realize their plans within the framework of a standard foreign policy.[146]

As a result of the decision taken at the Copenhagen Summit held on 22 June 1993, the integration process of *CEEC* into *EU* states began. Conditional integration policy towards *CEEC* has become a major tool in promoting the implementation of reforms.[147] A *Pre-Integration Strategy* towards the states was adopted in 1994. This strategy included three main elements. The legal framework strategy was based on the European Treaties. The economic basis was the *PHARE* program, which provided the necessary financial and technical aid. The *PHARE* Program was the basis for the necessary reforms and, since 1997, has become the primary tool for *the Pre-Integration Strategy*. The *PHARE* Program provided finance for forming the necessary institutions in these countries and was used for investment. National Programs for each of these countries were developed as part of the Pre- Integration Strategy. The candidate countries should adapt to the *EU acquis communautaire*.[148] Since countries that provided this assistance were aware that the outcome of the reforms carried out, they would become members of the *EU,* and they were provided with financial assistance during the difficult economic situation. Reforms in these countries were held very successful.

The third base was presented in the form of a "structural dialogue" forum, which was to bring together both member and candidate states. The main objective of the *Pre-Integration Strategy* was to prepare the *CEEC* for the conditions of work in the framework of the common market within the *EU*.

It is worth noting that the *Pre-Integration Strategy* in the previous enlargement of the *EU* has never been developed. However, it held the *EU* countries' acceptance for the first time, which had a different political and economic system. These countries would have to complete the transition to forming democratic institutions and a market economy as soon as possible. As a result of the implementation of the pre-integration process, it was signed by the European Treaties with all countries that completed the membership process. As can be seen, all subsequent actions and their final results were clearly defined, and the candidate countries for full membership in the *EU* knew what to expect based on large-scale and not widespread reforms. In general, in the process, the former *Eastern Bloc* countries were the subject of the programs developed for them on the part of *NATO* and the *EU*. One side has advanced relatively stringent requirements in the relationship between the parties, while the other has rigorous and successful implementation. Candidate countries were not only adopting the *EU acquis communautaire* in the national legislation, but they also had to meet the political and economic objectives of the *EU*.

The candidate countries were ready to follow these requirements as these countries understood that the result of the implementation of these requirements was the entire membership that met their interests and eventually would allow these *Small Powers* to increase their capacity and strengthen their position in the international arena, getting an opportunity to speak with one voice within *NATO* and the *EU*. As a result, their expectations were destined to happen. In 2002, the *EU* completed the negotiations with candidate countries, except Bulgaria and Romania. On April 16, 2003, Accession Treaties were signed with these states. On May 1, 2004, Poland, Hungary, Czech Republic, Slovakia, Slovenia, Latvia, Lithuania, Estonia, as well as Malta and Cyprus, became the *EU* members.[149] Bulgaria and Romania joined the organization later, on January 1, 2007, respectively, becoming the 26th and 27th members of the organization. Before joining the *EU,* these *Small Powers*, former members of the *Eastern Bloc*, have become full-fledged members of *NATO*.

Relations with the Former Yugoslavia

Several other policies of the EU and NATO were conducted concerning the second group of countries that gained independence after the breakup of Yugoslavia, which became known as the *Western Balkan* countries. These countries were Croatia, North Macedonia, Bosnia-Herzegovina, Serbia, and Montenegro. Albania was also considered the *Western Balkans*, which was not part of Yugoslavia. The term was created to separate these countries from Bulgaria and Romania, which were also in the Balkans, but in contrast to the countries of the former Yugoslavia, were included in the integration process with the *EU*. After the collapse of the *Communist Bloc* and the Soviet Union, the events in Yugoslavia evolved in a different scenario than those observed in the *CEEC*. Without a doubt, one of the reasons this scenario was quite a different and specific structure of the country compared to other socialist countries. Yugoslavia had a federal structure; the republics had the right to secede and had great potential and a more liberal economy. The collapse of the *Socialist Bloc* has also led to the disintegration of Yugoslavia. However, unlike Czechoslovakia, where this process has not led to a severe problem, Yugoslavia processed into a bloody war between the former republics. Even before the country's collapse in the late 80s, when President Slobodan Milosevich came to power, the rise of nationalism in all the Union republics began to be observed. After the elections in Yugoslavian republics, which were held in the '90s, except for Serbia, on the senior positions, the pro-independence leaders were elected. There were desperate attempts to save the country, but they were unsuccessful. Thus, on 25 June 1991, Slovenia and Croatia were the first to declare independence. Immediately after this, the bloody conflict in Yugoslavia began.

The *EU*'s stance towards Yugoslavia has been quite cautious. Initially, this organization supported the country's territorial integrity. This EU position was understandable since she feared possible instability that could erupt during the collapse of Yugoslavia and the emergence of new countries on the map. The *EU* Commission announced it was ready to contribute to forming a new Yugoslavia based on democratic principles. It would mediate the dialogue between the central government and the republics' leaders. At the same time, the *EU* has declared that in the event of a successful resolution of controversies, cooperation between the *EU* and Yugoslavia can achieve a level of partnership. The *EU* had talked about the signing of *Association Agreements* with both Yugoslavia and the *CEEC*.[150]

It indicates the possibility of an identical approach to Yugoslavia, which was undertaken concerning the *CEEC*.

However, such a position of the *EU* continued until December 1991, after which it began to change. Ethnic conflicts and the separatist movement took full size and reached an irrevocable point. At the same time, the *EU*'s position influenced the action of Germany, the leading actor in this organization, under pressure from public opinion. It recognized the independence of Slovenia and Croatia.

This action led to the European Commission's recognition of the independence of these countries.[151]

In 1992, North Macedonia and Bosnia and Herzegovina also declared their independence. Not agreeing with this development, the central government in Belgrade sent the Yugoslav army first to Slovenia and then to Croatia and Bosnia and Herzegovina.[152] At that time, the war had started in the region, which led to these countries' final political and economic collapse.

From the first days of independence, the former Yugoslav republics were in the midst of the conflict; in this regard, the *EU* has been unable to implement the programs that were proposed for the *CEEC*, except in Slovenia, where the focus of the conflict was extinguished at the beginning. In contrast, *CEEC*, *NATO*, and the *EU* countries did not offer these countries full membership while offering assistance in the transition period. Countries that were the focus of military action cannot be brought to the integration process. The military conflict in Yugoslavia also harmed the security of the *EU*. This organization tried to take action and form a different policy towards the *Western Balkans*. However, the *EU* needed more opportunities and alternative tools to achieve its goals. Diplomatic steps taken by the *EU* were unsuccessful because they did not support preventing military action. Arms embargoes have only aggravated the situation because Serbia inherited the Yugoslav Army's weapons, while Croatia, Bosnia, and Herzegovina did not have such an opportunity. In this way, the Serbs managed to occupy large areas in Bosnia and Herzegovina.[153]

Curiously, at an early stage, the EU was encouraged by the rapid developments in the region (the collapse of the *Eastern Bloc*, the creation of the EU, and its *Common Foreign and Security Policy*) and felt that it had become an essential actor in international relations. In this way, it could independently resolve the conflict that broke out in Yugoslavia. It was believed that the Europeans had to solve the problems that occurred in Europe. At the same time, the EU had hoped to resolve the conflict without the intervention of the only *Super Power*- the US.[154]

However, the *EU*'s desire to act as a coherent international actor in matters concerning security is faced with the opposite position of the countries, the core members of this organization. Such *Great Powers*, such as France and England, based on their national interests, were opposed to direct intervention in the conflict despite the presence of military capabilities. As for Germany, which was initially undertaken an active policy in the region, it was not able to intervene in the absence of military capabilities because of provisions of its constitution.[155]

On May 27, 1992, the *EU* European Commission decided to use trade sanctions against Serbia and Montenegro. In August of the same year, the Commission recognized the territorial integrity of Bosnia and Herzegovina, thereby assuming unacceptable occupation of its territories during the conflict.[156] In addition, the *EU* together with the *UN* attempted to resolve the conflict in that country and has produced and offered *the Vance-Owen Plan*.[157] However, this plan was not destined to be realized, and it failed to resolve the conflict by only using economic instruments that needed improvement and adequate improvement. There was a need for political and military tools. However, as it was mentioned, the *EU* member states were opposed to military intervention.[158] This situation did not allow the EU to resolve the conflict in Yugoslavia and failed in its purpose. The conflict in Bosnia and Herzegovina was possible to complete only after the intervention of the US and *NATO*. After the massacre committed over Bosnians by Serbs in Srebrenica, the US and *NATO* decided to launch airstrikes on the positions of Bosnian Serbs to force them to suspend hostilities and come to the negotiating table.[159] In addition, the US contributed to creating a military alliance between Bosnians and Croatians and began supplying them with the necessary military weaponry. The active participation of *Super Power* yielded results. Thus, in the conflict between the parties, a balance has become possible to create.[160] The US actions have brought the expected results, which led to the signing in December 14, 1995 *Dayton Agreement* between the parties of conflict.[161]

In general, it is worth noting that despite the failure of the *EU* in an attempt to resolve the conflict that broke out after the collapse of Yugoslavia, it was only possible to solve with the intervention of *the Super Power* of the US and *NATO* forces. Once it became clear that the *EU* and some of its members would not achieve an end to conflict and this mission laid the US. Thus, although the *Western Balkan* countries were not included in the integration into *NATO* and the *EU*, these countries were still in the sphere of influence and interests of the significant Western *Great Powers*. As a result, they could curb Serbian nationalism and contribute to the achievement of peace in Bosnia and Herzegovina.

After the peace agreement and its enforcement on the part of *NATO* and the US were provided, the *EU* had to play a more active role in promoting political and economic reforms in the *Western Balkans* countries. In May 1999, the *Stabilization and Association Process* program started to be implemented by the *EU* to support reforms in the countries of the *Western Balkans*. This program was developed since, at that time, the EU had no idea of membership for the Western Balkans countries. The process included countries such as New Yugoslavia, Croatia, Bosnia and Herzegovina, North Macedonia, and Albania.[162] Within the framework of *the Stabilization and Association Process*, as a result of the successful implementation of the reforms on the part of these countries, the *EU* intends to sign a *Stabilization and Association Agreement*. The results of this agreement allow countries that have signed it to achieve deeper integration with the *EU* in the economic sphere. On the part of the *EU*, it was given to know to these countries that in case of successful implementation of the reforms, they could become candidates for membership in this organization. It was expected development of regional cooperation and providing financial support to countries in the region.[163]

In addition, the *EU* has developed the *Community Assistance for Reconstruction, Democratization and Stabilization Program* (*CARDS*) for the region countries, intending to facilitate the successful implementation of reforms. It is worth noting that in its functions, *CARDS* was similar to the *PHARE* program, which was developed for the *CEEC*. The difference was only in the fact that as the result of *PHARE* implementation, *CEEC* became members of the *EU*, while the *CARDS* such a possibility was not provided. Since the countries in the *Western Balkans* region were in a different situation than the *CEEC*, the *EU* has decided to conduct a phased preparation of these countries for membership, first recognizing their candidates for membership and then beginning the process of integration itself. The prospect of *EU* membership has become attractive for countries in the *Western Balkans*, and the full implementation of the reforms in these countries took place very actively. The first country to sign a *Stabilization and Association Agreement* with the *EU* became North Macedonia; Croatia followed her.[164]

In October 2005, the *EU* started negotiations with Croatia on its membership. In July 2013, the country became the 28th member of the *EU*. Croatia's cooperation with the *EU* took work as a process to achieve membership in the organization. It was necessary to realize the demands made by the *EU* on this country. Croatia realized that the reforms were in its interests and that its results would be rewarded through membership in *NATO* and the *EU*, which were entirely consistent with its national interests. Croatia has agreed to cooperate, and it would seem, in such delicate matters as extraditing several of its citizens to the International Criminal Tribunal for the Former Yugoslavia. Besides the future benefit of the membership, Croatia also resolves the border dispute with Slovenia: on a shallow bay in the northern Adriatic. Thus, the parties came to a constructive decision for the negotiations and agreed to seek international arbitration.[165] As seen in the examples, the conditional accession tool was implemented by the *EU* to resolve a territorial dispute between the neighboring countries successfully. In short, Croatia also has a border dispute with Serbia and Montenegro, but since these countries are not members of the *EU*, the debate still needs to be resolved. In any case, Montenegro is implementation of reforms in order to be able to integrate into the *EU*, following an agreement signed with Croatia's readiness to resolve disputes through international arbitration. Thus, the appeal of membership in the *EU* makes the conditional accession tool and contributes to the successful resolution of regional disputes.

Despite the generally successful implementation of the process, given that it consists of several stages, it generally slows down the completion of the integration process for the region's countries. For some countries, the region's *EU* membership seems a very distant reality, which slows down the speed of reforms. Currently, the closest to *EU* membership are Albania, Montenegro, and North Macedonia (This country changed its name in 2018 due to the *Prespa Agreement* signed with Greece. The main reason for this is the position of Greece, which requires the former Yugoslav Republic to change the name of its country in order to avoid confusion with the Greek province of Macedonia. By the way, precisely because of Greece's position, Macedonia is recognized by the international community as the Former Yugoslavian Republic of Macedonia. In addition, even though the country has changed its flag and constitution, but refuses to change the country's name.[166] Thus, Greece plays a vital role in further integrating North Macedonia into the *EU*. Only after the agreement with Greece was it possible for North Macedonia to become a member of *NATO* and a candidate for membership to *the EU*. The example of this country once again indicates how attractive *NATO* and *EU* membership is and what countries are ready to do to achieve it). Albania, as well as Croatia, in 2009, became a member of *NATO*, which, behind the scenes, was a prerequisite for accession to the EU, and in 2014 received the status of membership candidate. Montenegro joined the alliance in 2016 and became the *EU* candidate for membership in 2010. It is the only country in the *Eastern Block* that received candidate status to *the EU* before the *NATO* membership. It is explained by the fact that Montenegro gained independence later than other republics of the former Yugoslavia (2006). By then, the *EU* had decided on a policy towards the *Western Balkans*. As for North Macedonia, it became a member of *NATO* in 2020 and received candidate status in the same year. In addition to Albania, Montenegro, and North Macedonia, Serbia received candidate status in March 2012.

Serbia is still not a member of *NATO*, but only in the negotiation process with the alliance. The participation of Serbia in negotiations with *NATO* and the *EU* deserves special attention. The fact is that this cooperation takes place in light of Serbia's disagreement with the *Great Powers* on the Kosovo issue. The disagreements between Serbia and Kosovo began after Kosovo's administrative status was eliminated, on which territory the majority of the population consists of Albanians. Kosovo was a part of the Serbia Republic during the existence of Yugoslavia in the status of an autonomous region. With the collapse of Yugoslavia, Kosovo also declared its independence on September 22, 1990.[167]

However, unlike the union republics of the former Yugoslavia, Kosovo's independence at that time was only recognized by Albania. The fact is that Kosovo, as an autonomous province under the Constitution of Yugoslavia, has not the right to self-determination. In 1998, the tension between Serbia and

Kosovo increased due to the Serb army launching military operations on the territory of Kosovo. Serbs attacked Kosovo cities such as Likoshani and Prekas using military aircraft, helicopters, tanks, and other heavy weapons.[168]

However, Serbia was not expected that the international community's reaction concerning its Kosovo actions would be radical. On 24-25 Mart 1999, *NATO*, since its expansion, for the first time in its fifty-year history decided to intervene in the conflict and the beginning of air strikes on Serbia.[169] The significance of the military intervention of *NATO* is that the organization and the member countries of the alliance took this decision without the need for such a case *UN* Security Council decision. In addition, in the event of aggression against its members, NATO, created for collective security, launched a military operation out of its area, going beyond its primary mission. *NATO* intervention also included a desire to create new goals after the Cold War. After the Serbian army and the police were forced to leave the territory of Kosovo, *UN* Security Council formed an interim administration under its mandate.[170]

This decision eliminated Serbia's sovereignty over Kosovo. The process has acquired an irreversible trend for this country. After almost ten years exceptional management, on February 17, 2008, Kosovo unilaterally declared its independence.[171] It was the second declaration of Kosovo's independence, but unlike the first time, many international community countries have recognized it. Among the countries that have recognized Kosovo as an independent state became the United States and *Great Powers* in the *EU*, such as Germany, England, and France. At the same time, Serbia itself refuses to recognize Kosovo's independence, considering it part of its territory. In turn, not all *EU* member states have recognized Kosovo's independence. The organization is divided into two parts: Spain, Greece, Slovakia, Cyprus, and Romania have refused to recognize Kosovo's independence.[172] Without a doubt, each country followed its national interests, thus breaking and unified approach to the issue of the *EU* itself.

On February 4, 2008, the *EU*, two weeks before the unilateral declaration of Kosovo independence, commissioned the *European Union Rule of Law Mission in Kosovo* (*EULEX*) to ensure peace.[173] The *EU* was also looking for ways to start implementing programs designed for the *Western Balkans* in Kosovo after the recognition of independence.

Changes in the position of Serbia towards the *EU* began after pro-Western parties came to power in this country. At the same time, after the parliamentary elections held on January 21, 2007, the *EU* insisted on the creation of the Democratic bloc of pro-Western parties.[174] Serbia new Prime-Minister Mirko Cvetković, announced that "One of the first moves of the new government will be to submit the *Stabilization and Association Agreement* with the European Union to the parliament for ratification."[175] Since December 2009, citizens of

Serbia received the right to visa-free entry in the countries of the Schengen Area. At the same time, in the same month, Serbia applied for *EU* membership. In turn, the *EU* contributed to the beginning of a direct dialogue between Serbia and Kosovo, intending to develop cooperation between the parties to achieve the goals of integration into the *EU* and improve people's living conditions. On April 19, 2013, Serbia and Kosovo, in the presence of the High Representative of the *EU* for Foreign Affairs and Security Policy Catherine Ashton, signed an agreement on the "First agreement of principles governing the normalization of relations."[176]

This fact is significant in that processes carried out by the *EU* towards Serbia are supported by the leading Serbian Progressive Party, which advocates an ideology of national conservatism. The party was founded in 2008 by former members of the Serbian Radical Party. This example once again proves the Western Balkans' interest in *EU* membership, which these countries can be obtained only in the case of implementing several requirements, some of which are serious dilemmas. However, even in this case, Serbia prefers to continue the integration process. The same applies to other countries in the region.

In general, even though the countries in the region implement the criteria in different ways and their progress towards membership, for objective and subjective reasons, different from each other, the process continues. The conditional accession tool of *the EU* continues to be effective in achieving its goals through the organization and implementation of reforms by the countries of the former *Eastern Bloc* countries region.

EU relations with Newly Independent States (NIS)

The third group, representing countries of the former Soviet Union or *Newly Independent States* (*NIS*), gained independence in 1991. In the face of the United States, *NATO*, and the *EU*, it is worth noting that the West did not immediately determine what policy to conduct concerning these countries. At first, the region's perception was based on the policy pursued concerning Russia. Separately, there needed to be a strategy concerning the NIS at the time. The reason for this circumstance was that initially, the *West*, as in the case of Yugoslavia, did not want the Soviet Union secession in the belief that this would lead to instability with unpredictable consequences for the vast territory. The *West* believed it would be possible to promote the expense of reforms, restructuring the Soviet Union, and achieving its democratization and liberalization. However, it became clear that the process of disintegration of the Soviet Union was inevitable, and this strategy was not to materialize.

In turn, Russia, which could not quickly recover after the collapse of the Soviet Union, announced the *NIS* as its "*near abroad*" and tried to preserve its influence in the region. This policy was announced in February 1993 and became the "*The Monroe Doctrine of Russia.*" In addition, immediately after the collapse of the Soviet Union, the former republics, except the three Baltic countries which have been adopted in the sphere of influence of the *West*, established the *Commonwealth of Independent States* under the patronage of Russia. By this, it is understood that Russia is not only formed its political and economic control over the region but also that it will not allow the interference of third forces.[177] Russia explained its policy as a critical action to protect the Russians, who live beyond the borders of Russia on the territory of former Soviet republics. In fact, in all the former Soviet republics, the Russian military base presence continued to be (at that time, as the Russian military units in the countries of the former *Eastern Bloc* were withdrawn before 1994 with the support of the US and *NATO*) and undertook roles in the internal and foreign conflicts in which *Small Powers* of *NIS* were involved.[178]

Regarding the *EU*, it recognized the independence of *NIS* on December 31, 1991, but only in 1993 began the first contact with these *Small Powers* when the *EU* began to assist the countries in the region, which were in a complex political and economic situation. By providing various kinds of assistance, the *EU* hoped that it would be able to ensure relative stability in these countries. As of this assistance, the *EU* has understood that it is necessary to establish a format in which it would be more effectively provided. Thus, the *EU* has developed a program of *Technical Assistance to the Commonwealth of Independent States* (*TACIS*). The program provided technical and financial assistance for the countries of the former Soviet Union.[179] Moreover, it had properties similar to *CARDS* and *PHARE*, developed for the *CEEC* and the *Western Balkans*. However, in contrast to these programs, whose implementation results provided membership and candidacy for membership, respectively, *TACIS* did not set any final objectives before the partner countries. In other words, the EU was trying to implement significant reforms in the *NIS* (at least in those which were located in Europe and theoretically had the opportunity for membership in the *EU*) in order to the formation of democratic regimes and market economies without the promises of their prospects for integration. Until 1995, the relationship between the *EU* and the *NIS* was limited *TACIS* program and even had no legal basis. They realized that the *EU* had decided to develop a new legal instrument that would apply to the *NIS*. That legal instrument was the *Partnership and Cooperation Agreement* (*PCA*). *PCA* was the essential document for implementing the *TACIS* program over *NIS*. In addition, the agreement included the basis of trade between the parts. It also included paragraphs on political dialogue and economic relations.[180]

The program itself was applied until 2006. In late 2006, the *EU* had doubts about the effectiveness of this program. In April 2006, the EU Audit Committee reviewed the *EU*'s *TACIS* program and its follow-up, concluding that the allocated € 4.2 billion of the funds had been spent inefficiently. As a result, European Parliament demanded to suspend the program. Instead *TACIS* program, the *EU* has developed a new initiative, the *European Neighborhood Policy* (*ENP*). *ENP* was developed in order to create stability, security, and welfare in the region neighboring the *EU*.[181] This program aimed to develop the *"zone of development and good neighborliness"* between the *EU* and *NIS*. The development of this project represents the creation of a buffer zone for the countries close to the EU regimes with Russia. Thus, the program did not offer full membership in the organization, as in the *CEEC* example, and no candidacy for membership, as in the case of the *Western Balkans*. Thereby, concerning the question of a possible *EU* integration for *NIS*, nothing has changed, as well as the fact that all *EU* programs concerning this group of countries have evolved separately. On the other hand, if the *EU* wanted to include countries of the former Soviet Union in the accession process, likely, it would not develop new foreign policy instruments and use those that have been successfully tested in the *CEEC* or the *Western Balkans*.

The *EU* did not want to continue to further the integration process in an eastern direction, and *ENP* was supposed to be a tool that would facilitate the continuation of political and economic reforms by the *NIS*.[182] *ENP's* difference from *TACIS* program lies in the fact that the partner countries, in the case of successful implementation of this program, will have a similar status to members of the *European Economic Area*. Countries will be able to integrate at this level in the economic sphere, however, without the prospect of political integration.[183]

Countries of the former Soviet Union geographically located in Europe, including Russia, were invited to participate in the program. Thus, the countries of Central Asia, which also applied for *the TACIS* Program, were not included: relations with them were built in the framework of the *PCA*. Although the program included only European countries, it was possible to assume that the *EU* had plans to start the accession process with them. However, also it coincided with those that *NIS* is located on the perimeter of the external borders of the *EU*. In other words, a significant factor that this initiative developed is that the EU geographically encircles these countries.

Another proof that the *EU* was not planning to continue the integration process, which would include a *NIS,* is the fact that the same initiative, but under the other title, began to implement in respect of countries located in North Africa and Asia on the southern and eastern coast Mediterranean Sea. The *EU* initiative for the Mediterranean was developed in 2008 and was a continuation of the Barcelona Process and, in many aspects, in common with the *ENP*.[184]

Given this feature of the program, there was a problem with the success of its implementation since it needed to be clarified how *Small Powers* of *NIS* would voluntarily implement the *EU* demands without the prospect of membership. As the case in other initiatives the *EU* has put forward concerning the countries of the former *Eastern Bloc*, it was necessary to implement the conditions because reforms were not widespread in the context of the interests of these countries and their regimes. As a consequence, without specific promises from the *EU*, *NIS* does not have no much enthusiasm connected to the program and does not want to pursue reforms actively.[185]

At the last *EU* enlargement to the east, another condition was the membership in *NATO*. So, it is interesting to see the development trend of this Alliance's relation with the *NIS*. Here, *NATO*'s actions were similar to those of the *EU*. In general, at the initial stage of *NATO*, as has been said before, all the countries of the former *Eastern Bloc* and the Soviet Union developed a common platform for dialog- *NACC*. Then, the program, which also included all these countries, - *PfP*. All countries, members of *NACC* and *OSCE*, were invited to participate in this initiative. Some *NIS* participated in this initiative with great enthusiasm, as these countries believed that *PfP* could play the role of a phased preparation for *NATO* membership.

However, as in the case of the *EU*, *NATO* in the first decade of the 2000s has developed a new initiative for the countries for which this alliance was not planning to provide membership. Thus, at the Prague Summit in 2002, the *Individual Partnership Action Plan* (IPAP) was adopted. The initiative included the cooperation between *NATO* and its partners in many aspects, starting with the restructuring defense system, structural changes, and human rights.[186] However, this initiative did not include full membership in the alliance based on the successful implementation of its terms. As has already been assumed, *IPAP* was developed and proposed *NIS*, while the *NATO* and *CEEC* re lations developed within *Membership Plan* (*MAP*).

Although the *MAP* did not guarantee membership in the alliance, this program prepared partner countries for accession to this organization. *MAP* was develope d in 1999 (before the *IPAP*, which confirmed once again that the latest initiative was designed for countries concerning which *NATO* had no plans for membership) to facilitate the aspiring countries to achieve compliance with *NATO* standards and prepare for possible future membership. That same year, the first members of the former *Eastern Bloc* were admitted to *NATO*: the Czech Republic, Poland, and Hungary.[187]

Thus, the *EU* and *NATO* conducted a parallel policy towards the *NIS* and complemented each other, forming a new opportunity for this group of countries, on the one hand, to bring them to a new level of political and economic relations, on the other hand, does not offer them full membership and form a zone of friendly states. The proposals from these two structures shall reflect the expectations of *NIS*. These states wanted to integrate into NATO and the EU fully, and the degree of success of reforms following the programs was directly dependent on the perception of the *NIS*. In other words, those *Small Powers* saw these programs as a step towards membership in *NATO* and the *EU* (it did not correspond to reality), with a greater willingness to reform than those who did not take it well.

With the development of the *EU*'s relations with the *NIS* under the *ENP* program, this structure is understood that the countries of the former Soviet Union, which are located in Europe, should be presented with different programs than those that have been developed for the countries of Northern Africa and Western Asia participating in the *New Neighborhood Policy*.

Thus, the new initiative was designed to *NIS* for such *Small Powers* as Ukraine, Belarus, Moldova, Azerbaijan, Georgia, and Armenia. The *EU* strategy towards these countries was the same: this structure would not offer membership to the former countries of the Soviet Union. However, it decided to offer more new opportunities than those that were in the preceding sentences.

The new initiative was called *Eastern Partnership* (*EP*). For the first time, this program was announced at the *EU* Prague Summit, which took place in May 2009. Poland proposed this initiative with the support of another *EU* member, Sweden. As in the case of the *ENP*, *EP* implies a transfer of laws and regulations of *the EU* to these *Small Powers*. At the same time, the *EP* provides an opportunity to develop political and economic cooperation. With the implementation of reforms, these *Small States* were structurally closer to the *EU*. Countries, after the implementation of all the reforms needed to develop values such as democracy, the rule of law, the complete transition to a market economy, sustainable development, and good governance.[188]

In order to achieve its goals, the *EU* has developed and introduced a new tool for political cooperation- *Association Agreement* (*AA*). *AA* allows *Small Powers* of *NIS* to develop the mobility of partner states' citizens, which would be achieved in the first stage due to the visa facilitation and readmission agreements, and, subsequently, by a visa-free regime.[189] The *EU* considers that the proposal could be an attractive partner for the *EP*, as it ensures full integration at the level of citizens who can visit freely and stay in the *EU*. It provided excellent opportunities for the citizens of these countries, besides the desire for *NIS Small States* to join the *EU*, primarily due mainly to give the opportunity for free access to the *EU* countries and the initiative it provides.

In addition, the *EU* also offers a certain level of economic integration with these countries. So, based on the implementation of reforms within the *EP* between the *EU* and partner countries, the *Deep and Comprehensive Free Trade*

Area (*DCFTA*) will be established. It will increase the trade turnover between the parties and increase and diversify exports from here *Small Powers* of *NIS* in the *EU*. The *EU* also does not remain the loser: exporting products and services in the *EP* countries will also increase.

Thus, it should be noted that for the part of the *Small Powers* of *NIS* reform, opportunities offered by the *EP* are very attractive. Countries have strengthened the infrastructure, strengthened the political and economic foundations of the state, and citizens have the opportunity to diversify their activities. Last but not least, the financial support of the *EU*, which as part of this initiative, is also essential to partner states. It should be noted that the economic situation in many countries of the former Soviet Union is still not up to standard and has not even reached the level of well-being they were when they were part of the Soviet Union. At the same time, with few exceptions, these countries do not have the necessary resources, which would allow them to change their economic situation fundamentally. Therefore, economic injections are essential for these countries. In turn, the *EU* is also considering financial and economic aid as a tool for the success of the reforms in these countries.

Even though, at first glance, *EP* may seem very attractive for *NIS Small Powers*, in practice, it turned out differently. The EU did not get the results obtained in implementing similar programs in the *CEEC* and the *Western Balkans*. As mentioned above, one of the reasons is the *EU*'s refusal to grant full membership. However, there are other reasons related to the specifics of these countries and the period of development since independence. Some of the great importance also play the geopolitical characteristics of the region in which these countries are located.

CHAPTER 4
The Emergence of New Small Powers after the Collapse of the Soviet Union and International Policy

Russian dominance in NIS

After the collapse of the Soviet Union, fifteen new states appeared on the world map. Russia declared itself the legal successor of the former *Super Power* but considerably weakened, at the same time, yet still could influence international processes, especially about the region of the former Soviet Union. Russia inherited the Soviet seat at the *UN Security Council* and has become adaptive to the new realities of the global system. With the formation of the new unipolar world order, Russia lost the status of *Super Power* but is still a *Great Power* whose status was also recognized by the *West*.

Besides Russia, the other fourteen states qualify as *Small Powers*. These *NIS* include states with a large territory, such as, for example, Kazakhstan, which is the ninth country in the world, and Ukraine, which became the largest state in Europe. All Central Asian countries have large territories, as well as Belarus. At the same time, the Baltic countries: Lithuania, Latvia, and Estonia; the South Caucasus countries, Azerbaijan, Georgia, Armenia, and Moldova, have small areas. In short, the largest country in this group is Azerbaijan, whose territory is only 86 600 km².

There is also a difference in the population figures. In short, besides Russia, most people at the time of the Soviet Union lived in Ukraine. In this country, the population consists of 52 million.[190] Behind Ukraine were Uzbekistan and Kazakhstan, whose populations in 1991 were respectively 20.6 million[191] and 16.6 million[192]. In the rest of the *NIS Small Powers*, in 1991, the population differed between one million and seven, not even reaching up to ten million.

Even though Ukraine, Kazakhstan, and Belarus at the time of the collapse of the Soviet Union had in their territory's arsenal of strategic and tactical nuclear weapons, the number of units consisted of 3000 and therefore could be considered nuclear powers, it did not change their status as *Small Powers*. These three countries have become owners of weapons of mass destruction by coincidence; it is impossible to assert that they controlled it. During the Soviet Union, the deployment of nuclear weapons was carried out on the territory of a single state, with a view to the strategic objectives of *Super Power* defense. After the collapse of the Soviet Union, a new situation was created, which concerned the main actors of international relations, especially the United States. Despite the generally passive US involvement in the fate of the *NIS*, this state has actively contributed to withdrawing all nuclear weapons from these *Small Powers* to Russia. The *West* wanted the number of countries possessing nuclear weapons to remain the same. Especially if these states, which needed more experience of statehood or independence, faced many political and economic problems.

Furthermore, there was the likelihood that these countries' arms could be sold or stolen. Thus, the United States contributed to the fact that these three *Small Powers* of *NIS*, on May 23, 1992, put their signatures under the *Lisbon Protocol*, under which these countries pledged to return nuclear weapons to Russia. By the end of 1996, the transfer of weapons was completed.[193]

Draws attention to the date of the signing of the Protocol, only six months after the collapse of the Soviet Union, this problem has been resolved at the legal level. This fact speaks about the US actions in matters of efficiency, which it was directly interested in. It again points to the fact that, in general, the *West* does not wish to penetrate the *NIS* region actively.

In 1991, *NIS* appeared in the formation of a new world system. At the same time, the importance played by the fact that they were part of one of the poles of the bipolar world and now had to change the whole system inherited from the Soviet Union radically. The new system possesses the values of the *West*, such as democracy, market economy, and human rights. Now, in a unipolar world, with no clear alternative, there is a general expectation that these values are ubiquitous globally.

The *NIS* assumed such a perception of the world. Logically, this perception is correct, considering the dynamics of the development of events. Consequently, these countries' formation and building of statehood were based directly on response to this reality. All *NIS Small Powers*, after independence, announced that the course of national development was the construction of a democratic society and the transition to a market economy. These *NIS* rely on the full support of the *West* in the face of the sole *Super Power*, the United States and other *Great Powers*, and structures such as *NATO* and the *EU*.

The West considered this perception of reality for *NIS* reasonable and correct. In short, on September 4, 1991, US Secretary of State James Baker announced five principles to guide action concerning emerging republics. Self-determination is consistent in following democratic principles, recognition of existing borders, support for democracy and the rule of law, respect for human and minority rights, and respect for international law. In this way, the United

States has stated that only if the new republic would follow these principles, then they could expect cooperation and assistance from this country.[194]

In addition, these *Small Powers* were not abandoning an adaptation to the new realities. They had sincere expectations and desired to implement reforms and complete the state formation as soon as possible. At the same time, *NIS* realized that the process should be gradual, and it would be dangerous to completely sever all of the relationships that formed between these countries, as it was in the Soviet Union. *Small Powers* of the former Soviet Union feared facing even more severe political and economic problems. The traditional relationship will be terminated until new ones have been created. It proves further developments.

Thus, on December 8, 1991, in Białowieża Forest (Belarus), three states-founders of the Soviet Union, signed the relevant treaty in 1922; Russia, Ukraine, and Belarus announced the termination of the state as a "subject of international law and geopolitical reality." At the same time, it announced the establishment of the *Commonwealth of Independent States* (*CIS*).[195] The new structure has been created to regulate the cooperation relations between the former Soviet republics. It is important to note that *CIS* is not a supranational structure, and participation in it is voluntary.

Because of a new geopolitical reality, the leaders of the former Soviet republics of Central Asia, Kazakhstan, Uzbekistan, Turkmenistan, Kyrgyzstan, and Tajikistan, on December 13, gathered in Turkmenistan capital - Ashgabat to discuss the future fate of their countries. During the meeting, the leaders declared their readiness for accession to the *CIS* as the founders of the organization.[196]

As a result of this statement, it was decided to hold a meeting of all interested former Soviet republics in Kazakhstan's capital –Alma-Ata. As a result, eleven former Soviet republics responded to the call and met on December 21, 1991. In addition to the three countries, the founders of *CIS* and the five Central Asian countries, Kazakhstan, arrived at the presidents of Azerbaijan, Armenia, and Moldova. Only four states were absent: Lithuania, Latvia, Lithuania, and Georgia. The three Baltic countries gained independence in September 1991 when the Soviet Union recognized their independence. Immediately after independence, these republics had the opportunity for active cooperation and integration with the *West*. As for Georgia, at the moment, it carried out differently from the other *NIS* and believed that *CIS* did not meet its national interests.

The result of this meeting was the signing of the *Alma-Ata Declaration*, which defined the principles and functions of *CIS*. With the signing of this agreement, the process of converting the former Soviet republics into independent states was also completed, and then its international recognition started. On December

25, 1991, as a logical completion of the previous events, the president of the Soviet Union, Mikhail Gorbachov, resigned. By early 1992, most of the states representing the international community have recognized the independence of the *NIS*.[197]

After forming a legal framework for cooperation among themselves, the *NIS* actively joined in the search for new contacts in the international arena to start a dialogue. First of all, these *Small Powers* were looking for assistance during the transition period to build a democratic society and market economy, as these countries have declared in their declaration of independence. However, the expected contribution has yet to be received. Western aid was limited to providing humanitarian assistance and loans to *Small Powers*.

As stated earlier, the US, *NATO*, and the *EU* focused on *CEEC* and the *Western Balkans* and were uninterested in *NIS*. The international community needed more time to prepare for the region's rapid change of events. It needed ready-made solutions to these countries' political and economic problems. In addition, the *West* needed more resources to be distributed equally among the former *Eastern Bloc* members. In this way, the *EU* concentrated on a narrow geography, promoting reforms in the countries close to its borders. The same can be said about the United States. At that time, the US focused on the Middle East because of the Iraq-Kuwait war. The United States and its allies have recently completed a major military operation, "Desert Storm," to defeat the Iraqi army. All the attention of the only *Super Power* was concentrated in the region, which had a strategic importance.[198]

As for the *NIS*, after the collapse of the *Eastern Bloc* and the Soviet Union as the main enemy of the *West,* the region's importance began to decrease. For the US, in addition to the question of the existence of nuclear weapons in the former Soviet republics, the acceleration of economic reforms in Russia was more interested.[199] The US believed that if the reform were successfully carried out in this country, it would positively affect the other *NIS*. Russia was the largest republic of the former Soviet Union, actually forming its basis. Now being the only *Great Power* that appeared on the map of the Soviet Union, it still has a pleasing effect on the *NIS*, as well as the strong economic ties. The United States also recognized the independence of all the former Soviet republics except Georgia. In this country, the civil war began, and therefore the recognition of the country and the establishment of diplomatic relations were only possible in May 1992. In February 1992, the US Secretary of State James Baker visited Uzbekistan, Moldova, Azerbaijan, Turkmenistan, and Tajikistan, following the process of establishment of diplomatic relations with these countries.[200]

In 1993, Bill Clinton was elected as the US President; the administration of which was to form a new foreign policy concerning the *NIS* since the end of the

Cold War. Thus, during the Clinton administration, the leading architect of the policy toward the former Soviet republics was Ambassador-at-Large and Special Adviser to the Secretary of State Warren Christopher on the *NIS* -Strobe Talbott. The policy proposed by him was briefly described as a *"Russia first"* policy, with which Russia was considered to be the main partner, and the interests of *NIS* were completely ignored.[201] Talbott believed that this approach would contribute to the success of liberal reforms in Russia, which in turn would promote reforms in the former Soviet republics.

As a result, Russia has been recognized for its leading role in the whole space of *NIS*. This situation was suited entirely to Russia. Given the lack of interest of the *West* in the region, Russia has not had great difficulty controlling the situation. As mentioned before, the *West* was more interested in supporting *EEC*. These countries received full support in the transitional period, ending with full integration into *NATO* and the *EU*. As for the post-Soviet space, the *West* policy was different, and it was declared and recognized a unique role of Russia in this region. In this way, Russia was freely pursuing policies following its expectations and interests.

Thus, almost the whole post-Soviet region (except for the three Baltic States: Lithuania, Latvia, and Estonia) was recognized as a sphere of interest of Russia. From the beginning (1991), the *West* had intended to build such a relationship with Russia, in which this country would not feel defective because of loss of *Super Power* status. Thereby, Russia retained influence over the former Soviet republics. In February 1993, Russia announced a new foreign policy, the *"near abroad policy"* doctrine towards the former Soviet republics, announced this region a sphere of its interests.[202]

Thus, Russia-led order doctrine declared its responsibility for the fate of twenty-five million compatriots (mainly Russians) who had remained outside of its borders after the collapse of the Soviet Union and living as minorities in the *NIS*.[203]

For the first time, the doctrine was offered in the early 90s of the last century by the Minister of Foreign Affairs of Russia. The "*near abroad*" policy is Russia's statement and its dominant position over *NIS*. Such a statement had no objection from the *West* and even received some support. In addition, the *West* believed that the confrontation with Russia on this issue needed to meet its interests in achieving more important goals of the reform process in the country. In addition, the West also understood that Russia's loss of the status of *Super Power* could not pass without severe consequences for her. As a result, Russia's desire to maintain its dominant position in the region, in which the *West* at that time had no interest, was seen commonly.

Russia's position and expectations were perceived in the *West* adequately. In turn, the parties had agreed upon some gentleman's agreement, according to which the former *Eastern Bloc CEEC* countries were released from Russian influence and military control. Immediately, these states proclaimed the "*return to Europe*" as the main goal of foreign policy and expressed interest in joining the Euro-Atlantic structures. This interest was enthusiastically perceived in the *West,* and the *CEEC* started to be provided with assistance to be prepared for their transition to democracy and the full integration into *NATO* and the newly created *EU* (1992).[204]

As a result, the *West* is quite passively built relations with *NIS*, not wishing to be bound by any responsibilities. Even those programs that have been proposed to *NIS* had minimal objectives. For instance, *NATO* only 1994 developed a new *PfP*-program of practical bilateral cooperation with individual Euro-Atlantic partner countries. The program contributes to the reforms in the partner countries through a mix of policies, programs, action plans, and other arrangements without giving them a perspective of full membership.[205] The *EU*, which built its relationship with *NIS* through the *TACIS program* only in 1996, has developed a legal framework for cooperation with these countries: *PCA*, the main goal of which was to strengthen partner states democracies and developing economies through collaboration in different areas through political dialogue.[206]

As mentioned, *PCA* also did not provide *EU* membership for these countries. Limited technical assistance without the offer of a conditional membership to the Euro-Atlantic structures (as it was in the case of the *CEEC*) didn't give the expected results. Over time, the difference between *CEEC* and *NIS* in implementing reforms has become more apparent.

Following this, Russia has issued the status of guarantor of security in the post-Soviet space. Russia began signing bilateral military agreements with several *NIS*, which eventually transformed into the signing of the *Tashkent Treaty on Collective Security* in 1992. Besides Russia, the treaty was signed by Kazakhstan, Uzbekistan, Tajikistan, Armenia, and Kyrgyzstan. In 1993, an agreement was joined by Azerbaijan, Georgia, and Belarus (later, Georgia, Azerbaijan, and Uzbekistan left the organization whose name changed to *Collective Security Treaty Organization (CSTO)*). According to the signed agreement, Russia was able to keep its military bases in almost all *NIS*.[207]

At the same time, Russia had an opportunity to control the settlement of all sorts of conflicts that erupted in the South Caucasus, Moldova, and Tajikistan. In contrast to the *Western Balkans*, the West, where the US, *NATO*, and the *EU* took an active part in preventing war, took a very passive position regarding the conflicts in the *NIS*. All Western initiatives are confined to providing a political and legal assessment of the conflicts, both at the *UN* level and on the platforms of other international organizations. Subsequently, after the cessation of the active phase of confrontation and to achieve a cease-fire, some *Great Powers* became involved in the negotiation process to resolve regional conflicts in international organizations. However, despite the presence of Western countries, Russia plays the main role in the conflict resolution process.

It cannot be said that these processes are enthusiastically perceived by the *NIS's Small Powers* regarding the Russian doctrine, directly related to the *NIS Small Powers,* which were only in a passive role, unable to oppose Russia's intentions. At the same time, these countries eventually realized that the *West* would not be to support *NIS*, tacitly agreeing with the actions of Russia.

In the absence of specific Western policies towards the region, attempts to come to power democratic forces in several *NIS* have been ignored. In particular, the leadership in Georgia and Azerbaijan in the early 90's pro-Western, anti-Russian forces came to power, which strongly spoiled relations with Russia. As a result, these regimes could not last long in control, and the countries faced political instability and escalated conflicts in their territories. Regimes in these states have changed, and new governments with more pragmatic relations with Russia and the *West*, clearly assessing the situation in the international arena, have come to power. Developments in Azerbaijan and Georgia showed that the *West* was not ready and did not want to confront Russia because of the *NIS*, about which they had no distinct interests. In turn, *NIS Small Powers* also began to soberly assess the situation, namely, the West's and Russia's actual influence in the region. A pragmatic approach to foreign policy demanded *that NIS Small Powers consider* Russia's interests in the area and avoid possible conflicts with this country. The *NIS* realized that Russia's influence on the world level after the collapse of the Soviet Union seriously diminished. However, this influence in the former Soviet Union region was still preserved. Even though the US and the *West* became dominant power worldwide, Russia maintained its position in *NIS*. Even if it considers that the Western countries and organizations have increased their interests in the *NIS*, in any case, they were not ready to compete with Russia. They retreated in the case of a possible confrontation.

Formation of New Regional Organizations in NIS

Despite the unconditional acceptance by the *West* of Russia's influence over *NIS*, *NIS Small Powers,* even in the absence of adequate support from the US, the *EU*, *NATO*, and other countries representing the *West*, they still tried to distance themselves from Russia.

At the same time, these countries have tried as much as possible to develop a more balanced foreign policy, drawing the attention of an increasing number of international actors. By the mid-90, a group of countries- members of *CIS* tried to break away from Russian dominance. In particular, this policy sought to adhere to the *NIS Small Powers*, located geographically in Europe. These countries have been very passive members of *CIS*. At the same time, Russia continued the attempt to save the integration process between the former republics of the Soviet Union within the framework of this organization. This situation is suited only to some countries. Some *NIS* was trying to avoid the possibility of making and implementing decisions that would not coincide with their interests. In addition, they also tried to find ways to develop relations with the *West*. Over time, the number of common points between all members of the *CIS* began to decline, which led to the formation of a new process, namely the sub-regional cooperation between some of the *NIS* with close interests.

Consequently, in 1997, four *NIS Small Powers* - Georgia, Ukraine, Azerbaijan, and Moldova, were established a new regional organization *GUAM,* known by the abbreviations of these countries. It was expected that the organization would facilitate the transit of energy resources from Central Asia through the South Caucasus to Europe. The probability of realizing this objective had increased since 1999 when Uzbekistan joined the organization. However, in 2005, referring to the changes in foreign policy, this country withdrew from the organization.[208] The creation of *GUAM* coincided with the expansion of *NATO* eastward. In 1999 Poland, Hungary, and the Czech Republic allied. Thus, *NATO* approached close to the borders of the former Soviet Union, namely, the edges of Ukraine and Moldova. Therefore, these countries were looking for ways for closer cooperation with *NATO*. This assumption was confirmed by the fact that, as mentioned before 1999, Azerbaijan, Georgia, and Uzbekistan withdrew pro Russian *CSTO* military alliance. Moreover, in 1999, at the *NATO* Summit in Washington, members of *GUAM* expressed the desire to integrate into the European and Euro-Atlantic structures.[209]

It is worth noting that at that time, except for Ukraine, three of the four members of *GUAM* faced a problem of separatism in their territories. Moreover, the countries believed that Russia was the main reason impossibility of achieving territorial integrity and solving conflicts. Unresolved conflicts allowed Russia to control the situation in these countries. In addition, Ukraine had been in a confrontation with Russia on the issue of the status of the Black Sea Fleet, which is based in Sevastopol, and on the Crimean Peninsula.[210]

Another sub-regional organization, which appeared in the former Soviet Union region, is the *Shanghai Cooperation Organization* (*SCO*), founded in 2001. Russia, China, Central Asian countries, Kazakhstan, Uzbekistan, Tajikistan, and Kyrgyzstan founded the organization.[211] Despite *GUAM's* desire to create a closer relationship with *NATO* and the *EU*, it has not received appropriate attention, and eventually, *GUAM's* activity began to wane.

In contrast to the *GUAM*, in addition to the members of the *NIS Small Powers*, its members are Russia and China. The organization was founded to create a common platform for the two countries with a view to their possible cooperation in Central Asia. The Central Asian countries have been objecting to this cooperation, as the basis for the agreement was precisely this region.

It is worth noting that the organization was formed based on the "Shanghai Five," created in 1996 by Russia, China, Kazakhstan, Tajikistan, and Kyrgyzstan. The *SCO* is designed to ensure security and stability in the region. In 2015, the organization expanded, and its members became India and Pakistan.[212]

One of the reasons for establishing the *SCO* was a desire to prevent the possible presence of the *West*, especially the US, in Central Asia. This problem is common to Russia and China, as both countries believe that the Central Asian region is a weak point in ensuring their national security. It was the basis for cooperation between the two countries.

In general, the *West* itself, as mentioned earlier, was not particularly interested in penetrating the region. The situation in the region has changed since September 11, 2001, when the terrorist attacks organized by the *Organization of Al-Qaida* in the US took place. It was found that the leaders of this terrorist organization were in the territory of Afghanistan. After the Taliban government refused to grant the organization leaders, the US military, together with its allies from NATO, on October 7, 2001, launched an operation, "*Enduring Freedom*," in this country. Due to the start of operations, the Central Asian region's importance has increased dramatically for the US and *NATO* from a geopolitical point of view. The location of Central Asia would allow the US and its allies to provide logistical support to their troops, which participated in the operation in Afghanistan. In turn, after a tacit approval of Russia, which could not contradict, the five Central Asian countries have opened access to their airspace for the US and *NATO* forces. The US began to use military airfields in Uzbekistan, Kyrgyzstan, and Tajikistan.[213] However, it is worth noting that the US involvement in Central Asia was limited to only using military airfields for operations in Afghanistan. Subsequently, this limited presence came to an end.

"Color Revolution" in the NIS

In the early 2000s, several *NIS* faced a new phenomenon, which directly influenced the further development of these countries. Political events held place, which led to the change of government and the arrival of new leadership, standing up for democratic reforms in their country.

The first of these transformations took place in Georgia, where after the parliamentary elections on November 2, 2003, members of the opposition, united in the bloc "*National Movement*," said that the elections were rigged and started mass protests. The opposition demanded revising the election results and the resignation of President Eduard Shevardnadze. Following November 22, the opposition, led by their leader Mikheil Saakashvili stormed the parliament building in Georgia. It disrupted the first meeting, which began the change of the former Shevardnadze government. The confrontation has been called the *"Rose Revolution,"* as a symbol for the protester's opposition was chosen a rose. Shevardnadze was forced to resign, and after the early elections held in January 2004, Saakashvili became the new president of the country.[214]

Roughly the same scenario took place in another *NIS Small Power,* Ukraine. Here, the beginning of the confrontation with the country's opposition leader was in the second round of presidential elections, held on November 21, 2004, when the opposition called on supporters to begin civil disobedience. The opposition leader, Viktor Yushchenko, said the presidential elections were rigged. On the same day, Maidan approached the protesters in the central square. Acts of civil disobedience in Ukraine were called "Orange Revolution," as protesters, in solidarity and distinction, used clothes and attributes in orange color. The confrontation resulted in recognition by the Parliament and the Supreme Court of the results of the invalidated second round of presidential elections. On January 10, 2005, the Central Electoral Committee of Ukraine declared Viktor Yushchenko as the winner of the presidential elections.[215]

The expectation that the parade of "*color revolutions*" could spread to other republics of the former Soviet Union more and more intensified. The *NIS* authorities believed that the processes in Georgia and Ukraine were not spontaneous, and the change of regimes was viewed with the *West's* support, first and foremost by the US. In this case, they worked through the scenario in which the acceleration of democratic processes in the *NIS Small Powers* was ensured through a change in leadership and the coming to power of pro-Western governments.

The events in Kyrgyzstan were also customarily considered a "*color revolution*." The situation was also developed, as in Georgia and Ukraine. In February-March 2005, parliamentary elections were held in the country, which were recognized as fraudulent. It has led to widespread discontent and upheaval of the regime at that time. On March 24, opposition supporters occupied the building of the government. In a tribute to the traditions of the revolutions in Georgia and Ukraine, the protesters have chosen a tulip flower to symbolize their opposition. That is why the regime changes in Kyrgyzstan were called the "*Tulip Revolution*." President Askar Akayev was forced to leave the country and was granted asylum in Russia. Instead, Kurmanbek Bakiyev was elected as a president.[216]

Riots also occurred in Uzbekistan, in Andijan, on May 13, 2005. Given that in three *NIS Small Powers*, the governments have changed in a relatively short period, these events were seen as a continuation of the process, supported by the *West*. Riots broke out after the trial of a group of businessmen accused of involvement in banned organizations. Supporters of convicts began a protest in Andijan, which escalated into a confrontation, resulting in the seizure of the prison and freed prisoners. Following this, the protesters held a rally in front of the Andijan administration. The rally turned into an armed confrontation between the protesters and government forces, killing many people. The Government of Uzbekistan has seen in these disorders the Western attempts to change the country's leadership, which required the US to leave the Karshi-Khanabad Air Base. In November 2005, American planes left the base. In the same year, Uzbekistan withdrew from *GUAM* and, in 2006, again became a member of the pro-Russian military alliance, the *CSTO*.

It is worth noting that, unlike Kyrgyzstan, the new authorities which came to power in Georgia and Ukraine pronounced anti-Russian and pro-Western orientation in foreign policy. The new authorities have openly declared their wish to integrate into *NATO* and the *EU* entirely. This desire was so clear that in Georgia, in official places, along with the national flag, the *EU* flag was begun to hang. Georgia was actively involved in all the initiatives proposed by the *EU* and *NATO*.

In turn, the relationship between Russia and these two countries deteriorated. Russia saw the desire of Ukraine and Georgia to cooperate closely with the West as the *West*'s intervention in the sphere of interest and influence of Russia. After the arrival to power of President Putin in 2000, as the basis of its foreign policy, Russia adopted the restoration of former positions. In particular, this applied to the *NIS*. As a result, Russia could not accept that several countries within its sphere of influence could change their foreign policy orientations. Russia took these intentions as an open challenge to these countries and the *West* regarding its interests in the former Soviet region. As a result, a perception of reality has led to complications in the relations between Russia, Ukraine, and Georgia. Over time, these relations have become even worse.

Geopolitical Rivalry in the Post-Soviet Region

Along with existing organizations in *NIS* that have been created under the leadership of Russia, such as the *CSTO* and the *SCO*, covering mainly security issues, the integration processes in the economic sphere also began to form. In short, in 2001, between some *NIS*, the *Eurasian Economic Community* (*EurAsEC*) created.[217] The first goal of this organization was to create a deeper economic integration process between the members of the *CIS*. The organization's founders were from Russia, Belarus, Kazakhstan, Tajikistan, and Kyrgyzstan. In 2006, Uzbekistan joined the organization.[218] However, as it has been shown in other examples by the specificity of this country the foreign policy, it withdrew from the organization in 2008.[219]

In 2010, with Russia's active steps, the integration process was accelerated, and based on the *EurAsEC, Customs Union* was established. The first members of this integration stage were Russia, Kazakhstan, and Belarus. In 2012, the three countries of the *Customs Union* established the *Eurasian Economic Union (EAEU)*. In 2014, the organization joined such *NIS Small Powers* as Armenia and Kyrgyzstan.

On January 1, 2015, an agreement on establishing *EAEU* occurred. Within *the EAEU*, freedom of movement of goods, services, people, and capital was ensured, as well as pursuing a standard policy in the sectors of the economy. At the moment, there are five members *EAEU*.[220] In addition, the most viable candidate for membership in this organization is Tajikistan.[221] For the remaining *NIS Small Powers*, for various reasons, membership in this organization is not considered.

It should be noted that attempts to deepen the economic integration process between the *CIS*-were sluggish in the first ten years. Things began to change only after 2010 when Russia considered as one of the priorities of its foreign policy strengthening of integration processes with *NIS Small Powers*.[222] At the same time, this process did not accidentally coincide with the beginning of the implementation of another regional project -the *EU Eastern Partnership*. It is worth noting that Russia is very negatively perceived of this program, considering that it is at odds with its geopolitical interests, and the *EU* is trying to penetrate the traditional sphere of its interests in the *NIS* region. This fact especially applies to the countries that have experienced "color revolutions." In short, after pro-Western governments came to power, Ukraine and Georgia declared their wish to integrate into the European and Euro-Atlantic structures fully. Expressing their intentions and, simultaneously, the background of these states deteriorate their relations with Russia.

In addition to these countries, its desire for close cooperation with the *EU* also expresses Moldova. Moldova has common roots with one of the *EU* member states, Romania. In this connection, political forces in Moldova advocate the association with that country. As for other states, varying degrees of development of relations with the *EU* are willing by Azerbaijan and Armenia. Belarus held a more passive role in developing relations with the *EU* within the framework of the *EP* program. It was facilitated by the fact that regarding Belarus President Alexander Lukashenko, the *EU* imposed sanctions, limiting him and several officials from entering the country as members of this organization. Especially these sanctions intensified after the scandalous presidential elections and mass protests in Belarus in 2020. Besides, Belarus is in close relations with Russia, creating with it the *Union States*. At the same time, Belarus is the founder of Russian integration initiatives.[223] As an industrial country without energy resources, the Belarusian economy is heavily dependent on oil and gas from Russia at prices well below market. Only in this case can Belarus produce competitive products in the international market.

It should be noted that *NIS Small Powers*, characterized by vibrant pro-Western orientation, faced the harsh reaction of Russia concerning these countries. Russia led sanctions on the import of goods from Georgia, Ukraine, and Moldova. Introduced a visa regime for citizens of Georgia, but for the rest of *NIS*, travel to the territory of Russia is free.

The peak of the confrontation between Russia and Georgia has become the event of August 2008, also known as the "five-day war." On August 8, 2008, Georgian forces launched a military operation in South Ossetia to restore its territorial integrity. On the same day, Russia joined the conflict on the side of the separatist regime in South Ossetia. The Russian troops also entered the territory of another separatist entity in Georgia- Abkhazia.[224] On August 13, 2008, the active phase of confrontation was completed; the Medvedev - Sarkozy plan was adopted, which was entitled the names of the presidents of Russia and France, Dmitry Medvedev and Nicolas Sarkozy, who took the lead in this document.[225]

As a result, the Russian troops began to control the territory of South Ossetia and Abkhazia. On On 26 August 2008, Russia recognized the independence of South Ossetia and Abkhazia and established diplomatic relations with them. It is worth noting that in addition to Russia, the independence of these territories is recognized only by Venezuela, Nicaragua, Nauru, and Syria. Vanuatu first recognized Abkhazia and then withdrew it. Recognition by these countries of the separatist entities contributed by Russia.[226] Abkhazia and South Ossetia are totally dependent on financial injections from Russia;[227] also, in their territory, Russia formed a military contingent. Thus, Georgia's pro-Western orientation resulted in a confrontation with Russia to establish its control over the breakaway regions. It is worth noting that, despite the open annexation of the Georgian territory, the *West*'s reaction was very restrained. Thus, in the first days after the confrontation, only the US condemned Russia's recognition of two breakaway regions of Georgia, and it was limited to.[228] None of the *Western Great Power* was about any support for Georgia in restoring its territorial integrity.

Ukraine must also pay a high price for its pro-Western orientation and willingness to integrate into *NATO* and the *EU*. Relations between Russian and Ukraine began to deteriorate during the time of the Ukrainian President Viktor Yushchenko. President Yushchenko declared the Euro-Atlantic vector of development of Ukraine's foreign policy. Therefore, the intensity of relations with *NATO* and the *EU* has increased. It led to the aggravation of relations with Russia. In 2008, Ukraine was expected to get the opportunity to join the *MAP* at *NATO*'s summit in Bucharest in April 2008. However, Ukraine was refused; several countries members of NATO were opposed. In turn, Russia has stated that in the case of Ukraine's joining the *MAP*, Russia would consider the possibility of denunciation of the *Treaty of Friendship, Cooperation, and Partnership* between the two countries.[229] The confrontations were both in the political and economic spheres. It also concerned Russian gas supply to Ukraine and conditions of payment, revision of conditions of basing the Russian Black Sea Fleet in Crimea in Sevastopol.[230]

However, the peak of the confrontation had at the time of the next President of Ukraine, Viktor Yanukovych. Yanukovych was elected as the president of Ukraine in 2010, after which the relations with Russia began to improve. During this period, trade between the two countries increased, and several disputes earlier resolved have arisen. At the same time, Russia offered Ukraine to join the pro-Russian Customs Union. Ukraine refused the offer, wishing to participate only as an observer. In parallel with this, Ukraine continued to develop relations with the *EU*. In September 2013, the Cabinet of Ministers approved a draft of *an Association Agreement* with the *EU* under the *EP*.[231] Russia has stated that in the case of the connection of Ukraine to the *EU* initiative, Ukraine could not join the *Customs Union*. As a result, in November 2013, Ukraine suspended preparations for the conclusion of an *Association Agreement* with the *EU*, which led to mass protests. Relations escalated in February 2014 when Ukraine's parliament suspended President Yanukovych from power. In turn, Russia declared the illegitimacy of the decision. Yanukovych left Ukraine and found refuge in Russia.[232] Following, a confrontation started between the South-East of Ukraine, traditionally supportive of Yanukovych, with the rest of Ukraine, which was on the side of the pro-Western opposition, which came to power. In March 2014, the Donetsk and Lugansk regions, populated mainly by Russians, declared Donetsk and Lugansk People's Republics.[233] A military confrontation began.

In turn, the protests also began in Crimea, which has a population of most Russians. On May 17, 2014, unilaterally, a declaration of the independence of Crimea and Sevastopol was announced. A day later, Russia announced the annexation of Crimea to Russia.[234]

Despite the military confrontation in the east of Ukraine and the annexation of part of the territory of Russia, the Western reaction to these events was not on the level that was required by this fact. The US and the EU, as well as some partner countries, have not recognized the legitimacy of the annexation of Crimea to Russia, considering this action as an act of aggression, occupation, and annexation of the territory of Ukraine. Western countries and organizations recognized the territorial integrity of Ukraine. In contrast to the passive position, which made the *West* during the crisis in Georgia, this time, economic sanctions against Russia were introduced.[235] However, at that moment, this has yet to lead to the solution of the Ukrainian problems.

Another *Small State* that wants to cooperate actively with the *EU* is Moldova. These countries, Georgia and Ukraine, faced pressure from Russia. Complications of the parties have begun since the independence of Moldova. Moldova faced a separatist movement in Transnistria, populated mainly by Russians. The Russian army intervened in the region, which stopped the war, and became a guarantor of the status of the unrecognized Transnistrian republic. Every year, Russia provides regular financial assistance to the region.[236] Currently, the conflict is frozen, and the Russian peacekeeping forces are placed in the region. Transnistria is a card to pressure Moldova when relations between the two countries are complicated. After Moldova began to actively cooperate with the *EU* in the framework of the *EP*, it increased pressure on Moldova. Thus, the self-proclaimed Transnistrian republic appealed to Russia to recognize its independence and continue to join the country.[237] This appeal to Russia from Transnistria occurred after November 2013, when Moldova initialed an *Association Agreement* with the *EU*.[238] Transnistria is not the only region that can be used as a pressure lever on Moldova. An autonomous unit of Gagauzia is situated in the south of Moldova, where more than 80% of the population are Gagauzes. In 2014, Autonomy held a referendum, according to which the participants supported the accession to the pro-Russian Customs Union. The supporters of joining the EU consist of only 2.7% of the votes. Given that the country has supporters of accession of Moldova to Romania, it voted in favor of the possible independence of Gagauzia autonomy, if Moldova ceases to exist as a state.[239]

Russia limited access to traditional Moldovan products like wine, fruit, and meat in its market. The last such restriction was introduced in the summer of 2014. Russia does not hide that this decision is since the Moldovan parliament ratified the agreement on association with the *EU*. Russia explained its decision by the fact that the Moldovan market is now open to European goods and that in the Customs Union market, a ban on Moldovan products does not occur re-export of these goods. Besides, Russia threatened to interrupt energy supplies to Moldova and stop Moldova`s migrant workers from entering Russia, which also harmed the welfare of Moldovan citizens, whose significant income consists of money transfers from Russia.[240] It is a severe impact on the economy of Moldova. At the same time, this restriction does not apply to Transnistria and Gagauzia.[241] Russia is the leading market for Transnistria and Gagauzia products. Thus, Moldova's sensitive export products are used as the political and economic lever of pressure from Russia.

Selection of Foreign Policy by NIS Small Powers Stationed in Europe

Six *European NIS locations* found themselves at the crossroads of two competing and opposing integration processes. On the one hand, the *EU*'s *EP* program and the other, *EAEU*, proposed by Russia. It is worth noting that the *NIS Small Powers* gravitate towards closer relations with the *EU*, even though the *EP* does not offer full membership for these countries. *NIS Small Powers* believe integration with the *EU* is more responsible for their national interests than a closer relationship with Russia. In addition, they think that *EAEU,* despite its economic component, is a political tool designed to strengthen Russia's position in the post-Soviet space.

As a consequence, a number of these countries, as it was mentioned above, in spite of confrontation with Russia, for which they had to pay a heavy price, continued a policy of rapprochement with the *West* and its institutions. These countries sincerely believe that the insistence these countries will not be the adoption in *NATO* and the *EU*. In this way, they will be justified for all the hardships and costs these countries faced. At this point, the group of countries that continue the integration process within the *EU* Eastern Partnership framework includes Ukraine, Georgia, and Moldova. All three countries have signed the *Association Agreement* with the *EU* and continue to develop relations with this structure. By the way, all these countries are members of *GUAM*.

However, there are more behavioral models of *NIS Small Powers* in Europe. There are two other options for foreign policy The second group of countries, Belarus and Armenia, became members of the *EAEU*. As mentioned earlier, Belarus is economically dependent on cheap energy supplies from Russia and closely integrated with this country. Regarding Armenia, the situation is somewhat different. Initially, this country is actively cooperating with the EU in the framework of the *EP* by participating in the preparation of the document on the *Association Agreement*. Negotiations continued for three years, and it was expected that Armenia would sign the document at the EU Summit in Vilnius in November of 2013. However, during the visit of Armenian President Serzh Sargsyan in Moscow, on September 3, 2013, after a meeting with Russian President Vladimir Putin, the country decided to join the *EAEU*. Until the last moment, Armenia hoped to carry out active cooperation with the *EU* without messing up its relations with Russia.

Given that this country is in a political and economic dependence on Russia, Armenia is thus trying to balance its foreign policy and diversify its financial support. However, Russia's positions on Armenian expectations were precise: Russia demanded Armenia identify its path. As a result, Armenia has chosen the pro-Russian integration project.[242]

The third group only consists of one state - Azerbaijan. Due to a successful energy policy and diversification of its export transportation corridors, this country had the opportunity to pursue a more independent foreign policy. As a result, Azerbaijan can choose its priorities in foreign policy, given the complex geopolitical situation in the region where Azerbaijan is located and the conflict with Armenia over Nagorno-Karabakh. As a result, 20% of its territory in 2020 was under occupation; this country has a more balanced approach to the proposed regional integration projects.

The first preference of Azerbaijan in building relationships with other actors relates to forming a bilateral format of cooperation. Participation in one of the proposed integration processes does not meet the national interests of Azerbaijan. In short, Azerbaijan does not consider the EP program as the stage for a full-fledged integration into the *EU* as it currently represents Ukraine and Georgia. Given that the project's cost does not meet the interests of Azerbaijan and geopolitically, it becomes a cause for the deterioration of relations with Russia. That's why Azerbaijan refused to sign the *Association Agreement* and called on the *EU* to develop a new format for the further development of relations between the two sides.

Regarding the *EAEU*, Azerbaijan also does not believe that the integration process meets its interests, preferring to form a relationship with each member individually. For Russia, the leading actor *in EAEU*, this position of Azerbaijan is acceptable. Russia likes to have a deal with "neutral" than pro-Western Azerbaijan. That is why the relations between Azerbaijan and Russia continue to develop, both in the political and economic spheres.

CHAPTER 5
Three Small Powers of the South Caucasus Region: Azerbaijan, Georgia, and Armenia and Factors that Affected Their Foreign Policy

The Main Features of the South Caucasus Region

Azerbaijan, Georgia, and Armenia are the three countries that form a region of the South Caucasus. Although this region is small in size, it has a strategic location. The South Caucasus is located on the border of Eastern Europe and South-West Asia, representing a natural bridge between the two parts of the world. This location is essential, as the South Caucasus is an alternative Russian corridor linking countries of the Black Sea region and Central Asia. In addition, these regions represent an additional link between the EU and countries of the Far East; it is the largest producer and market in the Eurasian region.

This region has geographically defined borders from the North region girded ridge of the Greater Caucasus, on the West by the Black Sea, and from the East, the Caspian. Just from the South, there is no apparent natural border, though here, mainly the Aras River separates it from Iran. International agreements with these countries determine the southern border of the region with Türkiye and Iran.[243]

The total area of the South Caucasus is 186 000 km2. 16.8 million people live in the region. Among the three states, the most significant area has Azerbaijan. Its area is 86,600 km2. Azerbaijan has most of the population in the part. In April 2022, the population consisted of 10.1 million people. It accounts for 46.5% of the total area and 59% of the region's total population. The second largest is Georgia, with an area of 69 700 km2 and a population of 3.68 million. The smallest country in the region is Armenia. Its area is 29,700 km2, and this country has the smallest population, slightly less than 3 million people. At the same time, in contrast to Azerbaijan, where there is a steady increase in population, the number of people living in Georgia and Armenia is decreasing yearly. Here, it occurs because the mortality rate in the country exceeds fertility. Armenia's population decreases because this country has an active migration to other countries.

Major nations make up a high proportion of the population in the country. Thus, the overall balance of Azerbaijanis of the total population in Azerbaijan is about

91%, and 84% of the Georgians live in Georgia, Armenia; this is a mono-ethnic nation, where the proportion is 98% of the total population.

The economic potential of these three countries is also different. The most economically developed country in the region is Azerbaijan. The country has deposits of oil and natural gas through the exploitation of which the country has been developed. Parallel to this, attention is paid to developing the economy's agriculture, transport infrastructure, and ICT sectors as alternatives to the energy sector. The development of the non-oil sector is essential, especially after the fall in oil prices in 2014 and the reduction of the country's income. In 2015, twice the manat's devaluation (Azerbaijan national currency) occurred. Thus, held in February 2015, a 50% depreciation of manat reduced nominal GDP by 8.0% in Azerbaijan.[244] Despite this, Azerbaijan has significant cash resources accumulated in the *State Oil Fund of Azerbaijan Republic* (*SOFAZ*). As for 2022, the fund is concentrated at about 45 billion US dollars. Even though the post of the economy has declined, GDP continues to grow. Overall, in the year 2015, the GDP increased by 1.1%,[245] including non-oil industrial production, grew by 8.4%.[246] Azerbaijan's GDP in 2021 amounted to 54.6 billion US dollars.[247] It is worth noting that the proportion of the economy of Azerbaijan in the South Caucasus in 2010 was 75%.[248] In 2014, this figure was even more- 77.7%.

Concerning the economy of Georgia and Armenia, they develop significantly slower than Azerbaijan. At the same time, both countries, unlike Azerbaijan, are members of the *World Trade Organization*. (*WTO*). At the same time, Georgia's economy receives additional revenues from transportation through its territory of oil and gas produced in Azerbaijan to the world markets. Georgia has had the opportunity to receive dividends on Azerbaijan's energy policy. In addition, the Azerbaijani oil company *SOCAR* is Georgia's largest investor and taxpayer. Georgia's GDP was 18.7 billion US dollars in 2021. In the same year, Georgia's GDP grew remarkable 10.4%.[249] The main growth was observed in such sectors as construction and mining.[250]

In turn, the Armenian economy grew by 5.7% in 2021. Armenia's GDP in 2021 amounted to 13.98 billion US dollars.[251]

It is interesting that, despite the region's small size and the three countries located there, all three countries, along with ethnic and religious composition, have no common roots. In short, Azerbaijan's population has Turkic roots, and the main religion, followed by its citizens, is Islam. The majority of the people, about 75%, belongs to the Shia branch of Islam, and others, to the Sunni.[252]

Georgians ethnically belong to the Kartvelian language family. Most Georgians are Christians, referring to its Orthodox branch. Georgians have their autocephalous Eastern Orthodox Church. Its jurisdiction covers the entire territory of Georgia and all Georgians, wherever they live, if they recognize its authority. More than 80 % of Georgians call themselves Orthodox.[253]

As for the Armenians, this nation belongs to the Indo-European language family. Believers Armenians in the majority are Christians and have their own independent church-Armenian Apostolic Church, which, unlike Georgia, is a non-Chalcedonian church.[254] Therefore, even though the Georgians and Armenians are Christians, they belong to different concessions.

The region of the South Caucasus is neighbored by countries such as Russia to the north, Iran to the south, and Türkiye to the southeast. At the same time, only Azerbaijan and Georgia share a common border with Russia. Azerbaijan and Armenia have borders with Iran and all three countries - with Türkiye. However, Azerbaijan has a border with Türkiye only through the Nakhchivan Autonomous Region, which is, in turn, divided from the mainland by Armenia.[255]

The proximity of these countries has a significant impact on the local people. Historically, in different periods, the country has impacted the people of the South Caucasus. For the last two hundred years, countries in the region were part of the Russian state at the beginning part of the Russian Empire and then the Soviet Union. It mainly has much in common with its neighbor Azerbaijan, which shares a common ethnic root and culture with Türkiye, religion, and history with Iran.

Besides the main neighbors, through the Black Sea, Georgia is also adjacent to the countries such as Ukraine, Bulgaria, and Romania. In turn, through the Caspian Sea, Azerbaijan is bordered by Kazakhstan and Turkmenistan.

After the collapse of the Soviet Union, the South Caucasus region was included in Europe, although the adoption of such a decision was mainly political. The Azerbaijan and Georgian territories are only partly located in Europe, while Armenia is entirely in Asia. As to the *"European identity"* of these countries, the perception among the Europeans themselves (mainly the EU member states) was not unambiguous, and the debate about where the border of Europe is why these countries are often referred to as Asia today. All three countries are members of the Council of Europe and have a dynamic relationship with the EU. Curiously, the first European organization into which the South Caucasus countries entered was *UEFA*.[256]

Factors Influencing the Formation of Foreign Policy of the South Caucasus Countries

All three South Caucasus countries are *Small Powers* with limited resources. At the same time, after the collapse of the Soviet Union, these countries are faced with acute political and economic problems. In this case, the possibility to shape their foreign policy has been limited because of the availability of a small resource. In addition, these countries, at first, needed more trained diplomats.

In general, the main factor that influences the formation of foreign policy is the region's geographical location. This factor plays geopolitical and geo-economic importance in the shape of the foreign policy of these countries.

First and foremost, it is worth noting that all three South Caucasus countries are landlocked states. Only Georgia, which has an outlet to the Black Sea, can go through the Bosporus and Dardanelles straits to enter the Mediterranean Sea. The availability of this feature is essential for the economy of Georgia. Primary trading operations in this country are made through ports on the Black Sea. For Georgia and other South Caucasus countries, the Black Sea coast is the exit to the world markets. In short, Azerbaijan, whose main export is oil and natural gas, has access to the Georgian port of Supsa, which relates to Baku with an oil pipeline. Via this pipeline, oil is supplied to the port and from there by tanker ships on the world markets. At the same time, *SOCAR* rent another Georgian Port- Kulevi, through which they export Azerbaijani oil and oil products.[257]

The lack of access to the open seas is significant for Azerbaijan and Armenia. In short, Azerbaijan, which, as mentioned above, has significant reserves of oil and gas to export to world markets and uses the territory of neighboring states. Thus, to ensure stable export of its energy resources, Azerbaijan, both politically and economically, is dependent on its neighbors. In this regard, Azerbaijan needed to implement appropriate policies to reduce this dependence. In this case, the basic strategy is diversifying Azerbaijan's export corridors.

As for Armenia, since it is in conflict with Azerbaijan over Nagorno-Karabakh, borders with two neighboring states, Azerbaijan and Türkiye of its four (this country is bordered by Azerbaijan, Türkiye, Iran, and Georgia), are closed. Türkiye closed the border in April 1993, following the 822nd *UN Security Council* resolution, after the Armenian armed forces occupied the Azerbaijani Kelbajar region.[258]

Therefore, for Armenia, developing transport routes with Georgia and Iran is imperative. It is especially true of Georgia because the territory of this country is a link between Armenia and Russia, its strategic ally and main economic partner. In addition, since 2015 Armenia has been in the *Eurasian Economic Union*, the primary member of which is Russia.[259] The lack of a common border with other members of *the Eurasian Economic Union* also adversely affects the formation of economic relations with key partners. This fact becomes relevant as Georgia participates in another integration process, which contradicts the Eurasian Union. This country is on the verge of entering into a free trade area with the EU, which will lead to the fact that both Georgia and Armenia will be forced to revise the regime of crossing the shared border.

Up to 70% of its imports Armenia received through the territory of Georgia. The importance of the northern route to Armenia began to be felt after the deterioration of relations between Russia and Georgia after a rail bridge near the Georgian city Gori was destroyed, [260] and Russia closed the border checkpoints Lars, Nizhny Zaramag, and Psou. The closure of the checkpoint at the Georgian-Russian border harmed exports of Armenian fruits and vegetables to the Russian market. [261]

Thus, the South Caucasus countries are susceptible to their geographical location, which directly affects the formation of political and economic relations in the international arena. At the same time, as was shown by the example of the complications of relations between Russia and Georgia, these countries are also very sensitive to changes in the situation in neighboring countries. Another example of this circumstance is the temporary lifting of international economic sanctions on Iran. It enabled countries in the region to develop relations with Iran actively. Hitherto, these features have been minimal. Azerbaijan, jointly with Russia and Iran, is actively implementing the *"North-South"* international transport corridor. Because of during the Donald Trump administration period in the US, sanctions against Iran were reintroduced again, so a number of shared projects between Iran and the South Caucasus countries were shelved.

The region is also an important transport corridor between the EU and the Far East. In short, if you draw a vertical line on the Eurasian continent, from the White Sea to the Persian Gulf, this line will intersect only Russia, South Caucasus (Georgia and Armenia or Azerbaijan), and Iran. Thus, the region is an alternative to Russia and Iran for ground transportation routes. At the same time, it can be used as an alternative to sea transport via the Suez Canal. Consequently, the *"West-East"* transport corridor has been developed under the *EU TRACECA* project.

In addition to transportation projects formed within the framework of the *EU* programs, the region attracts the other prominent actor in the Eurasian region- China. In recent years, the country has been actively shaping transport infrastructure in the Eurasian region, mainly Central Asia, providing these countries with the necessary loans and investments. China is interested in the infrastructure developing in the South Caucasus region, mainly in the territories of Azerbaijan and Georgia. Thus, the first tentative transportation between China and the part of the Black Sea began, which may be eventually increased.

The traffic between the *EU* and countries of the Far East is expected to increase after the new railway line *Baku-Tbilisi-Kars railway*, which connects the South Caucasus to Türkiye and further to Europe, is put into operation.

Regional Conflicts and Their Impact on the Foreign Policy of Regional States

One of the critical factors influencing the foreign policy of the South Caucasus *Small Powers* is regional conflicts, countries in the region inherited from the Soviet Union. All countries of the region are involved in different conflicts. Thus, two separatist entities in Georgia, Abkhazia and South Ossetia, seek to secede from Georgia. While Azerbaijan and Armenia till 2020 were involved in the conflict around Nagorno-Karabakh. These conflicts impede cooperation within the region and prevent more active implementation of these Small Powers' political and economic interests.

One of the internal conflicts in Georgia is associated with South Ossetia. The separatist movement in this region of Georgia, located in the north of the country, began in 1989. It is worth noting that Ossetians in Soviet times lived in two administrative units in the North Ossetian Autonomous Republic, located in Russia, and the Autonomous Region of South Ossetia belongs to Georgia.

Statements of South Ossetia to secede from Georgia started at a time when Georgia began to declare its withdrawal from the Soviet Union. South Ossetia declared its wish to withdraw from Georgia on August 20, 1990, and proclaimed on the South Ossetian Soviet Democratic Republic within the USSR. In December 1990, the Georgian parliament began to consider the question of the elimination of the autonomous status of South Ossetia. On December 11, 1990, in Tskhinvali (capital of South Ossetia), in ethnic clashes, three people were killed, leaving Georgia and introducing a state of emergency. It started a new round of escalation of the situation in the region.[262] On December 21, 1991, South Ossetia declared independence.

The armed confrontation continued up to the time when Eduard Shevardnadze came to power in Georgia. Shevardnadze, with the initiative of Russia, on June 24, 1992, signed a ceasefire agreement. Ten days before the region entered a peacekeeping force composed of Russian, Georgian, and Ossetian battalions.[263] Attempts have been made to resolve the conflict, but it has not yielded concrete results. When President Michael Saakashvili came to power in Georgia (2004-2013), he, in his election program, promised the resolution of conflicts on the territory of the country. In addition to other methods of conflict resolution, the military option also was present. Georgia agreed to the military operation in South Ossetia on August 8, 2008, the day when passed the opening ceremony of the Summer Olympic Games in Beijing. On that day, the Georgian troops entered Tskhinvali and announced the restoration of Georgia's territorial integrity. In response, Russia sent troops into South Ossetia and along with it, and in Abkhazia.[264] The basic thesis of Russia for the legalization of intervention was the protection of its citizens (until then, Russia has granted its citizenship to inhabitants of Abkhazia and South Ossetia), and the safety of the

Russian peacekeeping forces.[265] As a result of the intervention of Russia, Georgia troops were forced to retreat from the entire territory of South Ossetia. 25 August 2008, Russia recognized the independence of South Ossetia and established diplomatic relations with it.[266]

As for Abkhazia, the region located in northwest Georgia, near the shores of the Black Sea, during the existence of the Soviet Union, she has had the status of an autonomous republic within Georgia. On April 25, 1990, South Ossetia announced that it was seceding from Georgia and declared itself as the Abkhaz Soviet Socialist Republic within the USSR, a status she had enjoyed before connecting to Georgia SSR in 1921. However, this decision did not comply with the Constitution of the USSR and the Georgian SSR. In April 1991, Georgia declared independence, while Abkhazia declared its desire to remain part of the Soviet Union.

After the demise of the Soviet Union, Georgia, as well as other fourteen republics that became independent states, has been recognized by the international community. Due to Abkhazia was not a union republic, it did not have the right to self-determination. In the summer of 1992, the controversies between the parties escalated. On August 13, 1992, Georgia sent troops into Abkhazia. Active military operations continued until September 30, 1993.[267] It is worth noting that on the side Abkhazians fought volunteers from Russia.

During the Soviet period, 525 thousand people lived in Abkhazia. Only 17% of the total population, or 93,200 people, were Abkhazians, while Georgians consisted 240 thousand of people.[268] It would be naive to believe that they could repel the Georgian army. In addition, with the presence of the Russian militaries and military infrastructure bequeathed from the Soviet era, Russia has encouraged the North Caucasus peoples in their support of his Abkhazian "brothers." In 1993, the Abkhaz separatists, with the help of Russia, could supplant military units of Georgia.[269] Following the suspension of hostilities, the UN issued a mediation initiative with the participation of representatives of Abkhazia, Georgia, and Russia. Negotiations began to conduct, which were completed with the signing of an agreement on the peaceful settlement of the conflict.[270] The signing of the agreement did not lead to the final resolution of the conflict and did not eliminate the hostility between the parties. The region introduced the *CIS* peacekeeping contingent, composed of Russian troops.

The situation in Abkhazia changed dramatically after the "five-day war" in South Ossetia, after which, on 25 August 2008, Russia, as in the case of South Ossetia, recognized the region's independence. In response, the Georgian parliament adopted an agreement under which South Ossetia and Abkhazia declared the occupied territories.[271]

Russia also contributed to the fact that Venezuela, Nicaragua, Nauru, and Syria recognized the independence of these transformations. Today, these two entities entirely depend on Russia's political and economic support. Given the circumstances, neither Abkhazia nor South Ossetia can function as a full-fledged state. The international community recognizes the territorial integrity of Georgia, including the two breakaway territories. In turn, Georgia has no control over the country's whole territory, which violates its sovereign rights. Considering the newly formed realities, it is also difficult to state that the conflict is resolved, which can only satisfy some.

Regarding the Nagorno-Karabakh conflict, after the collapse of the Soviet Union, it became international. As in the case of the conflicts in Georgia, it also originates in the Soviet era. In February 1988, Armenians living in Nagorno-Karabakh Autonomous Region decided to detach from Azerbaijan and join Armenia.[272] That was the reason for the beginning of the long-term conflict. Following Azerbaijan Supreme Soviet (a legislative organ of the Azerbaijan Soviet Socialist Republic) announced that this decision violated the Constitution, both a republic and the Soviet Union, and rejected the decision. It was discussed in the Supreme Council of the Soviet Union, and the decision was that Nagorno-Karabakh should remain part of Azerbaijan. Not satisfied with this decision of the Supreme Soviet of the Soviet Union, Armenians began to attack the Azerbaijanis living in Armenia and Karabakh.[273]

In September 1991, the Nagorno-Karabakh Armenians, given the changes that had occurred in the Soviet Union, unilaterally announced the creation of the Nagorno-Karabakh Republic. Following the Supreme Council of Azerbaijan on 26 November 1991, according to the Constitutions of the Republic and the Soviet Union abolished the autonomous status of Nagorno-Karabakh.[274] Despite the declaration of the independence of the region and the holding of a referendum in December 1991,[275] Any state, including Armenia, has not recognized Nagorno-Karabakh. The reason for this is that the region constitutionally had not been able to declare its independence, as it was in the case of the fifteen Soviet republics, including Azerbaijan and Armenia. A military confrontation between the two countries continued after 1991. Armenians, who were better trained and equipped, were able to achieve some success in the conflict and supplant Azerbaijanis from Nagorno-Karabakh. Soon, the Armenian armed forces, with the support of Russian soldiers, in addition to Nagorno-Karabakh, occupied seven surrounding regional districts. The entire population of these regions, which were the Azerbaijanis, avoiding physical destruction, was forced to leave their homes.[276]

Armed clashes continued until 1994, when on May 12, in Bishkek, the parties had agreed on a cease-fire. As a result of the conflict, 30 000 people lost their lives. Many refugees and IDPs were formed on both sides of the conflict: 300

000 Armenians left Azerbaijan at the time, and more than 800 000 people were forced to leave Armenia and the occupied Azerbaijani territories. About 20% of Azerbaijan's territory was occupied by Armenian military forces.[277] Since then, the *OSCE* Minsk Group has undertaken a mediation mission to resolve the conflict. This group is represented by three co-chairs, representing three countries: Russia, US, and France. Periodically, they were offered several conflict resolution models, which have yet to be implemented for various reasons.

Despite the ceasefire, violation of it continued periodically. The escalation of these violations has become active hostilities between April 2-5, 2016, and has received the name "a four-day war." As a result of the military confrontation, for the first time in 24 years, it changed the status quo on the front lines, and the Azerbaijani military units managed to release and gain a foothold in a number of strategic heights. Only after the intervention of Russia was the ceasefire restored, and the commanders of staffs of Azerbaijan and Armenia met in Moscow and signed a ceasefire agreement.

It has become clear that the formed balance between Azerbaijan and Armenia, with the help of Russia, is broken in favor of Azerbaijan, and the status quo needs to meet the realities of the new situation. And as will explain later, during the 44-day war, Azerbaijan restored its territorial integrity.

The Energy Factor in the Foreign Policy of the South Caucasus States

Another factor that affects the foreign policy of the South Caucasus region's *Small Powers*, as well as its geopolitical and geo-economic formation, is Azerbaijan's oil and natural gas resources. In this case, this factor is primarily decisive for Azerbaijan. However, for Georgia and Armenia, it also has a particular influence. Given that there has been a confrontation between Azerbaijan and Armenia, then Armenia is not directly involved in energy projects. The fact that Azerbaijan purposefully isolates Armenia from transport projects pending the resolution of the Nagorno-Karabakh conflict. At the same time, due to the closure of borders, Armenia has yet to acquire oil and natural gas from its geographical neighbor. On the other hand, Georgia is actively involved in the energy strategy of Azerbaijan. Through the territory of this country, the main transport corridors for the export of Azerbaijani oil and gas have passed.

As mentioned earlier, the South Caucasus is in the interests of Russia, which, like other *Small Powers* of the former Soviet Union, is part of its "*near abroad policy*" doctrine. This development did not coincide with the interests of the South Caucasus countries, especially Azerbaijan and Georgia. In the first years of independence, Georgia has conducted anti-Russian and pro-Western foreign policy, spoiling its relations with Russia. Russia has supported the separatist regimes of Abkhazia and South Ossetia. Georgia wanted more active involvement of the *West* and its regional institutions.

The same can be said about Azerbaijan. Azerbaijan's relations with Russia were not at the ideal level, with the result that, in the Nagorno-Karabakh military confrontation, Russia supported Armenia, which led to significant territorial losses. Azerbaijan, unlike Georgia, had a critical trump card in the form of the availability of energy resources. Azerbaijan hoped that using this factor would form a new balance in the region, which would also help ensure its territorial integrity. Initially, the energy factor in Azerbaijan has been used to solve economic problems (though it was not in the last place) and achieve existing policy objectives. First of all, Azerbaijan was trying to attract the *West* to the South Caucasus region to create balance, the growing influence of Russia.

This task took work. Complete negotiations and signing the contract at the beginning of the exploitation of oil fields in the Caspian Sea were possible only during the period of the third president of Azerbaijan, Heydar Aliyev, when Azerbaijan signed the "*Contract of the Century*" with international energy companies. Unlike their predecessors, Aliyev managed to prevent a coup,[278] supported by Russia, and began forming the balanced foreign policy of the country for which the necessary conditions were created. The signing of the "*Contract of the Century*" was the first stage of forming the energy strategy and the balanced foreign policy of Azerbaijan. For clarity, the definition of the Azerbaijan balance policy should be stressed that Azerbaijan (along with forming relations with the *West)* did not want to aggravate it with Russia.

However, the energy factor in Azerbaijan's foreign policy and the formation of the geopolitical situation in the South Caucasus region was more comprehensive than the start of oil production. An important component was the creation of its export transportation routes. For countries that do not have access to the open seas, there is a reality that their access to world markets passes through the territory of neighboring states. Neighbor countries may use this factor to achieve political and economic dividends. Consequently, the basic rule for the energy security of any country that does not have access to the open seas is the maximum to ensure the diversification of transport routes. In other words, it is to create alternative export corridors. For Azerbaijan, the availability of such alternatives, for geographical and political reasons, is minimal. In this regard, optimizing the formation of energy transport routes that would meet its national interests is necessary.

In addition to the creation of alternative ways made it possible to reduce the potential geopolitical risks and dependence on neighboring countries, it allowed Azerbaijan to strengthen the sanctions measure against Armenia to obtain from that country to liberate the occupied territories and agree to resolve the Nagorno- Karabakh conflict within the territorial integrity of Azerbaijan.

Therefore, Azerbaijan deliberately chose a transport path that would bypass Armenia, although geographically, to gain access to the Mediterranean Sea, the territory of Armenia is the shortest route and hence commercially attractive.

This development fully meets the interests of Georgia, as the isolation of Armenia from regional projects has turned the country into a hub of export pipelines to transport oil and natural gas from Azerbaijan. Thus, the availability of energy resources in Azerbaijan became a game changer for himself and Georgia, which has become part of the energy strategy.

With the implementation of new regional energy projects and the solution of geopolitical problems, geo-economic goals are also begun to form. Energy transportation projects allow the region to strengthen its relations with the countries of Southeast Europe and the Black Sea region, creating these countries' integration processes. At the same time, Azerbaijan's energy projects play an essential role in shaping the EU's energy security, which also contributes to strengthening relations.

Relations with Russia

As previously stated, a key actor in the South Caucasus is Russia. The level of relations with this country is essential for the region. Russia had unlimited influence on the developments in the South Caucasus region. With geopolitical interests in the South Caucasus, Russia was trying to prevent attempts of the regional countries in search of closer ties with the *West*. As in other regions of the former Soviet space, Russia's interests in the South Caucasus are closely linked to its geopolitical context. The main task of Russia in the South Caucasus is complete control of the region, preventing the possible wishes of the region for integration with Euro-Atlantic structures and institutions. Thus, Russia does not want the Western presence in the region.[279]

As a result, the *Small States* of the region need to fix their foreign policies and national interests following the expectations of Russia. If the action of any of the *Small Power* of the South Caucasus is contrary to the interests of Russia, it leads to a complication in relations with this country. This development could mean for *Small States* in the region big problems.

It is worth noting that since the independence of the South Caucasian countries, Russia has controlled the situation in the region. Russia has different pressure tools concerning the *Small Powers* in the region and possibly tries to increase and enhance them. The maximum bar control for Russia is to ensure these Small Powers' political and economic dependence. This goal, however, was provided only concerning Armenia. Other countries have a slightly different structure of relations with Russia. However, this does not mean that Russia is not trying to control these countries.[280] Along with other methods of control of the South

Caucasus region, the most effective tool is the preservation of the status quo in the unresolved regional conflicts, which limit not only the free action of these countries but even brings the loss of sovereignty, both in terms of control of part of its territory and opportunities independently make decisions in the national interest.

This control does not require more diligence because Russia has no geopolitical rivals in the South Caucasus. The US and other Western countries have restricted their interests mainly to economic objectives, namely the development of energy and transport projects. Thanks to the support of the US made possible the realization of these projects since Russia could not resist the only remaining *Super Power*. Regarding the geopolitical interests, they were limited to only the use of the territories of Azerbaijan and Georgia as a springboard for providing logistical support for NATO troops to conduct military operations in Afghanistan. However, neither the US nor NATO is considering the possibility of strengthening its position in the region by creating a military base in one of the countries of the South Caucasus or admission to the alliance.

The perception of *the Great Powers* and the international community towards the region is based on the fact that the essential duties to the South Caucasus *Small Powers* have been met. These countries 1991 were recognized as full actors of the international community. The current international system guarantees the preservation of their independence. Thus, the South Caucasus countries have no fear of a possible forced disappearance from the world map, as happened with these countries in 1920-1921, when the Red Army occupied them.[281] However, even though the international community also recognizes the territorial integrity of these countries, no collective security instruments have been used to maintain it. As a result, Georgia and Azerbaijan faced the problem of separatism and occupation of their lands.

At the same time, although the Western countries and institutions are interested in strengthening democratic principles in the South Caucasus countries and are ready to contribute to their formation by various methods, including sanctions and structural support, they are not prepared to respond to the geopolitical challenges. In this case, countries in the region are forced to react and deal with these challenges, resulting from efforts to encourage the formation of Western values in the South Caucasus. At the same time, taking into account that Azerbaijan is a mainly Muslim country, some of these kinds of challenges for it come from Iran.

The Iranian interests coincide with the interests of Russia, namely the prevention of the possible presence of the *West* and its institutions in the South Caucasus. Iran, as well, and Russia sees the region as its "*soft underbelly*" and beware that *Small Powers* of the South Caucasus will allow the *West* to organize its military presence. It is no accident that Iran (in the issue of defining the legal status of the Caspian Sea) has a destructive position and remains the only country which not ratified *the Convention on the legal status of the Caspian Sea* (2018).

As for Türkiye, although its relations with Azerbaijan are at a strategic level, a few factors limit its action in the region. First, the traditional policy of non-interference and the preservation of the status quo was formed during the time of the first president of Ataturk and defined as "*Peace at home, peace in the world.*" Once again, this thesis was confirmed by the fact that after Türkiye began to abandon the traditional foreign policy course, it actively supported Azerbaijan during the "*44-day war*" in 2020, which played an essential role in achieving victory on the part of Azerbaijan.

Another limiting aspect of this country is the responsibility of Türkiye to NATO, of which this country is a part. Türkiye is forced to shape its policies towards the region in the context of the common interests of the Alliance. However, as its foreign policy course changed, its relations with the Alliance also underwent correction.

After the Party of Justice and Development came to power in 2002, the new Turkish government began gradually evading the traditional course in foreign policy, which also impacted the South Caucasus region. However, the lack of a shared vision and long-term strategy towards the region initially does not make Türkiye a competitor to Russia. This statement remains true even during the complications of relations between the two countries. At that time, Türkiye's interests were not focused on geopolitical problems and were limited to the economic sphere. But even in this case, the South Caucasus was not a priority region for implementing its economic interests. Even though Azerbaijan, Georgia, and Türkiye are significantly actively developing relations in the economic sphere, they are limited to mainly the implementation of energy and transport projects. At the same time, these projects' main initiator and implementer was Azerbaijan, not Türkiye.

In general, for *the Small Powers* of the region, there are three possible options for developing relations with Russia, depending on the chosen foreign policy. The first version of such a relationship involves the formation of a foreign policy that would be fully coordinated with Russia's interests. In this case, the *Small State* has to give up the desire for active cooperation with the *West*, primarily the US, *NATO*, and the *EU*. Since Russia perceives all of these actors as geopolitical rivals in the South Caucasus region, it is possible that the struggle for the region does not pass directly between Russia and these actors; Russia is using all likely pressure directly on the South Caucasus *Small Powers*. It is due not only to Russia's inability to expostulate with the US and *NATO* directly but also the lack of interest and willingness of these actors to participate in this because the region is not essential for them. In this case, the main impacts from Russia are because of the ongoing pro-Western politics *Small Powers* of the South Caucasus get themselves.

Moreover, Russia is trying to use both "*soft power*" and force, including military intervention, as tools of influence. Essential tools are the impact of economic instruments, especially the energy factor. Russia, which has abundant energy resources, uses this resource to achieve its goals, especially in the countries of the former Soviet Union. Thus, Russia can use privileged prices for energy supply, primarily natural gas, for close allies.

With complicated relations with Russia, *NIS Small Powers* must purchase gas at a higher price. For some *NIS*, it is an essential factor; therefore, they face a choice in determining their priorities. A number of *Small Powers* of the former Soviet Union (under the impossibility of diversifying its energy imports) chose the path of least resistance and preferred to coordinate their national interests with Russia. In this case, it concerned not only importers but also oil and gas exporters. Countries with immediate access to the world markets which pass through the territory of Russia also adjust their foreign policies according to the interests and expectations of Russia.

The second option, about *NIS* with Russia, is a policy of the least resistance. These states produce their foreign policy following Russia's national and regional interests. The small regional NIS *Powers* must consider possible integration with Western institutions. However, after 2000, Russia also hoped that these *Small Powers* would actively participate in the integration process proposed by that country. Russia believes the best option to achieve its interests in the former Soviet Union is to achieve the maximum impact on *Small Powers* regarding security, politics, and economy.

Therefore, *Small Powers* of the South Caucasus, in the selection of this option of building relationships with Russia, should clearly define what their national interests, as the close cooperation with this country, will allow their implementation is, and whether this *Small Power* will be able to prevent possible unwanted heavily dependent on Russia. Therefore, it is essential to be clear about the main priorities and determine how the country is ready to give up specific interests. As time has shown, since the independence of the *NIS*, it is generally the least desirable option for developing relations *with Small Powers*.

The third option to build relations with Russia is following a policy of neutrality and balancing. In other words, *Small Powers* adhere to an equidistant policy concerning all the major actors in the region to avoid being involved in a possible confrontation between them. At the same time, following these policies maximize opportunities to realize own interests. Regarding specifically the South Caucasus region, since for *Small Powers* in the region, there are two possible options for the integration of formation of relations, namely the

EU's *EP* program and pro-Russian *EAEU*, then this kind of policy demands equidistant steps towards them. In other words, in order to avoid complicating relations with prominent geopolitical actors in the region, *the Small Powers* of the South Caucasus shall refrain from involvement in integration processes proposed by the *West*. At the same time, to avoid possible dependence on Russia, this *Small Power* shall also seek opportunities not to participate in the integration process which runs this country.

In order to conduct this type of policy, countries need to have a specific resource, which would allow involving more actors in the region, which in turn are also involved in forming a balance between them. In addition, pursuing predicted for the main actor's foreign policy is very significant to the course of this state. The need for this is to convince the *Great Powers* that the steps taken by *Small Powers*, in any case, do not run counter to their interests. Otherwise, the possible misperception of reality may lead to a miscalculation of the situation arising from key actors in the region and further actions that may result in a high price for the *Small Powers*. Consequently, *Small Powers*, which base their policies on balancing forces, must constantly ensure that information on their activities concerning existing or new situations is stable.

It is worth noting that although the South Caucasus is composed of only three states, there are three proposed options for relations. In short, the biggest of the South Caucasus country, Azerbaijan, adheres to the policy of balance in its relations with the main actors in the region. Through this kind of policy, Azerbaijan also refused to participate in integration processes, preferring the formation of bilateral ties with the main actors. This format is also in the national interest of this state.

Georgia pursues a pro-Western foreign policy, whose ultimate goal is full integration into the Euro-Atlantic and European structures, especially for Georgia, which was confirmed during Michael Saakashvili's presidency. Despite the fact that it came to change, the government is looking for ways to improve relations with Russia, foreign policy priorities of the country remained unchanged.

As to Armenia, despite attempts to pursue a balanced foreign policy of this country, its dependence on Russia continues to grow.

CHAPTER 6
Azerbaijan: Foreign Policy is Designed to Maintain the Balance

Formation of Foreign Policy during the First Years of Independence

The processes in the Soviet Union allowed Azerbaijan to gain its independence in 1991. Like other former Soviet republics, Azerbaijan became part of the international system, which shaped the form of her state-building and vector of further development. As a result, Azerbaijan has announced Western values as the basis of her constitutive principles.[282] Foreign policy priorities have been determined following the realities in which this government was formed. It is worth noting that the lack of experience of statehood also affects the conduction of foreign policy.

Azerbaijan falls under the category of small states. The country, by size, is only in 110th place in the world among the currently existing states. Meanwhile, the population was just over seven million at the time of the restoration of independence (now 10,1 million (2022). At the same time, Azerbaijan is the largest state in the South Caucasus. Along with this, Azerbaijan is adjacent in the north to the largest country in the world, and the former *Super Power*- Russia, and in the south, another important regional player - is Iran. At the same time, Nakhchivan (which has no connection with the rest of Azerbaijan, separated from it by Armenia) neighbors another significant regional actor- Türkiye. These three countries have historically influenced the formation of modern Azerbaijan.

As mentioned before, like the other two South Caucasian *Small Powers*, Azerbaijan has had-relations with Russia for almost two hundred years. Russia and Azerbaijan were part of a single state (firstly as part of the Russian Empire (1813-1918) and then the Soviet Union (1920-1991)), and together with this country, were affected by the process of Westernization and secularization, which resulted in the formation of the modern secular society in the country.

As for Iran, Azerbaijan also has historical ties to this country. Azerbaijan was a part of different empires that emerged on Iranian territory for a very long time. As a result, the majority population in Azerbaijan, as it is in Iran, belongs to Shia Islam, treated to the Twelver (Ithna'ashariyyah) branch. Moreover, in Iran, there are significant numbers of Azerbaijanis, whose population, according to the different sources, varies between 18 and 27 million.[283] To determine the exact number is virtually impossible because Iranian' official statistics are not published detailing ethnic structure.

Regarding the mutual features with Türkiye, the peoples of both countries have common ethnic and cultural roots. Not coincidentally, a catchphrase, was said by the third Azerbaijani President, Heydar Aliyev: Azerbaijan and Türkiye are *"one nation, two states"* has become a motto of these relations.[284] Consequently, common modern history with Russia, the past with Iran, and the ethnic and cultural unity with Türkiye are key factors in forming the Azerbaijani society and its identification.

One of the most important factors which affected Azerbaijan's foreign policy was the long-term, protracted Armenian-Azerbaijani Nagorno-Karabakh conflict. Azerbaijan faced separatism of Armenians living in Nagorno-Karabakh who demanded unification with Armenia. Inherited from the Soviet Union, this confrontation escalated into war in 1991-1994, leaving the entire Nagorno-Karabakh and seven adjacent regions[285] were occupied by Armenia.[286] Those occupied territories could be liberated only in 2020, during *the 44-day war*. Incidentally, the conflict with Armenia has profoundly affected the construction of its foreign policy and the ability to realize the national interests of both states.

The increasing influence of a conflict between the two countries is that after the collapse of the *Eastern Bloc* and the Soviet Union, the former republics of the Union, with the tacit consent of the *West*, entered the Russian sphere of influence.

Concerning Azerbaijan, the primary tool of Russia to deter this country from closer cooperation and integration with the *West* became the Nagorno-Karabakh conflict. As a result, when the Cease-fire Agreement between the sides of the conflict was agreed in May 1994, in Bishkek, Armenia controlled 20 percent of Azerbaijani territories.[287] The attempts and desire of Azerbaijan to return to these territories through negotiations or military operations have so far failed. One of the main reasons for this is that Russia wants to preserve the status quo that was formed to be able to pressure both Azerbaijan and Armenia. *"No war, no peace"* status[288] quo has become a geopolitical lever with which Russia is allowed to solve several issues at the same time: namely, it can maneuver in the South Caucasus, maintain control over regional states, and prevent the possible political presence of the *West*. Even in 2022, two years after the *"44-day war"* ended and Russia is mediating for *Cease-Fire Declaration* between Azerbaijan and Armenia, this country is still using the same approach: wanting to maintain its presence in the region (after the *"44-day war,"* the Russian peacekeepers dislocated in the Karabakh region), Russia is trying to prevent a final solution to the conflict. In a word, although Azerbaijan and Armenia are ready to sign a *Peace Treaty*, Russia is adjusting the status of Karabakh, which Azerbaijan refuses to provide after winning the war.

Thus, until 2020, neither Azerbaijan nor Armenia could achieve the desired result in this conflict. Although Armenia de facto controls the region, Nagorno-Karabakh is not recognized as an independent state by any country, including Armenia. At the same time, despite the fact that the international community recognizes the territorial integrity of Azerbaijan, de facto, the country had no control over the occupied territories. For a very long time, attempts to change the status quo could lead to even more disastrous consequences, as the struggle for the change of status would be conducted with Armenia and Russia, for a *Small Power*, which as Azerbaijan, due to the limited resources and capacity, confrontation with this state is impossible. Azerbaijan seeks to balance Russia's influence in the region at the expense of efforts to attract other significant actors (in this case, the *West*) in the South Caucasus, but their interests were limited. The maximum that Azerbaijan has managed to achieve is to reduce the degree of pressure Russia has on the situation regarding the implementation of the geo-economic interests of the country. Namely, it was performed by the performance of energy projects and the creation of regional transport routes. It became possible through the involvement of Western companies and states in implementing these projects.

Even the beginning on April 2, 2016, a new confrontation on the front line, which was later named "*the four-day war*," as a result of which Azerbaijan was able to release a number of strategic heights in the Nagorno-Karabakh, it was not a full-scale war, or blitzkrieg, and was only a tactical reconnaissance. For the first time in 24 years, Azerbaijan was able to release part of the territories associated with good planning, preparation, and choosing the right time. Azerbaijan understood that the existing status quo must change concerning what military operation was carried out. At the same time, Azerbaijan was aware that Russian intervention should not be expected under partial military operations. Given that Russia is currently interested in the situation in Ukraine and Syria, and in this country, there is an economic downturn due to the sharp fall in oil prices and Western sanctions; the country would not wish to complicate the relations with Azerbaijan. As a result, Russia would only assist in a ceasefire and adopted a new situation to the indignation of the Armenian side.

As mentioned above, in the beginning, just after the independence, Azerbaijan's international system perception existed in the context of the main developments held at the beginning of 90-ies. The victory of the *West* in the *Cold War* for Azerbaijan was represented as unconditional, the result of which the unipolar world was formed. Western values such as democracy, market economy, and human rights were to be distributed across the planet as the uncontested. In this case, a corresponding policy was expected to be held by the US and its allies. At first glance, this assures there is nothing wrong, if not underestimating the fact that the impact the Western interests at the planetary level had not an equal degree for different regions. For the post-Soviet space, it was significantly lower. In addition, the *West* recognized the leading role of Russia in the post-Soviet region, suggesting that the transition process in the country would be successful, and it brought impact to another former Soviet republic. However, Russia has sought to strengthen or at least re-establish its role in the international arena while forming its perception of the world.

During the first years of independence, the Azerbaijani leaders could not take all of these factors into account, and as a result, they had to pay a hefty price. Azerbaijan hoped that during the transition period, it would receive the necessary assistance from the *West* and eventually become a wealthy member of the international community. As a new state, it has not been able to accept all of the features of the global system, and the full support of the *West* was seen as a matter of course. However, Azerbaijan did not get the expected response like the other NIS. The lack of interest from the *West* in the former Soviet republics has led to a situation in which Azerbaijan had to solve the political and economic problems in its way. The condition deteriorated because this country faced the adverse effects of political instability and economic collapse. Since independence, between 1991-1993, three governments with opposing views on domestic and foreign policy have come to power in Azerbaijan. Lack of experience in governance and inability to determine the actual events in the international arena have led to an even more difficult situation in the country.

The main mistake was that the actual condition of the international situation could not be correctly analyzed. Consequently, the attempts at foreign policy and its priorities during the first two presidents of Azerbaijan, Ayaz Mutalibov and Abulfaz Elchibey, have led to Azerbaijan has soured relations with Russia. This fact had very negative consequences for Azerbaijan. Being the only force that formed the framework for the activities of the *NIS* in the post-Soviet space, Russia tried to control its actions to avoid not desired for her developments. In this case, countries that did not meet the expectations of Russia were subjected to pressure and "punishment." In the case of Azerbaijan, the confrontation with Russia began already during the reign of the first president of Azerbaijan, Ayaz Mutalibov. Even though Mutalibov was trying to maintain friendly relations and led pro-Russian foreign policy, Azerbaijan's wish to attract Western energy companies to develop oil fields has strained relations between the two countries.

Thereby, Russia, which until a specific time maintained a neutral stance on the Armenian-Azerbaijani Nagorno-Karabakh conflict, wanted to "punish" Azerbaijan to support Armenia in the conflict. Thus, Armenian armed forces, with the support of the *366th infantry regiment* of the former Soviet army, staged a massacre in the Azerbaijani city *of Khojaly* on the night of 25 to

February 26. As a result of the bloody strife, more than 600 civilians were killed, hundreds injured and maimed, and hundreds of people were missing.[289] As a result, on March 6, 1992, President Mutalibov was forced to resign.

After Mutalibov, the Popular Front came to power, the party and the leader Abulfaz Elchibey of which, known for its anti-Russian and pro-Western (through close relations with Türkiye) foreign policy,[290] That only exacerbates the relations between Russia and Azerbaijan. In turn, the superiority of Armenia over Azerbaijan in war became her loyalty to the regional leader- Russia. Armenia's support is because Russia understands to maintain the desired status quo in the region, which should be a balance between Azerbaijan and Armenia. It is a fact that Azerbaijan's potential is much higher than Armenia, so Russia began to exert more significant assistance to Armenia. Russia also started considering the relationship between the two South Caucasian countries through the Armenian prism. As a result, in June 1993, the Elchibey government fell at the outbreak of the self-styled Colonel Surat Huseynov rebellion in the second city of Azerbaijan Ganja with the Russian support.[291] Thus, a few days before the unrest, the Russian *104th infantry regiment* stationed in Ganja left the city six months ahead of schedule, leaving behind all of their weaponry and equipment.[292] As a counterargument, Elchibey invited Heydar Aliyev, a veteran of the Soviet policy, to Baku, which at the time was chairman of the *Majlis* (Parliament) of Nakhchivan Autonomous Republic. After arriving at Aliyev in Baku, he was appointed chairman of the Azerbaijani Parliament. In turn, Elchibey left the capital and went to his native village, Keleki, in Nakhchivan. Despite calls for the President to return to his duties, Elchibey refused to return to Baku. As a result, a referendum was held on August 29, 1993, on the vote of confidence in the President, following which, Elchibey was no longer President.[293] In October 1993, the next presidential election, Heydar Aliyev became the third president of Azerbaijan.

Foreign Policy During Heydar Aliyev

After Heydar Aliyev came to power, Azerbaijan gradually managed to change the situation in its favor and began to apply a balanced foreign policy. In the early stages, Aliyev made attempts toward rapprochement with Russia. Still, it did not change the Russian perception of the status quo in the region, which was formed during the period of the Popular Front government. But, even though Azerbaijan has taken a more constructive position towards Russia that did not lead to a significant change in its foreign policy, the Russian pro-Armenian approach in the South Caucasus region balance of power continues despite of new Azerbaijan authority position. In 1994, Azerbaijan also joined the pro-Russian military alliance- *CSTO*. However, five years later, Azerbaijan did not renew its participation.

Russia does not consider it necessary to adjust its foreign policy towards the small newly formed country, believing that it, in any development, will be able to control the country and quickly achieve its interests in the region. However, as the events show, Russia's this approach toward Azerbaijan must be corrected. Azerbaijan's new government has forced actively looking for ways to attract the attention of the West in the region. Aliyev clearly understood that resolving the Nagorno-Karabakh problem requires considering many internal and external factors. As for external factors, it was needed to achieve the involvement of different actors and decrease the absolute influence of Russia in the region. With this, achieving an optimal condition for Azerbaijan to solve the Nagorno-Karabakh conflict and strengthen the state's independence will be possible. For this purpose, firstly, achieving stability in the country was necessary. However, achieving stability with the cessation of hostilities was possible. Initially, it was essential to stop the military confrontation with Armenia, which did not bring any results but losses. In this connection, it was able to negotiate a ceasefire with Armenia. By the way, Russia is very actively involved in achieving the ceasefire. For Russia, maintaining the status quo in the conflict is in its interests. As mentioned earlier, it turned into a perfect tool for pressure on the two conflicting states depending on a given situation requires it. Thus, the occupation of Azerbaijani territories would persist, but Armenia's control of these territories would not have a legal basis. In 1994, the Ceasefire Agreement, with the participation of Russia, was agreed.[294]

After completing the first stage, to achieve the balance, Aliyev realized that it was necessary to change the perception and attitude of the Western states towards Azerbaijan. To this end, playing with only Azerbaijan's trump card was essential - energy resources. This card could be successfully played to achieve the goals of Azerbaijan's foreign policy.

Azerbaijan is historically known to have rich oil and gas deposits. Here, for the first time in the world, the oil began to extract by industrial methods. After independence, energy again began to have strategic importance in the economic and political sphere of the country. The energy factor has become a vital tool in the foreign policy of Azerbaijan and the achievement of national interests in the international arena. For *Small Power*, such as Azerbaijan, the energy availability factor will enhance its capacity and action. As shown in time, the skillful use of this factor will play a role in changing the game's rules for Azerbaijan and the region as a whole.

Attracting Western energy companies to operate oil fields could be achieved, and changing priorities in the foreign policy of the Western states' governments.[295] Aliyev believed that the participation of Western energy companies would be the reason for this change since implementing multi-billion-dollar contracts would be considered strategically important for the governments that represent these companies. This perception was not groundless. There are many examples of how energy companies eventually became detonators of foreign policy changes in their countries. At the same time, Azerbaijan is trying to attract companies from different countries, reaching as far as possible geographical diversification to ensure the multinational project. It provides a balance of opposite forces in the South Caucasus region.

Politics of balance also implied the participation of Russian energy companies in energy projects. Heydar Aliyev took into account the unfortunate experience of predecessors and, along with the involvement of foreign companies, invited the *Lukoil* Company to join and sign a contract.[296] This decision allowed Aliyev to achieve support from several Russian officials who simultaneously neutralized those circles in the Russian establishment who were against it. Thus, Aliyev enlisted the help of Russian Prime Minister Viktor Chernomyrdin and partly Energy Minister Yuri Shafrannik. Although some groups in the Russian government were against Azerbaijan succeeded in deal an agreement with this company. An especially ardent opponent of this project was performed by Russian Foreign Minister Andrei Kozyrev.[297]

Despite the objections in the top echelons of authority in Russia, on September 20, 1994, in Baku, the "*Contract of the Century*" for developing the *Azeri-Chirag-Guneshli* offshore oil fields was signed.[298] During the Baku signing ceremony, the consortium members represented nine energy companies from six countries. Only the US was represented by four companies that have received political support from their government.[299] That was a profound success of Azerbaijani diplomacy. Although since independence, there was political instability that led to the change of several heads of state, economic collapse, and continued military operations in Nagorno-Karabakh, it was possible to attract energy companies to participate in the project. In addition, a contract was signed to exploit *Azeri-Chirag-Guneshli* offshore fields. However, the legal status of the Caspian Sea has not been approved, in connection with which Russia and Iran have expressed their protests. In June 1994, Russian President Boris Yeltsin signed the secret directive "*On Securing the Interests of the Russian Federation in the Caspian Sea*," which included measures of economic sanctions against Azerbaijan if this country continues its actions regarding the implementation of energy projects with Western companies.[300] But this did not become an obstacle to signing the contract.

But the signing of the agreement still needs to be a point of refraction and the formation of a new situation in the South Caucasus region. The Western companies only confirmed their participation in the project but have yet to make investments that would connect them with Azerbaijan more than put a signature. It was only the beginning of the process, and sustaining the next onslaught had to be possible. Geopolitical risks were still present, and it had to give a decisive rebuff. In short, although the contract had been signed, this situation in Azerbaijan still was critical. Surat Huseynov, who became Prime Minister of Azerbaijan, with Russian support this time, rebelled against President Aliyev. Aliyev appealed to the people on national television to prevent another state coup d'état. Thousands of people gathered around the presidential palace, forming a human shield. Thank to this support, another overthrow was averted.[301] Preventing another coup- d'état related to energy projects in Azerbaijan-could be the reference starting point for creating a balanced policy in Azerbaijan. It will allow the country to minimize geopolitical risks and have a more flexible foreign policy based on the national interest. For the first time since the beginning of industrial oil production in Azerbaijan, the energy factor was a blessing, not a curse.

After sometime after the signing of the "*Contract of the Century*," as was expected, the Western nations and institutions began to form their interests in Azerbaijan. By the way, the US is a perfect example of how the *West* has already started changing its perception towards Azerbaijan and reviewing its foreign policy priorities. In short, the first time these relations began to form was on February 12, 1992, when the US Secretary of State James Baker briefly visited Baku during a tour of the South Caucasus and Central Asia. By the way, initially, this visit was not planned but was included at the last moment at the insistence of the request of the Azerbaijani side.[302] So, James Baker stopped rather than visit Baku before his departure to the Turkmenistan capital-Ashgabat. During his visit to Baku, Baker mentioned that the US is interested in the further democratization process of the former Soviet Union republic and in preventing Iran's possible influence. In other words, the priorities of the US at the beginning of 1992 concerning the region, data were limited to these expectations.[303] The South Caucasus, including Azerbaijan, was beyond the interest of the US.

The lack of national priorities of the US in the region and Azerbaijan in particular, allowed the representatives of the Armenian lobby in the US Congress, on October 24, 1992, to approve *Section 907 to the Freedom Support Act*, according to which imposes a ban on the provision of government assistance of the US to Azerbaijan because of the sanctions against Armenia (though Azerbaijan itself is a victim of aggression).[304] The sanctions were adopted without any complications. Members of Congress have no clear idea about the situation in the South Caucasus region. In addition, Azerbaijan did not have lobbying representatives in Congress at that time, which could prevent this development. The adoption of sanctions was a clear example of the lack of a clear course in the US concerning the South Caucasus countries, making lobbying circles have solutions, the complete abolition of which has failed to achieve so far.

Only in 2001, after the tragic events of September 11, when the US suffered a terrorist attack by the ultra-radical Islamist group *al-Qaeda*, the US Congress approved a bill granting the US president authority to suspend *the Section 907th*.[305] The point is that *NATO* was needed logistical support, which provided by Azerbaijan, for the redeployment of its armed forces with the necessary equipment and inventory in Afghanistan. To this end, both states agreed on this issue during the visit of Defense Secretary Donald Rumsfeld in Baku on December 14, 2001. As a result of the negotiations, Azerbaijan supported the military operation and opened its airspace and airfields for use by the US and its allies. In January 2002, President George W. Bush, for the first time, decided to temporarily suspend *the Section 907th*.[306]

With the participation of American companies in the "*Contract of the Century*," the US government (at that time, the president was Bill Clinton) was to pay more attention to Azerbaijan. With the implementation of this energy project, the main objective was to determine the transport corridor through which oil would supply to the world markets. As mentioned earlier, Azerbaijan has no access to the open seas and therefore depends on neighboring countries to transport its energy resources. In this case, the US became a country that has played a vital role in determining the route for Azerbaijani oil. For example, the Clinton administration wanted to reduce Azerbaijan's dependence on Russia and to seek alternatives to this country's routes. This wish of the US coincided with the expectations of Azerbaijan, as it is the basis for a policy of balance. However, this balance was necessary to maintain relations with the region's countries. Such a task to Azerbaijan stood at determining the corridor for the export of "*early oil*." Azerbaijan's wish to diversify transport corridors coincided with the interests of the West. The Clinton Administration was actively involved in determining the route for the export of the "*early oil*" from the *Azeri-Chirag-Guneshli* oil field. It should be noted that "*early oil*" stands for the crude oil produced at the *Azeri-Chirag-Guneshli* oil fields that did not require extra costs to build infrastructure for exploitation. It should be exported at the end of the 90-ties before the main exploitation would start.[307]

The access of Azerbaijan to the world markets depends on neighboring states. It is especially significant because Azerbaijan is an exporter of energy resources, and their transportation is made via pipelines through the territory of third states. In this case, political and economic dependence and manipulation are probable on its neighbors. This circumstance is significant because it constructs the environment and opportunities for action in Azerbaijan in international areas. Therefore, dependency on other states can bring a high probability of losing the ability to conduct an independent foreign policy following national interests.

It should be noted that the options for energy exports through the territory of Armenia and Iran were immediately eliminated. Despite the fact that transit through Armenia and then Türkiye is the shortest, and therefore commercially attractive, because of the conflict over Nagorno-Karabakh and Armenia's policy of isolation from the Azerbaijani side, this option was not considered. What sways Iran against this direction was initially against the US government, which has become increasingly involved in implementing regional projects.

Thus, there are still export options through the territory of Russia and, second, through Georgia: the *Baku-Novorossiysk pipeline* and the *Baku-Supsa pipeline*. Both pipelines connect *the Azeri-Chirag-Guneshli* oil field via *the Caspian Sea's Sangachal terminal with the Black Sea's* Russian and Georgian ports. The first pipeline was supported by Russia, which considers that its choice also prejudges the fate and determines the direction of the main oil pipeline. In this way, Russia could compensate for the setback suffered by the country trying to prevent the signing of the "*Contract of the Century.*" Russia could control the flow of oil produced in Azerbaijan and send it to world markets. In this way, the country would receive geopolitical dividends from the control of crude oil exports from Azerbaijan and Western companies' activities in this country.

In turn, the US government supported the second route to prevent such a scenario. The United States believes that the choice of the construction of the *Baku-Supsa pipeline* will allow Azerbaijan and companies participating in the consortium to reduce its dependence on Russia. In this case, the United States is a somber approach to selecting the transport route to *"early oil."* An example of this is the fact that in October 1995, President Clinton sent a private letter to President Aliyev with the former adviser on national security, Zbigniew Brzezinski, expressing the US support for the construction of the *Baku-Supsa pipeline*.[308]

As a result, the choice of Azerbaijan was based on the formation and strengthening of a balanced policy. With the active participation of the US and the reluctance of Azerbaijan again to complicate relations with Russia, it was decided to elect both corridors to export "*early oil*." It was done to achieve the possibility of maneuvering. Shortly after the decision, both the pipeline went into operation. The effect of the *Baku-Supsa* pipeline was very significant: for the first time in the post-Soviet era, one of the republics gained access to the European markets without crossing Russian territory.[309] It allowed Azerbaijan, as the country has no access to the open seas, to diversify its export transportation corridors and the opportunity to choose the best, according to a certain length of time, and form an international conjecture route. Azerbaijan also wanted to reduce the likelihood of Russia's influence and dependence on this country. In this way, the government had the opportunity to make decisions on political and economic values without looking at the response of its northern neighbor. The only instrument of pressure preserved from Russia towards Azerbaijan was the unresolved Nagorno-Karabakh conflict. However, even this factor was not an obstacle to implementing regional projects in Azerbaijan following their national interests.

At the same time, the preference for bypassing Russian transport corridors was the base for determining the main transport pipeline. Thus, with US political support, the *Baku-Tbilisi-Ceyhan oil pipeline* (which crosses through the territories of Georgia and Türkiye to the Mediterranean Sea) has been chosen as a main transport corridor for exporting Azerbaijani offshore oil. With its support, the US provided a guarantee to ensure the implementation of the project and reduce the likelihood of possible geopolitical challenges and risks.[310] Implementing the *Baku-Tbilisi-Ceyhan oil pipeline* has had a substantial geopolitical and geo-economic effect, which exists to the present day. Azerbaijan's foreign policy has started to be formed on the strategy that will reduce of unwanted influence of *the Middle* and *Great Powers*, which have their interests in the South Caucasus. Azerbaijan became a dominant power in the region; nowadays, it is possible to implement regional projects with her participation. This circumstance is why Armenia has become an outcast from all regional projects. On July 13, 2006, the *Baku-Tbilisi-Ceyhan oil pipeline* was officially opened for operation.

Continuation of Balanced Policy

Azerbaijan is trying to pursue a pragmatic, predictable for the main actors in the regional policy and to prevent such acts that would lead to their irritation, even though Azerbaijan, when making foreign policy decisions based on its interests, this country will never act if the risks and geopolitical challenges outweigh the benefits. The dividend data should be guaranteed; otherwise, Azerbaijan avoids participating in dubious projects.

It explains the unwillingness of Azerbaijan to participate in constructing the *Nabucco* pipeline. The idea of the project, which owes its name to an opera written by the Italian composer Giuseppe Verdi, was first announced in 2002. The initiators of this project became two energy companies from Türkiye and Austria - BOTAŞ and OMV, which the Bulgarian Bulgargaz, Hungarian MOL, Romanian Transgaz, and German RWE later supplemented. The *Nabucco* project was initially conceived to transport natural gas from the Central Asian countries to the markets of Central and Eastern Europe states. This pipeline should be anchored in the Turkish Erzurum city. But for gas from Central Asia to fill the *Nabucco* pipeline, it needed to be transported across the Caspian Sea and through the South Caucasus region. However, if in the territories of Azerbaijan and Georgia, there was a laid pipeline - the *Baku-Tbilisi-Erzurum* gas pipeline, another route - via the Caspian Sea, it was necessary to build. But it was never implemented.

The consortium members should have perceived the *Nabucco* project as purely commercial. Consequently, the negotiations with the governments of Azerbaijan and Turkmenistan, which saw this project from a geopolitical perspective, failed. These countries wanted to implement the *Trans-Caspian* project with political support and security guarantees. Azerbaijan and Turkmenistan realize that this project fails to meet the national interests of Russia and Iran on the Caspian Sea and can cause them displeasure. The support needed about the one that gave the US made possible the realization of the project of the *Baku-Tbilisi-Ceyhan* pipeline, which Russia and Iran so opposed. In the case of *Nabucco*, the US did not openly support the project because of other priorities in foreign policy.[311] Lately, after realizing the reality of the situation, the place the US was trying to take by the European Commission, representing the *EU*. In January 2011, European Commission President Jose Manuel Barroso visited Baku and Ashgabat to assure everyone of the *EU*'s ability to act as a regional player.[312] However, foreign and energy policy is not subject to supranational relations within the *EU*, and remains at the intergovernmental level. As a consequence, the national interests of the *EU* Member States take precedence over the general. In this case, expect that the *EU* could provide security guarantees in the case of Russian or Iranian displeasure; it would be at least naive. That is why Azerbaijan refused to participate in implementing the *Trans-Caspian* pipeline and did not support the performance of the *Nabucco* project. As it became clear later, this project was only possible with Azerbaijan's support and participation. As a result, after the announcement of Azerbaijan and Türkiye to start construction of the *TANAP* pipeline with the purpose of pumping Azerbaijani gas to markets in Türkiye and Europe, the *Nabucco* stopped even their hypothetical existence.

The balanced policy approach of Azerbaijan can also be explained in its relations with the Euro-Atlantic organizations such as *NATO* and the *EU*. In 1994, *NATO* pioneered a new *PfP* program for cooperation with European countries and the former Soviet republics, which were not members of the organization. Azerbaijan actively took the initiative and became the second country after Austria signed an agreement with *NATO* on May 4, 1994. The program predetermined the new format of relations and cooperation between the Alliance and the newly independent states.

Active participation and interest in Azerbaijan were reflection of her perception of international Politics in the early 90s. At that time in Azerbaijan, there was still the belief that *NATO* conducts its policy towards the newly independent states with a view to their integration into the organization and assisting in the transition period. Azerbaijan also believes that this program is to prepare for full membership in the organization. Moreover, it fully meets the interests of its balanced policy.

This expectation cannot be called accidental. Since this program also included the *CEEC*, for which the West had a more specific target: full integration into the Euro-Atlantic structures. These countries have received full support from *NATO*, and eventually, between 1999 -2009, 12 countries in the region, which had been partners in the *PfP*, became full members of *NATO*. However, the expectations of Azerbaijan and other post-Soviet states still needed to meet. There was something else: even though all the countries of the former *Eastern Bloc* and the Soviet Union were members of the *PfP*, in the future, the *CEEC* was able to receive membership, while, as the next stage of cooperation for the countries of the former Soviet Union was the *Individual Partnership Action Plan*. As it became clear over time, the *PfP* program included two main goals: preparing *CEEC* for membership and retaining the former Soviet Union countries (including Russia) in orbit of the Alliance's constructible new perception of security. In addition, in 2008, at the Budapest Summit, *NATO* was denied candidacy for membership to two former Soviet republics -Ukraine and Georgia.[313]

The same can be said for the relations with other regional organizations, the *EU*. The *EU* originally developed different programs for *CEEC* and the former Soviet republics. For *CEEC*, the *EU* initially builds relationships that were to be completed with the full integration,[314] while the relations with the former Soviet republics were limited to providing technical and financial assistance.[315] Lately, the *EU* has developed a new legal instrument: *Partnership and Cooperation Agreement* (*PCA)*, which created the basis for relations between the *EU* and the *NIS*.[316] Azerbaijan signed *PCA* on 22 April 1996 in Luxembourg with Georgia and Armenia. By signing this document, which has been specially developed for the countries of the former Soviet Union, Azerbaijan already knew that the *EU* does not imply the country's full membership in the organization. Thus, one of the conditions for full integration into the *EU* for the countries of the former *Eastern Bloc* was their prior membership in *NATO*. All the *CEEC* in the first stage become members of *NATO* before entering the *EU*. Since *NATO* was not going to take Azerbaijan, therefore, the *EU* has also been closed for this country.[317] But at the same time, Azerbaijan's interest in signing such a document was more based on how to deepen relations with the *EU*, which has been seen as a continuation of the balancing foreign policy. It allowed for forming a legal framework with the *EU* to expand relations with it while taking into account the features of the agreement, not to spoil relations with its neighbors Russia and Iran, traces jealously every action of the *West* to deepen ties with the region's countries. Since *Russia also signed PCA*, this also reduces the possibility of geopolitical risks due to the signing of the contract on the part of Azerbaijan. At the same time, this agreement did not require Azerbaijan to any primary responsibilities while creating a legal basis for technical and financial programs under *TACIS*, which the *EU* has already implemented in the post-Soviet space.[318]

Another reason for signing the agreement was that Azerbaijan wanted to avoid keeping up with her neighbors in the region (especially Armenia) in expanding relations with this organization. However, the situation changed after the *EU* proposed a new instrument for ties with some countries of the former Soviet Union located in Europe, namely Ukraine, Belarus, Moldova, Azerbaijan, Georgia, and Armenia. It is worth noting that according to the *EC* Treaties, any European state can become an *EU* member.[319] However, as the *EU*, despite the wishes of *NIS* to become members of this organization, the *EU* is not planning further expansion to the *East*; it has proposed a new developed initiative -*Eastern Partnership*. This program offers some integration in the economic sphere, without the participation and inclusion of these countries in the *EU* institutions.[320] In other words, the main goal of this program is to create favorable for the organization's rings from neighboring countries, which share common values with the *EU* and to fulfill the role of a buffer zone on the possible geopolitical challenges from Russia.

Azerbaijan is very cautious about the program, which proceeds with conditions that do not suit the country. Unlike Georgia and Ukraine, Azerbaijan did not consider the *Eastern Partnership* as a stage for full integration into the *EU*. Moreover, from an economic point of view, this country would only win if it created the *Free Economic Zone* with the *EU*. Azerbaijan's main exports consist of more than 90 percent of oil, oil products, and natural gas, for the implementation of which engaging in any economic integration structures is optional because energy recourses are strategic product and quickly finds a consumer on the market. Besides, any economic integration has a downside: a number of sectors of the Azerbaijani economy could be adversely affected. It is one reason why Azerbaijan is still not a *World Trade Organization (WTO)* member.[321] The *WTO* membership is a prerequisite for creating a free economic zone with the *EU*.

However, the primary cause of passive acceptance of this *EU* initiative is the possible geopolitical risks the program brings. Namely, Russia's adverse reaction towards the *EU* and partner countries' reciprocal steps within this initiative. As for Azerbaijan, the government refused to accede to the *EP* initiative, which later turned out to be a geopolitical risk. Instead of this, the priority of Azerbaijan is to develop relations with the *EU* on a bilateral basis. One of the areas for such kind of cooperation is energy cooperation, which is very actively developed between the parties. On September 20, 2014, exactly twenty years after the signing of the "*Contract of the Century*," the ceremony of laying the foundation of the *Southern Gas Corridor* was held in Baku. The initial stage of this project was a *Joint Declaration on the Southern*

Gas Corridor signed between the *EU* European Commission and Azerbaijan in 2011 during the visit of European Commission President Barroso in Baku. However, the role of the *EU* in implementing this corridor is minimal; the main actors in its realization are Azerbaijan and Türkiye, who agreed in 2012 to start the construction of *the TANAP* (*Trans-Anatolian Natural Gas Pipeline*). Besides *TANAP* (which will pass through Turkish territory up to its border with Greece), *the Southern Gas Corridor* project includes the expansion of the existing *Baku-Tbilisi-Erzurum* gas pipeline and the construction of *TAP* (*Trans Adriatic Pipeline*, originating from the Turkish-Greek border passing on Albania, until Italy) to export Azerbaijani gas from *Shah Deniz* offshore field to the European markets.[322] The construction of the *TANAP* was completed on June 12, 2018, and the commercial operation of the *TAP on* November 15, 2020. Thus, Azerbaijani gas began to flow to European markets.

At the same time, Azerbaijan also stayed aside from the other regional integration project present in the region - the *Eurasian Economic Union*. It is known that; Russia initiated this project. Azerbaijan's approach to the project is identical to that applied to the *EU*, namely the development of bilateral relations rather than within this format.

Policy equidistant from the polar integration projects also strengthened Azerbaijan's accession in 2011 to the organization of the *Non-Aligned Movement*.[323] Azerbaijan indicates its priorities in foreign policy, consolidating the trend equidistant from ambivalent processes in the region. In general, Azerbaijan considers *the Non-Aligned Movement* organization as an additional platform for presenting and promoting its national interests. Since this organization involved 119 countries, it is the most comprehensive framework for dialogue after the *UN General Assembly*.

Participation in the *Movement* played a positive role in providing the necessary votes for the election of Azerbaijan to the *UN Security Council* as a non-permanent member. 117 member states of the *Non-Aligned Movement* voted in favor of the Azerbaijan candidacy.[324] Azerbaijan's membership in the *UN Security Council* in 2012-2013 was an excellent experience for the country's participation in decision-making in global affairs.[325] It has allowed Azerbaijan to reach a new level of relations in the international arena, which, along with the strengthening of the country's image, also enabled Azerbaijan to form a new relationship for a successful implementation of national interests. Thus, examples of Azerbaijan show how any *Small Power* can act at this level only if the correct calculation of its potential and capabilities are there. Participation in the *UN Security Council* demands that its members make decisions that, in the event of disagreement with the main actors in the system of international politics, can lead to a deterioration of relations with them and unwished consequences. The experience of Azerbaijan, the policy balance that has held this country since 1993, has allowed her to actively participate in such a high platform and vote on specific issues without the sensation of external pressure. As a result, it only strengthened the view of Azerbaijan as a country whose foreign policy is based on its interests and forces on this country impermissible.

At the same time, participation in the *United Nations Security Council* and the *Non-Aligned Movement* has allowed Azerbaijan to start building relationships with countries and organizations in regions such as South America, Africa, and Southeast Asia. At that time, with several country members of this organization, Azerbaijan had no diplomatic relations, and relationships of political and economic nature were at a minimum. The vector of these relations is the country's geopolitical and geo-economic interests. Additionally, the geo-economic denominator in Azerbaijan's foreign policy is critical. At the same time, developing economic ties and cooperation with more and more countries, Azerbaijan also has an opportunity to strengthen political consensus. An essential tool for the formation of this kind of relationship is still playing a creation of a regional energy and transport infrastructure.

Through the construction *of TANAP* and *TAP* gas pipelines, Azerbaijani gas is receiving countries like Greece, Italy, Albania, and Bulgaria. Following this is also possible to pump gas in such countries of the Balkans as Croatia, Serbia, and Montenegro.[326]

In this way, it is possible to build closer relations with countries whose characteristics are similar to Azerbaijan, and many of them are *Small Powers* in the international system. The countries through the territory which will pass these transport corridors are currently involved in various integration processes. Some of them are *EU* members. Thereby transport projects after their implementation may be the basis for inter-regional integration, and Azerbaijan directly occurs in its formation. The implementation of these transport projects will provide for the development of economic relations between the countries. Additionally, closer ties between the states located on the route of these regional projects and proposed by Azerbaijan also contribute to the *Baku-Tbilisi-Kars railway,* and it can be a base for further acceleration of cooperation and trade relations between the *EU* and the Far East states. This project will bring together two of the regions by rail and provide an alternative to the Russia corridor for freight transportation.[327]

Using proceeds from realizing transport corridors for all sorts of energy will allow Azerbaijan to diversify its economy and increase its importance internationally. In this way, from the format of the object of international relations, as usually a small state becomes, Azerbaijan is gradually turning into a subject of connections, which plays a crucial role in realizing specific geopolitical goals of regional importance.

The pinnacle of the course of a successful balance policy was the liberation of its territories by Azerbaijan from the occupation of Armenia during *the 44-day war*. For the first time in the post-Soviet space, one of the *Small Powers* managed to change the existing status quo in its favor. The determination of the moment of the start of the military operation was also the result of a precise analysis of the situation in the international arena. In a word, Azerbaijan first used force to liberate its lands in 2016. Then it was done in a limited manner, and after the intervention of Russia, the war was suspended.

In 2020, Azerbaijan secured the full support of Türkiye, which partially took on the mission of neutralizing possible negative consequences for Azerbaijan in the international arena. It is no secret that Russia was the primary *Great Power* that could intervene in the situation. In the example of Georgia, during its "*five-day war*" in South Ossetia in August 2008, the reaction of Russia turned out to be very tough, which led to the fact that, along with this separatist region, Russia also recognized the independence of Abkhazia. It is worth noting that before the start of the operation, Azerbaijan also clearly assessed the degree of tension in relations between Russia and Armenia, as well as Russia's involvement in the conflict with Ukraine and her participation in the Syrian crisis. In addition, Russia is facing a recession in its economy due to sanctions from the West and falling oil prices. Therefore, Russia needed to solve several problems at the same time.

Considering the current situation and the opportunities, Azerbaijan made the most of its chance. And after Russia proposed to accept a ceasefire statement, Azerbaijan could put forward its demands regarding the results of the war. Achieving its own goals, Azerbaijan also considered the interests of the main *Great Power* in the region. Russia's compromise on the issue of introducing Russian peacekeeping forces into the region is connected precisely with making decisions within the framework of a pragmatic perception of the world.

In this case, Azerbaijan is an example of how a *Small Power,* through a pragmatic analysis of foreign policy and the correct calculation of internal and external factors, can achieve its national goals in conditions of the contemporary international system.

The foreign policy of Azerbaijan may be referred to as the three *P's: pragmatism, predictability, and prevention*. Pragmatism in foreign policy is conditioned by the fact that Azerbaijan is trying to realize its interests in the international arena only if it allows its political and economic potential. In addition, Azerbaijan pays special attention to assessing the possible reaction of the main actors in the region so that not dealing with them is not the desired reaction. However, this in no way means that Azerbaijan refuses to implement the national interests if they do not coincide with the interests of other countries.

From time to time, specific differences in the views of Azerbaijan with all regional actors, such as Russia, Türkiye, Iran, the US, and the *EU*, have occurred. During the disputes, Azerbaijan generally did not give up its expectations and interests and continued its implementation. Moreover, such a position has formed the image of Azerbaijan as a country with which the desired result cannot be achieved by acting from a position of strength.

At the same time, Azerbaijan and any other small state cannot change the external factors. The positive or negative format of relations with the main actors in the international system depends on the perception of Azerbaijan's actions by these countries. However, Azerbaijan has built its foreign policy when to be able to predetermine the possible change of perception to reduce the risks of geopolitical challenges to the country's security. Due to the diversification of transport routes for the export of energy resources to the world markets, and the significant role that Azerbaijan plays in ensuring energy security in the region, the country has the opportunity to maneuver while maintaining a balance and avoid undesired immense cataclysms that could become a threat to the country. This course, which Azerbaijan has evolved over the years, will continue in the future unless there are any fundamental changes in the international arena, which can lead to a re-evaluation of external factors.

CHAPTER 7
Foreign Policy of Georgia: Towards Euro-Atlantic Area Integration

The Formation of Foreign Policy at an Early Stage

Back in the late 80s, nation-state revival began in Georgia. This process accelerated after April 9, 1989, when Soviet troops shot the mass demonstration in Tbilisi. As an echo of these events, in October 1990 in Georgia, the first in the USSR free parliamentary elections on a multiparty basis was held, won by a coalition of "*Round Table*," headed by former dissident Zviad Gamsakhurdia, who was elected a chairman of the Supreme Council of Georgia. The main task of the new leadership has become the country's independence. Subsequently, on March 26, 1991, Zviad Gamsakhurdia was elected as the country's first president. Under the rule of the nationalist forces, on April 9, 1991, the Supreme Council of Georgia adopted the Act on the restoration of the state independence of Georgia.[328]

Following the formal dissolution of the Soviet Union and the formation of the *CIS* in December 1991, Georgia was the only country that had not joined the new organization. The reason was an open anti-Russian stance of the government, which was identified with the Russian occupation of Georgia in 1921.

Zviad Gamsakhurdia and his companions headed the construction of the unitary state of Georgia, which caused disagreement among the national minorities, which have their autonomous entities: the Abkhazians and Ossetians. Differences existed with other national minorities living in Georgia. Nationalist doctrine Gamsakhurdia, "*Georgia for Georgians*," was the cause of the outbreak of civil war in the country.[329] Disagreements led to the destabilization of the situation in Georgia, which led to political instability. The instability within the country and inter-ethnic conflicts virtually paralyzed the country's foreign policy activity in the first months of independence.[330]

Despite all of this, the US recognized the independence of Georgia on December 25, 1991. It was only possible thanks to the fact that the US did not make a difference between the former Soviet republics and recognized them in one day. The following year, diplomatic relations were established on March

24, 1992. The first US envoy was the Chargé d'Affaires ad interim Carey Cavanaugh, who arrived in Tbilisi on April 23, 1992.³³¹

In December 1991, due to the armed conflict, there was a revolt against the country's president. Part of the National Guard, gone over to the opposition, headed by Jaba Ioseliani and Tengiz Kitovani, started a confrontation with the country's leadership; as a result, Zviad Gamsakhurdia was forced to leave the capital, Tbilisi, and then the country. To power in the country came the Georgian former Communist Party leader and Soviet Minister of Foreign Affairs Eduard Shevardnadze,³³² who took over as chairman of the State Council of Georgia in March 1992; in October 1992, he was elected as the head of the republic's parliament.

After Shevardnadze came to power, the beginning of the formation of the foreign policy of Georgia started. Georgia became a UN member only on July 31, 1992, due to the civil war, a few months later than the rest of the *NIS Small Powers*. At the same time, Shevardnadze understood that it was necessary to form normal relations with Russia. In this connection, on October 1993, Georgia was applying for membership in the *CIS*.³³³ By the way, membership in the *CIS* of Georgia has always been associated with relations with Russia. In short, in 2009, after relations between Russia and Georgia again soured, Georgia withdrew from the *CIS*.³³⁴

Parallel with this, internal stability started to form. A cease-fire agreement, on the initiative by Russia, ending the confrontation in South Ossetia, was signed on 24th June 1992. According to the agreement, peacekeeping forces consisting of Russians, Georgians, and Ossetians should be deployed in the conflict zone.³³⁵ At the same time, in May 1994, a cease-fire in Abkhazia was signed with the mediation of the UN and Russia. Consequently, 24-kilometer security zones, introduced by the UN and the Russian Federation peacekeepers, have been established. In addition, an agreement was signed on establishing Russian military bases on Georgian territory in 1995. It was not only the desire of Russia, which formed its military presence in the *NIS* within the framework of the "near abroad" policy; at that time, Georgia was also interested in placing troops. The Georgian leadership hoped to receive assistance from Russia to combat organized crime, as well as provide military reform, the fight against the uprising in Samegrelo with supporters of the disgraced president Gamsakhurdia and restoration of Georgian control over Abkhazia and South Ossetia.

Thus, in this period, relations with Russia were defined within the framework of the geopolitical interests of its northern neighbor, the presence of ethnic conflicts on the territory of Georgia, and Georgia's desire to ensure political and economic stability in the country. However, over time it became clear that Russia needed economic opportunities to sustain Georgia. Therefore, for financial support and assistance, Georgia began looking to the *West*, creating opportunities for the necessary conditions. Although Shevardnadze realized the need for a more balanced foreign policy, the Georgian elite and society aimed to strengthen relations with the *West*. Shevardnadze did not want Georgia's dependence on Russia.[336]

However, given that the US and other Western *Great Powers* had yet to shape national interests in the region and recognize the dominant role of Russia, Georgia failed to achieve the expected goals. However, in favor of Georgia played a factor that Eduard Shevardnadze, while being Minister of Foreign Affairs of the Soviet Union, participated in the process of German unification. Due to personal sympathy, Western countries, especially Germany, have provided economic assistance to Georgia. In the '90s, Georgia became one of the world's largest per capita American financial assistance and aid recipients. Georgia received about a billion dollars in the period of Shevardnadze.[337]

In any case, Georgia tried to develop relations with Western institutions. In April 1992, Georgia became a member of the *NACC*, and two years later, on 23 March 1994, one of the first *NIS* joined the NATO *PfP* initiative. Regarding the relations with the *EU*, Georgia has received financial and technical assistance under the *TACIS* program. However, even this support to this country had to be delivered through a cumbersome mechanism across Russia. Humanitarian aid was provided to these *NIS* primarily within the framework of the ECHO and Food Aid Operation programs.[338] At the same time, like other *NIS*, Georgia has received financial assistance. So, the *EU* has listed this country as 160 million Euro.[339] This amount was significant for the small budget of Georgia.

At the same time, due to instability in the country, Georgia only in 1995 signed agreements with the European Economic Community on regulating trade in the field of textiles,[340] unlike its neighbors in the region, Azerbaijan, and Armenia, which made it in 1993. No other proposals were from the *EU* at that time. Only years later, the *EU* developed a new legal instrument *PCA*, which Georgia joined on 22 April 1996 in Luxembourg, together with other countries of the South Caucasus.

At the same time, Georgia, as well as Azerbaijan, realized that to attract the West's attention to the South Caucasus region, it requires the successful implementation of energy projects in Azerbaijan. In this case, Georgia is getting a chance to become a transit country for energy exports from Azerbaijan to the world markets, which could bring her political and economic dividends. Georgia knew that because of the Nagorno-Karabakh conflict, Azerbaijan would not launch pipelines on the territory of Armenia, even though this route is shorter. Therefore, the chances that the export routes would pass through Georgia were great. In addition, it is necessary to take into account the close friendly relations between the two countries' presidents, Heydar Aliyev, and Eduard Shevardnadze, which arose in the days of the Soviet Union when the two leaders directed their republics.³⁴¹ In 1995 a new constitution was adopted in Georgia, according to which, in the same year, Edward Shevardnadze was elected as the second President of Georgia.³⁴²

As it was expected, Georgia has become the main direction for the creation of export transport corridors. The beginning Baku-Supsa pipeline began in 1999, and then the Baku-Tbilisi-Ceyhan oil pipeline and Baku-Tbilisi-Erzurum gas pipeline were built. Georgia has openly supported the construction of the route through Türkiye despite pressure from Russia. With the development of regional transport routes, relations between Azerbaijan and Georgia reached a strategic level. Both countries need each other. At the time, as Azerbaijan needed an alternative to Russia's transportation routes to world markets, Georgia, which does not have its energy resources, needed to diversify its oil and natural gas supplies. Thus, the relationship between the two countries has become interdependent.

The development of transport corridors was wider than constructing of energy pipelines. Georgia took an active part in the decision to establish the European transport corridor (*TRACECA*), and the author of the idea was Shevardnadze. The *TRACECA* corridor originated in the *West*, on the *EU* border in Varna (Bulgaria), passing through the ports of Odesa (Ukraine) and Constanta (Romania) and continuing through the Black Sea to the ports of Poti and Batumi, and into the transport network of the South Caucasus. The route then passes through the Caspian Sea (Baku-Turkmenbashi, Baku-Aktau) to reach the railway networks of the Central Asian states Turkmenistan and Kazakhstan, the transportation networks of which relate to Uzbekistan, Kyrgyzstan, and Tajikistan, and reaches the boundaries of China and Afghanistan.³⁴³

In connection with the *TRACECA* significance, the two leaders of *the Small States* of the South Caucasus, Azerbaijani President Aliyev and Georgian President Shevardnadze, in September 1997, prepared a joint proposal to the *EU* to organize a conference within the framework of the *TRACECA* for signing the "*Multilateral Transportation Treaty*." The *EU* held the initiative, and on September 8, 1998, the conference "*Revitalization of the Silk Road*" was held in Baku with representatives of 32 countries and 12 international organizations. At the end of this conference, the "*Transport Corridor Europe-Caucasus-Asia for the Development of International Multilateral Treaty*" agreement was signed.³⁴⁴ In order to develop its transport infrastructure Georgia began receiving financial assistance from the *EU*.

Parallel with these developments, Georgia, together with Azerbaijan, Ukraine, and Moldova, created *GUAM* in 1997,³⁴⁵ hoping that this organization will contribute to the creation of closer relations with the *West* and integration into Euro-Atlantic structures. At the same time, *GUAM* included the country whose territory extends *the TRACECA* route, which gives hope that the *EU* is also interested in this initiative and will support it. However, the expected dividends were to no avail.

An essential step in Georgia's relations with the *West* was its entry into the Council of Europe on April 27, 1999, becoming the 41st member of this organization. A notable was the performance of the Chairman of the Parliament of Georgia Zurab Zhvania, who said during the inauguration ceremony in Strasbourg: "*I am Georgian. Therefore, I am European*",[346] thereby again indicating the direction of the foreign policy of Georgia. A month after Georgia acceded to the Council of Europe, President Shevardnadze said in an interview with Western journalists, "*Georgia knocked at NATO's door in 2005*". On January 4, 2000, Georgian Minister of Foreign Affairs Irakly Menagarishvili described the priorities of Georgia's foreign policy. These were: "Developing relations with *NATO*, the *EU*, and other Western organizations, hosting the *TRACECA* transport corridor, and providing transit for Caspian oil and gas international markets."[347]

The desire for rapprochement with the *West* directly impacts Georgian-Russian relations. In November 1999, at the *OSCE* Summit in Istanbul, Georgia began to demand the withdrawal of Russian troops from the country's territory. Although signed in 1995 agreement on Russian military bases, according to which Russia received the right to use Georgian territory for 25 years, Georgia did not ratify it. Thus, in Istanbul, Russia and Georgia signed an agreement on gradually reducing Russian military presence in Georgia. However, Russia was not in a hurry with the withdrawal of troops, which was later the cause of tension between the two countries.[348] At the same summit, Georgia signed an agreement to build an oil pipeline to the main export of Azerbaijani oil Baku-Tbilisi-Ceyhan pipeline.[349] At the same time, this decision undermines the expectation of a monopoly position in the Russian oil exports from Azerbaijan through the Baku-Novorossiysk pipeline.

In general, this period may begin the deterioration of relations between the two countries, which is only getting worse in the future. It occurred despite attempts. Shevardnadze maintains a balance between the *West* and Russia. However, not all depended on this small country. At the same time, the events developed very fleeting. In short, on 25 January 2000, the Ministers of Foreign Affairs of Russia and Georgia signed a memorandum on cooperation in the fight against terrorism and extremism. This memorandum was meant for a military operation launched by Russia in Chechnya. However, by the end of this year, Russia accused Georgia of aiding Chechen terrorists' penetration through Georgian territory during the Chechen war. This accusation was marked by the fact that Russia introduced a visa regime for Georgian citizens.[350] Because there is a visa-free regime in the *CIS*, Russia's decision was a landmark.

An essential event for Georgia was this country's entry into the *WTO* on June 14, 2000. Thus, Georgia became the 137th member of the *WTO*. Georgia became the fourth country in the former Soviet Union (after Kyrgyzstan, Latvia, and Estonia), which became a member of this organization.[351] Thus, Georgia, not having the opportunity to develop their products through trade liberalization and increased competition in the market, had hoped to improve the living conditions of the country's citizens, which in this case, would have access to cheaper and better-quality goods and services.

After September 11, 2001, Georgia's importance for the US and *NATO* increased as it was the example of Azerbaijan. The US and the alliance saw the territory of Georgia as one of the transport links for the operating forces in Afghanistan. Thus, Georgia's geopolitical importance has grown for the *West*. At that time, for this *Small Power*, it was challenging to determine whether it would allow Georgia to create a new balance with Russia to reduce the pressure and the possibility of integrating into Western institutions.

At the same time, Russia threatened Georgia with an air strike on its territory, namely the Pankisi Gorge. This region borders Chechnya, where Kists and ethnical Chechens live, to destroy the bases of Chechen fighters. Russia is not only limited to warnings. Twice, in November 2001 and February 2002, she bombarded the territory of Georgia.[352] In response to the actions of Russia, Georgian President Shevardnadze appealed to the US for the expansion of military and economic aid to his country. In addition, it signed a strategic agreement with *NATO* that pushed Shevardnadze to announce his country's desire to join the alliance.

In February 2002, the Bush administration decided to send American troops to train Georgian soldiers to fight terrorism in the Pankisi Gorge. During Shevardnadze's visit to the US, military aid to Georgia was promised in October 2001. However, this idea's practical realization was after Russia's air strike on Pankisi Gorge. At the same time, the US reiterated its position regarding the recognition of the territorial integrity of Georgia and called on Russia to refrain from annexing this *Small Power*.[353] Assistance was provided in the framework of the program "*Georgia Train and Equip Program*," which was calculated at 18 months, ending in April 2004.[354] The total cost of the program amounted to 64 million US dollars. However, the US aid to Georgia also continued after the program's end. The continuation was "*The Georgia Sustainment and Stability Operations Program*," under which Georgian troops were preparing to attend *Operation Iraqi Freedom* stability mission.[355]

At the same time, the US credibility with the Georgian president also became exhausted. It explains that the US has become openly supporting young pro-Western politicians. Incidentally, it is worth noting that some of them were included by Shevardnadze in the party which he led: the Union of Citizens of Georgia. Through this, Shevardnadze wanted to strengthen the reformer's image in the West's eyes.

In short, the future president Mikheil Saakashvili was a member of parliament from the party, and since 2000, almost a year, was the Minister of Justice of Georgia. Another reformer, Zurab Zhvania, was a chairman of the parliament in the period between 1995-2001. Nino Burjanadze also was a member of parliament from the Union of Citizens of Georgia.

These three would be at the head of the "*Rose Revolution*" in Georgia, culminating in Eduard Shevardnadze's resignation. In Georgia, there was a change of power, with the result that, on January 4, 2004, with more than 96% of the vote, Saakashvili became the third president of Georgia.[356]

Foreign Policy During Saakashvili

The new government immediately declared that its priorities were to restore the country's territorial integrity, strengthen relations with the US, and integrate with *NATO* and the EU. In principle vector, Saakashvili's foreign policy differed little from that declared by Shevardnadze in recent years. However, Shevardnadze sought to achieve this goal and, at the same time, did not want to aggravate relations with Russia. Shevardnadze was not directly involved because these relations deteriorated in recent years. Being a *Small Power* from Georgia, it was independent of the level of relations between the two countries. In addition, an essential factor in forming relationships was that in 2000, Vladimir Putin became the president of Russia, who is more jealous of maintaining control over the sphere of influence, the *NIS Small Powers*.

In addition, Putin saw the *NIS* as a springboard for restoring former Russian strength, which the country did during the Soviet era. Therefore, even a slight roll of a *Small Power* of *NIS* to the *West* is negatively perceived by Russia. In addition, Shevardnadze needed help to correctly recognize the degree of the growth of interest of the *West* in Georgia and the South Caucasus since 2001. The mistaken belief was that if not the entire region, Georgia would gradually move from the sphere of influence of Russia to the *West*. Shevardnadze believed that the process could begin immediately after the completion of the *CEEC* integration into *NATO* and the *EU*. The *West* had no such plans, implementing only their interests, trying not to interfere with the Russian geopolitical expectations in the region. Misperception of the *West* would continue during the period of a new president - Saakashvili. The wrong analysis of the Western interest was associated with its activation in the South Caucasus region. It was associated with two events: the beginning of *NATO* operations in Afghanistan and the coalition forces in Iraq, and second, completed in 2004, the expansion of *NATO* and the *EU*. Following the *CEEC's* accession to *NATO* and the *EU*, the structures closed doors to the *NIS's Small Powers*.

The question arises: What should the other policy of these structures on new neighbors be? In addition, the South Caucasus countries have played an important role in providing logistic support in operations against terrorism in Afghanistan and Iraq; the troops of the South Caucasus countries are present in Afghanistan and Georgian in Iraq. It was clear that these countries needed to create a new format for the formation of relationships. The new post, Special Representative for the South Caucasus and Central Asia, occupied by Robert Simmons, was created by *NATO*. On October 29, 2004, Georgia, the first of the *NIS*, joined the new *NATO* initiative for these countries' *IPAP*. At the same time, Georgia considered this initiative a step to full membership in the alliance. A month later, in November 2004, *NATO* Secretary General Jaap de Hoop Scheffer paid a visit to all three South Caucasus countries.[357]

At the same time, on 17 December 2004, Georgia created the post of State Minister for European and Euro-Atlantic integration. For effective operation and implementation of tasks in the new structure, set up three departments: coordination of European integration, coordination of Euro-Atlantic integration, and coordination of the *EU* programs. In addition, two state commissions were established in 2005: "The State Commission for *NATO* Integration" and "Integration into the *EU* State Commission".[358] At the same time, in all state administrative offices, along with the national flag of Georgia, the *EU* flag began to hang, symbolizing Georgia's determination in wanting to achieve its foreign policy goals.[359]

Symbolic was also the visit of the US President George W. Bush in Georgia in May 2005.[360] The visit was regarded as open support by the only surviving *Super Power* to Georgia's aspirations of integration into *NATO* and the *EU*. In the same year, in September, President Saakashvili visited the US.

In September 2006, taking into account the successful implementation of the objectives within the framework of the *IPAP*, *NATO* granted a new format of "*Intensified Dialogue*" to Georgia.[361] This format of relations with *NATO* had only countries in the *Western Balkans* region, for which this program was a step to full membership in *NATO*. In turn, Georgia was the only country from the *NIS* that was given the opportunity.

This intensification of relations is not limited to *NATO*: This also applies to the *EU*. In June 2004, Georgia and Armenia, and Azerbaijan were included in the new *EU* program, *New Neighbourhood Policy*. All of these steps, on the part of *NATO* and the *EU*, were perceived by Georgia as the further expansion of the *West* to the *East*. This perception, as well as new initiatives of the *West* in the *NIS* region, irritates Russia.

The continued deterioration of relations with Russia accompanied the pro-Western orientation and actions in this direction Saakashvili administration. Unlike Shevardnadze, Saakashvili was worried less about this. Saakashvili did not avoid empty anti-Russian rhetoric, which was directed mainly to the internal audience, and the message was for the *West*.

Saakashvili was actively pursuing the policy of withdrawal of Russian bases from Georgia. In October 2006, the Russian Duma ratified an agreement on withdrawing troops from Georgia. In the short term, the complete withdrawal of Russian troops from the territory of Georgia was completed until November 2007.[362]

In parallel, Russia continued pressure on Georgia in order to affect change in its foreign policy priorities. In addition to the introduction of the visa regime for citizens of Georgia, since 2006, Russia imposed a ban on the import of Georgia's main export products: wine and mineral water.[363] Russia has also resorted to using its main instrument of pressure- energy- the principal for that period in its foreign policy of coercion. So, from January 1, 2007, the Russian company Gazprom raised the price of natural gas imported from Georgia from 64 US dollars per thousand cubic meters to 110 US dollars.[364] At that time, Georgia, which did not have energy resources, imported gas, mainly from Russia. In 2006, Georgia gained 1.44 billion cubic meters of Russian natural gas.

The exact price for Russian natural gas was also to pay Azerbaijan, which still needed to begin to produce its gas fully and acquire it from Gazprom. At the same time, Russia's main ally in the South Caucasus, Armenia, continued to pay 56 US dollars per thousand cubic meters.[365] In this way, once again, it can be seen that the decision to raise the gas price was economic and political, designed to subordinate *NIS* to Russia's interests. It is worth noting that prior to the increase in gas prices, Russia periodically, for various reasons, suspended gas supplies to Georgia.[366] Gazprom was not limited to the increase in gas prices in 2006. A year later, in January 2007, Gazprom announced the subsequent increase in prices for Russian gas, which now has been increased up to 235 US dollars per thousand cubic meters.[367] The next, more than two-fold rise in the price of gas negatively impacted the overall economic situation in Georgia. It was the price that Georgia could not pay, which could mean the country's energy crisis.

Initially, Russia proposed to keep the prices for Georgia to 110 US dollars per thousand cubic meters level in 10 years if the country agreed to sell the Russia-Georgia-Armenia gas pipeline, through which Russian gas enters the Armenian market. First, Georgia has given its consent to the sale. However, the US intervened in the case. That during President Saakashvili's visit to the US, has signed an agreement for the next five years, according to which Georgia would receive 295 million US dollars for the development of the Georgian economy.[368] In addition, the US government has allocated funds to rehabilitate this gas pipeline. As a result, Georgia has refused to transfer the Russian gas pipeline.[369]

In addition, Georgia was rescued by Azerbaijan, which increased its production of natural gas from the Shah Deniz field and began to export to Georgia and Türkiye for 120 US dollars per thousand cubic meters.[370] Azerbaijan's support has helped Georgia to avoid the economic crisis and reduce its dependence on energy supplies from Russia, and therefore of the potential negative economic and political consequences.

Another Russian instrument of pressure on Georgia, which later played the role of "time bombs," has become a massive provision of the breakaway regions Abkhazia and South Ossetia residents with Russian citizenship. As a result, 90% of the inhabitants of South Ossetia and 80 % of Abkhazia became owners of the Russian passports.[371] Thus, Russia has included these two regions in the direct sphere of influence. It also allowed her to create a buffer zone in the South Caucasus in the case of *NATO*'s possible expansion.

On April 8, 2008, Georgia, together with Ukraine, at the *NATO* Summit in Budapest, referred to the alliance with the request to begin negotiations on accession to the *MAP* for *NATO* membership. Before that, on January 8, 2008, in Georgia, a referendum was held, the results of which 77% participated citizens of Georgia voted in favor of joining *NATO*. However, at the summit, Georgia has yet to receive the expected response: despite the US and several other countries supporting Georgia and Ukraine, Germany and France, and some other alliance members voted against the provision of a formal invitation. At the same time, in adopting the statement after the meeting, it was noted that Georgia and Ukraine have the opportunity to become full members of *NATO* when they meet the requirements for membership in this organization, and *MAP* is the next step in relations with *NATO*.[372]

Despite *NATO's* assurances, until today, these two countries are even further away from membership in the alliance than it seemed in 2008. In addition, Russia negatively perceived the possible membership of Georgia in *NATO*.

One of the main reasons that the already tiny chance of membership of Georgia decreased became the "*five-day war*" between Georgia and Russia, which began military operations in Georgia to restore its territorial integrity. On the night of 7-8 August 2008, the Georgian army launched a full-scale attack in order to "*restore constitutional order*" in breakaway South Ossetia. In a short time, the Georgian army managed to maintain control over the entire territory of the region. However, immediately after that, Russia harshly reacted to the situation by accusing Georgia and declaring its readiness to use force against this *Small*

Power based on the principles of human security and the responsibility to protect.[373] At the same time, it was also stated that the need to protect the Russian citizens living not only in South Ossetia but also in Abkhazia. Russian President Dmitry Medvedev announced the start of an "*operation to enforce peace*" in the conflict zone. Russian troops were introduced in the region. Georgian troops were driven out of South Ossetia. On August 12, military actions in South Ossetia were suspended. At the same time, Russia sent troops to Abkhazia. As mentioned earlier, on August 26, Russia recognized the independence of Abkhazia and South Ossetia. In response, Georgia severed diplomatic relations with Russia. Events of the "*five-day war*" slowed down the process of Georgia's accession to *NATO*, which, in principle, Russia desired.

Saakashvili's administration initiated this military operation, hoping for the support of *NATO* and the US, believing that after Georgia took South Ossetia, the US, through diplomatic channels, neutralized possible Russian intervention. However, the expected did not happen. As a result, the Georgian forces were driven out.[374]

After the "*five-day war*," Georgia changed its security concept, adopted on 23 December 2011. According to her, following the new realities formed after the August 2008 war, Russia from the partner country, per the previous concept of security, has become a "*major threat and challenge*." Russia was recognized as the occupier of Georgian territories. At the same time, Georgia re-emphasized the country's intention to join *NATO*.[375]

Georgia after Saakashvili

The loss of territories, economic instability, and failure in foreign policy direction led to the fact that in 2012, during the parliamentary elections, Michael Saakashvili's party United National Movement lost, and the opposition coalition led by the Georgian businessman Bidzina Ivanishvili won the elections.

Ivanishvili only in October of 2011 began to participate in Georgia's political life actively, the cause of which was opposition to Saakashvili's policies. It was intended to create a political party and participate in elections. Interestingly, a few days after the announcement of the decision to start opposition activities, the authorities deprived Ivanishvili of Georgian citizenship. Therefore, he created a party initially headed by his wife, who at first was also deprived of citizenship but was able to regain it by a court decision.[376] In April 2012, the Georgian Dream coalition was established.

On October 1, 2012, the coalition, led by Bidzina Ivanishvili, got 85 seats out of 150 in parliament at the time, as the Saakashvili's United National Movement won the remaining 65 and went into opposition.[377] This development is very significant because for the first time in Georgia and the post-Soviet space, the change of power took place through elections. Following the elections, Bidzina Ivanishvili became prime minister of the country. This fact is significant also because according to the changes in the Constitution in 2010, the powers of the president will be reduced and reallocated between the parliament and the government. Thus, after 2013, Georgia had become a parliamentary republic, and the powers of the Prime Minister were to increase substantially. One of the reasons due to which the reform of the state system of Georgia was held, was that Saakashvili's presidential term was to be completed in 2013. According to the Georgian Constitution, he could not re-elect to this post, so in case of victory of his party in the parliamentary elections, Saakashvili could become prime minister of the country, while maintaining full power.[378] However, this was not to happen; United National Movement lost the election.

One of Georgia's new government's moves, led by Ivanishvili after coming to power, was the country's foreign policy adjustment. From the very first days of his reign, the new Georgian leadership completely abandons the provocative anti-Russian policy and rhetoric. In addition to these, other vectors of foreign policy concerning relations within the region and the Euro-Atlantic orientation remained unchanged. In short, concerning relations with its neighbors, Georgia has maintained balanced and good neighborly relations with Armenia, Azerbaijan, and Türkiye. At the same time, relations with Azerbaijan and Türkiye were considered strategic since, with these countries, Georgia implemented a regional economic project. Due to the successful implementation of the energy and transport projects, further relations between the two countries have acquired a trilateral format, which has spread to other areas of cooperation.

As it were during the reign of the previous presidents of Georgia, already become traditional, strategic relationships with the US have been preserved. At the same time, the new authorities of Georgia, as the main priority of foreign policy, chose partnership and friendly relations with the *EU*. The Saakashvili government previously desired further integration into *NATO* and the EU.

It is worth noting that Bidzina Ivanishvili, after a year stint as Prime Minister in November 2013, voluntarily resigned, handing the post to his ally Irakli Gharibashvili. However, even though Ivanishvili refused the post of Prime Minister, he retained control and influence on the formation of an overall strategy both in his party and the coalition. On November 17, 2013, Georgia's new president Giorgi Margvelashvili was elected. He received 62% of the votes and became the fourth president of Georgia. Margvelashvili was nominated for the presidency by the Georgian Dream coalition, but he is neither a member of the party or a coalition.[379] Thus, by the end of 2013, the Georgian Dream coalition controlled all senior positions in the country.

A few days later, the newly elected President of Georgia, Margvelashvili, presented at the Vilnius Summit of the *EU EP*, held November 28-29, 2013. During the summit, Georgia initialed the *Association Agreement* with the *EU*, completing a process begun by the Saakashvili administration. On June 27, 2014, the *EU*-Georgia *Association Agreement* was signed.

The signing of the agreement has not caused a stormy reaction from Russia, as could have been initially expected. Several reasons can explain it. First, relations with Georgia were superficial because of the continuing controversy on Russian intervention in South Ossetia and Abkhazia, the visa regime, and little economic relations. This state of affairs did not suit Russia, so she refrained from a sharp reaction. In addition, the Georgian government has changed, and the presidential term of Michael Saakashvili, an implacable opponent of Russia, was ended. In addition, the country's new authorities from the first days stated that they wanted to improve relations with Russia and avoid anti-Russian rhetoric, even if it was addressed to the internal public. At the same time, in this period, complicated relations between Russia and Ukraine, so Russia all the attention was focused on this country. Given Ukraine's geographic location, size, and population, for Russia, integration of this country into Euro-Atlantic structures would have more considerable geopolitical consequences than in the case of Georgia. In turn, the *West*'s actions concerning Georgia and Ukraine were parallel; thus, the concentration of Russian forces in question to prevent Ukraine's integration into Euro-Atlantic structures also applies to other *NIS Small Powers*, primarily Georgia.

An important aspect was the negotiation on the liberalization of the visa regime between the *EU* and Georgia. The result should be abolishing visas for Georgian citizens with biometric passports. In a relatively short period, Georgia has carried out all reforms outlined in the plan to liberalize the visa regime and accept all the conditions. The *EU* has promised to begin the process of the abolition of tourist visas. On March 9, 2016, the European Commission proposed to the Council of the *EU* and the European Parliament to abolish tourist visas for Georgian citizens who have biometric passports. It should be achieved by making Georgia on the list of countries whose citizens are entitled to travel without a visa for the Schengen countries.[380]

Although Georgia has fulfilled all conditions and received approval from the European Commission, in early June, the *EU* delegation discussed the liberalization of the visa regime with Georgia but postponed a final decision. Against were France and Germany. Some of the *EU* and German officials are concerned about Georgian organized crime groups, which may be amplified after the abolition of visas.[381] Also, this decision affected the growth of migration from the Middle East and Africa, which has become a severe problem for the *EU*. Finally, only on March 28, 2017, Georgia granted a visa-free regime to the *EU*.

Despite the current problems, Georgia was considering the adoption of a visa-free regime as the next step for *EU* membership. President of Georgia Margvelashvili expressed confidence that Georgia will join the *EU*.[382]

Along with the *EU*, Georgia continues to develop relations with *NATO*, actively participating in the programs offered by this alliance. Georgia provides logistical support for *NATO* operations in Afghanistan. This Georgian activity in this country is not limited to logistics: 860 of its soldiers are now there. It is significant because, not being a member of *NATO*, this country is presented with the third-largest contribution after the US and Germany. In addition, Georgia sent thousands of soldiers to Iraq, and hundreds of Georgian peacekeepers were sent to the Balkans; a new direction for this country became the Central African Republic, which also sent troops. Georgia is actively pursuing reforms following *NATO* standards.[383]

Even though Georgia has implemented large-scale *NATO* requirements under the different cooperation programs, *NATO* is still not ready to give *MAP*. Interestingly, Montenegro, which became the 29th member of *NATO* on June 5, 2017, had implemented far fewer demands than Georgia. However, this does not prevent her from becoming a member of *NATO*. Georgia's membership, especially, was opposed to Germany and France. The main reason for this is that these countries consider that the granting of the *MAP* could provoke Russia, which is currently already, expressed its concern about the possible membership of Georgia and Ukraine in the alliance.[384]

In addition, part of the territory of Georgia: Abkhazia, and South Ossetia are controlled by Russia; in this case, the alliance is not ready to clash with Russia.[385] Russia's annexation of Crimea and the subsequent violence in the east of Ukraine complicate the already tense relations between Russia and *NATO*. Each side accuses the other of interfering in the affairs of the *NIS's Small Powers*. By the way, when France and Germany vetoed granting Georgia *MAP* at the Bucharest Summit, held on April 8, 2008, at that time, Russia did not recognize Abkhazia and South Ossetia. But the concern was the same: the possible adverse reaction of Russia.[386] Therefore, relations with Georgia develop in various formats, except the *MAP*. *NATO* opened in Georgia the inaugural *NATO*-Georgia Joint Training and Evaluation Center in the Krtsanisi National Training Center outside of Tbilisi. The center's purpose is to train both Georgian and *NATO* troops. It was a gesture of *NATO*, which not wanting to give Georgia *MAP* but is trying to encourage the aspiration of this state.[387]

Since independence, despite the change of governments, Georgia was considered a priority for integration with the *West*. For her, it was the basis for forming its new post-Soviet identity. At the same time to achieve this goal, Georgia has implemented all the requirements set in front of it on the part of the Western institutions and states. Undoubtedly, these reforms are only possible with technical and financial support from the *West*. Between 2007 and 2013, the *EU* provided 452 million Euros under the *EP* program. In turn, the US, in the period between 2005-2010, provided 395 million US dollars via the Millennium Challenge Corporation. After the *"five-day war"* in October 2008, international donors, including the US, the *EU*, EBRD, World Bank, and others, have provided post-war assistance for Georgia worth 4.5 billion US dollars.[388]

Sometimes this desire of Georgia to dispense is costly, as happened in the case of the invasion of Russia in South Ossetia and Abkhazia. Georgia was at the center of the confrontation between its Western aspirations and the discontent of Russia, which considers the *NIS* region a sphere of its interests. At the same time, the *West* itself participated or supported Georgia directly, but not in the confrontation with Russia. Moreover, even though this opposition has managed it quite expensively, Georgia has not abandoned the process of adopting Western values; *NATO* and the *EU* are in no hurry to support the aspiration of Georgia precisely because these structures do not wish to spoil relations with Russia.

As seen in the example of relations with the *EU*, even though the *EU* initially promised a visa-free regime for Georgia, it had postponed several times. Even though Georgia has implemented all the requirements of this structure, several sovereign rights were abandoned in favor of this possibility. Moreover, the *EU* needs to provide complete freedom of movement for the citizens of Georgia. Abolition of the visa regime, which includes only Georgian tourists with a biological passport and gives the right to stay in the *EU* states only for 90 days, does not provide a right to work. However, even such a limited provision of rights is faced with doubts and reluctance from the members of this structure.

The same can be said about *NATO*, which is realizing that it needs some way to encourage Georgia's efforts and develop new tools for developing relations with Georgia, which may include everything but the eligibility for membership in the alliance. At the same time, in Georgia, the programs offered by the *EU* and *NATO* are considered the next step to full integration.

Thus, the purposeful implementation of a pro-Western foreign policy on the part of Georgia until that is not justified. This *Small Power* is still not achieved its goals because it does not depend on it. It needs the willingness of the *West* to respond to these expectations; it is likely, at least in the medium term, will not be realized. The main mistake of Georgia's foreign policy is that the government of this country, especially in times of Saakashvili's relations with the *West*, perceived wishful thinking. This perception formed the conviction that a stable and persistent implementation of the Western programs eventually paved the way for full integration into *NATO* and the *EU*. Thus, both *NATO* and the *EU* are also confronted with a difficult situation, not wanting and not being able to meet the expectations of Georgia. As a result, Georgia was on the way, which did not lead to its logical end. Along with the fact that Georgia has only partially realized their interests in relations with the *West*, the country still has a problematic relationship with Russia.

The complex relationship with one of the essential neighbors causes geopolitical and geo-economic problems that Georgia cannot solve. Consequently, if not with new problems, this situation threatens, at least with the need for more resolution of the current issues. Georgia believes that the solution to current and prevention of future problems can become a full integration with Western organizations. However, as has become clear, if such integration is to happen, then it will be after a very long time. It is, therefore, necessary to look for alternative ways. First, it is necessary to correct foreign policy following the realities within the region and in the international arena. The current government of Georgia understands that improving relations with Russia, first of all, is necessary for its economy. The primary market has traditionally been Russia for the export of the Georgian products.[389] However, between 2012-2016, when the Georgian Dream coalition was in power, it could not achieve significant progress in developing relations with Russia. The current establishment of Georgia understands it. Thus, Ivanishvili, in June 2016, stated that: "*The South Caucasus nation*" must absolutely "*join NATO and the European Union, but cautioned that it will first have to overcome Russia's disapproval.*" Ivanishvili proposes to continue to carry out reforms until it is: "*the right time, when Russia realizes, and when our allies see that it is time for Georgia to become a member of NATO and the EU.*".[390] Thus, the new authorities of Georgia, unlike Saakashvili's administration, see Russia's importance in its national interests.

Since Georgia still insists on membership in *NATO*, these relations will not improve. Russia attaches particular importance to the South Caucasus region in its security concept. For Russian interests, meeting any *Small Power* in this region, including Georgia, in *NATO* is categorically unacceptable.

Interestingly, Euro-Atlantic structures were reduced in popularity at that time among the population in Georgia, and the number of supporting accessions to these organizations had declined. Thus, according to surveys conducted in Georgia, between November 2013 and August 2015, support for integration with the *EU* decreased from 85% to 61%. At the same time, the number of those who are against the integration had increased from 10% to 21%. In turn, support for *NATO* dropped from 81% to 69%.[391] In parallel, the stronger the position of the pro-Russian parties, such as the Democratic Movement - United Georgia, the Alliance of Patriots of Georgia, the Labour Party, and Free Georgia, and non-governmental organizations, such as the Eurasian Choice of Georgia and the Eurasian Institute.[392]

The activation of pro-Russian groups was not only related to the activity of Russia but also connected with the passivity of the *West*. In this case, strengthening the pro-Russian forces' position in Georgia does not result in a possible balancing force. It could cause a confrontation between them since the polarity is newly observed in the actions of the political forces.

Thus, Georgia is conducting a pro-Western course and has not achieved the desired results. Since more than one of its intents and the appropriate actions are needed, the West's willingness needs to respond to these requests. The *West* is still being prepared to do it. At the same time, Georgia's persistence led to complicated relations with Russia, and now normalizing them will take much work. For this *Small Power*, it is now necessary to improve relations with Russia and build relations with the *West* from the perspective of the realistic paradigm, abandoning excessive idealism.

CHAPTER 8
Armenia and Political and Economic Dependency on Russia

Armenia Foreign Policy During Levon Ter-Petrosyan

The smallest in size and population of the South Caucasus countries, Armenia, is simultaneously devoid of significant natural resources but has no access to international waters. In turn, the country's geographical location would have allowed it to become a central transportation hub between *East* and *West* and between *North* and *South*. For example, Armenia could become the shortest route for oil and natural gas export from Azerbaijan to Türkiye. However, the country was out of these and other transportation projects because of the Nagorno-Karabakh conflict. Due to the conflict borders of this country with Azerbaijan and Türkiye are closed: the output to the outside world via Armenia carries out two other neighbors, Georgia and Iran. At the same time, Armenia is faced with a difficult situation when the geopolitical situation in the neighboring countries is complicated. Thus, when the anti-Iran sanctions were imposed, or when the Georgian-Russian border was closed by Russia in the mid-90s because of the Chechen war, and from the Georgian side, after the "*five-day war*" in 2008.

Given that Russia is the leading trading partner of Armenia and these countries do not have a common border, it negatively impacts the overall situation in Armenia. At the same time, the Georgian ports on the Black Sea are the main gateway for the export and import of Armenia. However, if the border with Türkiye had been opened, the transportation to this country would cost less.

It is worth noting that, unlike Georgia and Azerbaijan, Armenia has been in a relatively stable political situation in the first years after independence. This country was not a "storm" of the civil war or internal conflicts, while the conflict it was involved in did not occur within the borders of Armenia and occurred in neighboring Azerbaijan.

On October 16, 1991, the Armenian president Levon Ter-Petrosyan was elected, who, unlike their colleagues in the region, could hold on to power for more than one term. As the Georgian President of Gamsakhurdia, Ter-Petrosyan was not a representative of the Communist Party and came to power after the emergence of the Nagorno-Karabakh conflict. Even before the collapse of the Soviet

Union, since 1988, Levon Ter-Petrosyan was a member of the "Karabakh" committee, demanded the withdrawal of the Nagorno-Karabakh Autonomous Region from the jurisdiction of the Azerbaijan SSR and one of the leaders of the Armenian National Movement. Later headed the movement, he was elected to the Parliament of Armenia and its chairman.

From the first years of Armenia's independence, the main factor influencing the foreign policy of Armenia became the Nagorno-Karabakh conflict. Ter-Petrosyan, as well as the President of Azerbaijan Mutalibov, realized that in order to succeed in a military confrontation, it is necessary to have good relations with Russia and rely on its support. In addition, it should not have ruled out such factors as historically developed relations with Türkiye. In addition, in the first years of independence, Armenia has existed the perception of a "Turkish threat." It was primarily due to its geographical position. Located between Türkiye and Azerbaijan, Armenia formed the feeling of being under siege and insecurity.[393]

For the formation of this threat, Armenia itself has also contributed. In short, *"the events of 1915"* in the Ottoman Empire are perceived by Armenians as an act of genocide towards this nation and is a very sensitive issue for Armenians worldwide. At the same time, in the declaration of independence of Armenia, signed by Levon Ter-Petrosyan, one of the main points of the new state of activity was assumed as: *"Support of the task of achieving international recognition of the 1915 genocide in Ottoman Türkiye and Western Armenia"*.[394]

Under *Western Armenia*, here it means the territory of modern Türkiye; thus, main Armenian document relating to the formation of the state also appeared with territorial claims to its western neighbor.

In addition, it is worth noting that in the Armenian-Azerbaijani Nagorno-Karabakh conflict, Türkiye has supported Azerbaijan, which is ethnically and culturally close to her. So, close relations with Russia and its support were needed to balance these outgoing calls.

Initially, the observed anti-Russian sentiment in Armenia was more concerned with the desire to gain Armenia's independence from Moscow. In Armenia, the supporters of independence came to power. At that time, for any *NIS*, gaining independence implied a reduction of dependence on Russia. However, despite these sentiments, Ter-Petrosyan did not take a break in relations with Russia,[395] as it did in Georgia.

Russia's position on the Nagorno-Karabakh issue, the two countries, was initially balanced. Both countries joined the *CIS* at the Almaty Summit, trying to prove their loyalty to Russia. In the territories of both countries, there were Russian military bases left over from the Soviet times. As mentioned before, after Azerbaijan began to search for ways to cooperate with Western energy companies, Russia's position changed in favor of Armenia. Ter-Petrosyan skillfully took advantage of this situation, which became strengthened during the reign of the anti-Russian Popular Front in Azerbaijan.

However, Ter-Petrosyan himself, as much as possible, tried to avoid one-sided dependence on its northern neighbor. Therefore, Ter-Petrosyan tried to minimize the possible dominance of Russia in Armenia. Armenia is willing to form relationships with Russia in the security sphere. In turn, in the first years of independence, Armenia received economic and financial support from the *West*, and fuel from Iran.[396]

This kind of foreign policy, in which Armenia is trying to form equal relations with all the prominent regional and global actors, in other words, to sit simultaneously in several chairs, later became known as a policy of *complementarism*.[397]

On May 15, 1992, Armenia joined the pro-Russian military *Collective Security Treaty Organisation*. At that time, as the Russian military bases from Azerbaijan had been entirely withdrawn as early as during the reign of Abulfaz Elchibey, Armenia, on March 16, 1995, signed an agreement on the status of the 102nd Russian military base in Armenia in Gyumri. According to this agreement, the Russian base in Armenia will be placed for twenty-five years.[398]

At the same time, in about the same period, Armenia became the first of the South Caucasus *Small Powers*, which signed an agreement with *NATO* on joining the *PfP* program on October 5, 1994. Also, like other countries of the South Caucasus, Armenia in 1996 signed the *PCA* with the *EU*.

It is worth noting that if these actions in the foreign policy of Armenia are considered in the framework of *complementarianism*, there is a need to consider three aspects. Firstly, in the first years of *NIS*'s independence, every step they took in foreign policy led to the establishment of relationships rather than their development. Therefore, here we should talk about the balance of policy and attempts to act following the interests of various regional powers, but as the initial stage of forming relationships with different actors. Second, in the early stages of *NIS Small Powers'* relations with the *EU* and *NATO*, there was no subject of polarity between the *West* and Russia. Russia has actively cooperated with these structures in the framework of programs they proposed to the former Soviet republics. Therefore, Russia was not against the participation of *NIS* in cooperation with these organizations.

Moreover, the *West* has not shown much interest in the South Caucasus and Armenia. At the same time, relations between Russia and the US have developed rapidly. Third, since Armenia is a *Small Power*, this country cannot run development following her interests. Armenia has only used the opportunities that it provides and has yet to create them. In this case, talking about the policy of *complementarianism* is not true because if Western countries and organizations did not want to cooperate with Armenia, then she would not be able to conduct a multi-vector foreign policy.

As proof of this statement can be shown the relations of this state with Türkiye, which Armenia is also considered in the context of *complementarianism*. The Ter-Petrosyan administration was willing to develop relations with Türkiye. It is assumed that one of the reasons for the ban of Dashnaktyutsun party activities in Armenia is as a step towards rapprochement with Türkiye. In addition, Ter-Petrosyan avoids rhetoric that could negatively be perceived in Türkiye. Symbolic was the personal involvement of President Ter-Petrosyan at the funeral ceremony of the President of Türkiye Turgut Ozal, who died in 1993. At the same time, President Ozal died just two weeks after the closure of the Turkish-Armenian border.

Moreover, good relations with the Western neighbor were necessary to balance Türkiye during active hostilities with Azerbaijan over Nagorno-Karabakh. The geographical location of Türkiye also is not played the last role, which is a window to Europe for Armenia. Türkiye was one of the first countries to recognize Armenia's independence. In the first years of independence, several times, it was allowed to transport humanitarian aid from Europe to Armenia from its territory. However, after April 1993, Armenia occupied the Azerbaijani region of Kelbajar, located outside of Nagorno-Karabakh. Turkiye, in solidarity with Azerbaijan, closed its border with Armenia and ceased all relations until the occupied territories were liberated.

However, unlike Azerbaijan and Georgia, Armenia has the resources not in Georgia and Azerbaijan—namely, a strong, close-knit Armenian community residing in the Western states. A powerful representation of the Diaspora lives in the US and France. A large number of Armenians also live in Russia. Due to the presence of the Diaspora, Armenia had the opportunity to receive financial and economic aid, both directly from the Diaspora itself and from the states in which they are located, using their logistics activities.

Because of the Diaspora logistics activity in the US in 1992, the "*Freedom Support Act section 907*" against Azerbaijan was adopted. Azerbaijan could not receive government assistance from the US for about ten years. By the way, the US government's economic aid is an essential financial infusion in a very tight budget of Armenia. Serious financial investments for infrastructure projects received in the framework of *the Millennium Challenge Account Program*.[399] Thus, in terms of per capita, Armenia was the largest recipient of direct US aid after Israel. Since independence during the two decades, Armenia has received about 2 billion US dollars.[400] At the same time, Ter-Petrosyan and next president Robert Kocharyan's administrations used representatives of the Armenian Diaspora, who agreed to participate in the formation of the state. For example, Gerard Libardian, a US citizen, was a senior presidential adviser of Ter-Petrosyan and a key architect of Armenian foreign policy. Libardian played an essential role during the negotiations for the Nagorno- Karabakh conflict solution. Raffi Hovannisian was the first Minister of Foreign Affairs of the Republic of Armenia, and Vartan Oskanian, Minister of Foreign Affairs during Robert Kocharyan's reign, were also US Diaspora members.[401]

However, along with the provision of assistance, representatives of the Diaspora had the opportunity to intervene in the internal affairs of Armenia more actively. Compared with the Armenians living in Armenia, Diaspora has a more rigid position on foreign policy. It is mainly observed in the reign of Levon Ter-Petrosyan. The Armenian Diaspora has played a vital role in forming the strict policy towards Türkiye and then Azerbaijan. Given that Diaspora interests do not always coincide with the national interests of Armenia, President Levon Ter-Petrosyan tried his best to reduce their impact on the country. These efforts led to the fact that some circles began to say that Ter-Petrosyan "offended" Diaspora.[402]

In 1996, Ter-Petrosyan the second time was re-elected as president of Armenia. However, the primary opponents and observers deemed these elections rigged. In general, the popularity of Ter-Petrosyan in the country was rapidly falling. It was the reason for the difficult economic situation in Armenia. In order to strengthen its position within the country, Ter-Petrosyan resorted to the only option, namely, to begin to expand relations with its northern neighbor- Russia. In 1996 several agreements were signed in the military sphere. In addition, on 29 August 1997, the Armenian-Russian *Treaty on Friendship, Cooperation, and Mutual Assistance* was signed, the first that Russia signed with the *NIS*.

Ter-Petrosyan also noted the growth of the Armenian-Russian relations. The agreement includes mutual military support if one country is attacked or perceives a threat from a third party. At the same time, the parties undertake not to participate in military alliances or conclude agreements aimed against each other. Thus, Armenia received Russian support in case Azerbaijan desired to take revenge.[403] Although in May 1994, a cease-fire was agreed upon, the final *Peace Agreement* had yet to be signed. War could begin again as soon as Azerbaijan had completed the signing of agreements on energy projects and started their implementation. Thus, because of internal instability and a rapid fall in popularity, Ter-Petrosyan was forced to seek support on the side. The only option was to find such support from Russia, and Ter-Petrosyan got it. However, it happened because of further deepening relations with this country. Armenia entered deeper into Russia's orbit, which negated attempts to maintain a balanced foreign policy.[404] If Ter-Petrosyan were other opportunities and could get support from the *West*, he would not fail to take advantage of it.

In addition to a rapprochement with Russia, Ter-Petrosyan made a series of reshuffles in the government. In March, for the post of Prime Minister of Armenia, the Karabakhian Armenian Robert Kocharyan was appointed. Robert Kocharyan was the first "president" of Nagorno-Karabakh. Kocharyan's appointment to the Prime Minister post has served to improve relations with the Armenian Diaspora and was generally well received.[405] Ter-Petrosyan, by appointing Kocharyan, was hoping that participation of the "*Karabakh party*" in the administration would let them feel more clearly how the unresolved conflict affects the economy of Armenia.[406]

However, the leading cause of dissatisfaction with Ter-Petrosyan was his position on resolving the Nagorno-Karabakh conflict. The fact was that, at that time, Ter-Petrosyan was looking for ways of conflict resolution. Pragmatic Ter-Petrosyan knew that Armenia's future had to begin with forming relationships with Türkiye and Azerbaijan, and without resolving the conflict, it was impossible.

In 1994, Azerbaijan signed the "*Contract of the Century*," the parties negotiated an agreement regarding how the oil produced from the field would be exported to world markets. As mentioned above, the route through Armenia was not considered due to the Nagorno-Karabakh conflict. Ter-Petrosyan wanted to play proactive: it is believed that if a conflict with Azerbaijan is resolved, the Azerbaijani and Turkish border will be opened. The economic relations will restore, and Azerbaijan, in exchange for a peace agreement, will consent to export its oil through the territory of Armenia. For a country with no significant natural resources, the revenues from transport would be significant for its budget. In addition, Armenia would have access to the stable delivery of energy resources to cover its needs. At the same time, if the pipeline passes through Armenia, it also allows her to gain political advantage against Azerbaijan, as the country would fall into dependence on Armenia on the issue of stable transportation.

In this way, Ter-Petrosyan started talks with Azerbaijan regarding resolving the conflict. However, the negotiations included a compromise from the Armenian side, which were very unpopular among the population of Armenia. In order to change the situation, on November 1, 1997, Levon Ter-Petrosyan, published in the Armenian newspapers the article "*War or Peace: Time to get serious*." Ter-Petrosyan tried to initiate a serious discussion in the press about the possible ways to settle the Karabakh conflict. Ter-Petrosyan said that maintaining the status quo was impossible, and it was necessary to resolve the conflict only through peaceful negotiations. He emphasized that what Armenia rejects today, in the future, will not be possible to achieve. According to Ter-Petrosyan, for the resolution of the conflict, necessary compromises for both sides. It is a tricky business, and the leaders of both countries could be perceived as traitors.[407] Ter-Petrosyan considered that granting independence to Nagorno-Karabakh was unrealistic and urged society to be ready to support this compromise and conflict resolution.

Thus, Ter-Petrosyan, thereby trying to divide the interests of Armenia and Karabakh: for Ter-Petrosyan, Armenian national interests were superior to the interests of Karabakh.

In September 1997, the *OSCE Minsk Group* suggested "*a step-by-step*" solution to the conflict. The Presidents of Azerbaijan and Armenia considered this proposal a basis for further negotiations. Under the proposal, the first step is returning five occupied Azerbaijan regions and returning refugees. At the same time, it lifts the blockade against Armenia. In the second stage, the status of Nagorno Karabakh and the liberation of Shusha and Lachin would be negotiated.[408]

Ter-Petrosyan's wishes faced serious opposition from Prime Minister Robert Kocharyan, Minister of Defense Vazgen Sargsyan, and the Minister of Internal Affairs Serzh Sargsyan. Against Ter-Petrosyan also addressed the opposition Armenian intellectuals, the Diaspora, and the media.[409] Faced with strong opposition and pressure, President Ter-Petrosyan resigned without completing his second presidential term. Even though Ter-Petrosyan could stay in power longer than his colleagues- the first presidents of Georgia and Azerbaijan, Gamsakhurdia, and Mutalibov, the same way as they, he could not fulfill his obligations.

On March 16, 1998, the first round of the early presidential elections passed, which did not reveal the winner among the twelve candidates. On March 30, 1998, Armenia hosted the second round of elections. The primary battle for the presidency has passed between the acting president of Armenia, Robert Kocharyan, and the Speaker of Parliament and former head of the Armenian SSR, Karen Demirchyan.[410] As a result, gaining 58.9 % of the votes, Kocharyan became the country's second president.[411]

Foreign Policy in the Time of Robert Kocharyan

Immediately after the election of President Robert Kocharyan, it became clear that Armenia's foreign policy, especially in the settlement of the Nagorno-Karabakh conflict and relations with Türkiye, would be radically different from that of what was held by Levon Ter-Petrosyan. As a representative of the Karabakh Armenians and close to the Armenian Diaspora, it was more based on the interests of these two groups rather than Armenia's national interests, as it unsuccessfully tried to do the previous president. One more confirmation of this was that in February 1998, Kocharyan again permitted activities of the Dashnaktsutyun party. It was a gesture toward the Armenian Diaspora. Robert Kocharyan and a new administration were to go against the discussed compromises. Despite that, Kocharyan held talks with Azerbaijani President Heydar Aliyev, but they have not led to any conclusion.[412]

The negotiations process was also affected by the terrorist act on April 27, 1999, in the Armenian parliament. As a result of the attack, Prime Minister Vazgen Sargsyan, the parliament chairman Karen Demirchyan, and six deputies were killed. Both leaders wanted a solution to the Karabakh conflict. However, after their death, the likelihood of resolution probability is decreased.[413]

As a result, all of the energy transport projects have been implemented bypassed Armenia, and oil and gas pipelines passed through the territory of Georgia. Along with this, Azerbaijan, which is not achieving a resolution of the conflict and is faced with a situation in which Armenia is pursuing a policy to preserve the status quo in the conflict, has become following a policy of isolation of Armenia from all regional economic projects, which is implemented in the South Caucasus. In addition to the implementation of energy transport corridors bypassing Armenia, Azerbaijan prevented the active participation of this country in the *TRACECA* transport corridor. Azerbaijan has imposed a ban on the use of its territory for the goods which are transported from Armenia through the territory of this country or sent to that country.[414] It is entering this country in a geographical deadlock. This policy of Azerbaijan towards Armenia will be continued in the future.

In 2007, Azerbaijan, with Georgia and Türkiye, began construction of the Baku-Tbilisi-Kars railway, which had a geopolitical goal: to build a railway route bypassing Armenia. In this way, it would have remained irrelevant the Gyumri-Kars railway, which has existed since the days of the Soviet Union, but it has ceased to operate after the closure of the Armenian-Turkish border.[415]

Thus, Armenia was isolated entirely from regional economic projects, which were actively developing. Attempts to consolidate transport corridors passing through the territory were also unsuccessful. Despite the strong relations with Russia and Iran, regional transport projects initiated by these countries were not realized with Armenia but with Azerbaijan.[416]

As for Armenia's foreign policy in general, president Kocharyan like Ter-Petrosyan tried to pursue a policy of *complementarianism*. By the way, the author of this term was the Minister of Foreign Affairs during the reign of Kocharyan- Vartan Oskanian.[417]

Armenia was to develop relations with *NATO* within the *PfP*. However, she also enforced relationships with the pro-Russian *CSTO*. To a greater extent, the interests of Armenia's relations with *NATO*, since it is possible to obtain financial support that allows carrying out reforms in the military sphere. In the same vein, relations with the US developed, from which Armenia received significant financial contributions for its budget. From 1999 to 2001, President Kocharyan visited the US three times. At the same time, he was formally invited to this country only once, when President George W. Bush invited him to attend the summit in Key-West (Florida) for settlement of the Nagorno-Karabakh conflict.[418] Quite often, Armenia Minister of Foreign Affairs Vardan Oskanian has visited the US.[419] During visits to the US, the meetings with the Armenian Diaspora in this country were of particular importance, which continued to provide financial support to Armenia. Regarding the relations with the *EU*, in 1999, Luxembourg ratified the *PCA*. The Armenian delegation headed personally by President Kocharyan.[420]

However, opportunities for a balanced policy in Armenia were less. At the same time, dependence on Russia was growing. It coincided with President Vladimir Putin coming to power in Russia, who has come to pursue a more coordinated policy towards the South Caucasus. In addition to the fact that Armenia had close relations with Russia in matters of security, during Kocharyan, Russia's presence in the economy was sufficiently increased. Immediately after coming to power, Robert Kocharyan received a loan from Russia of 500 million US dollars. However, it was not possible to return this loan to Armenia. From this point in the economic relations between the two countries, a new formula, "*loans in exchange for property*," has formed. Armenia became pay for loans granted to Russia at the expense of enterprises controlling this state. On July 17, 2002, the two countries signed several agreements on the transfer of ownership of the Russian Federation and shares of Armenian enterprises to repay Armenia's state debt to Russia in the amount of 93 million US dollars. According to the document, the ownership of Russia moved by such companies as JSC "Mars" (which was valued at $ 56.29 million), CJSC "Yerevan Research Institute of Mathematical Machines" ($ 2.75 million), CJSC "Yerevan Research Institute of automated control systems" ($ 3.37 million), CJSC "Yerevan Research Institute of Materials Science" ($ 0.35 million), the property complex of Hrazdan Thermal Power Plant ($ 31 million).[421]

Lately, this practice has been continued. So, based on the practical realization of repayment according to the abovementioned scheme, 80% of the Armenian energy structure, including the Iran-Armenia gas pipeline, is controlled by Russia. In addition to several Armenian hydroelectric and nuclear plants, the rest of the infrastructure in the energy field was transferred to Russia in exchange for writing off the Armenian debt. Among them: the Sevan-Hrazdan cascade of Hydroelectric Power Station. The Russian company "Inter RAO UES" owns 100% shares of the monopoly in electricity sales - CJSC "Electric Networks of Armenia." Besides, "Rosneft" - is a monopolist in supplying oil products to Armenia. The Armenian-Russian JSC "Gazprom Armenia" is the exclusive seller of natural gas in Armenia. "Gazprom" himself took part in the construction of the Iran-Armenia pipeline. Rosatom owns Armenian Metsamor Nuclear Power Plant.[422]

In the non-energy sectors, the Russian commercial airline Sibir owned 70% of the Armenian airline Armavia. Russian state-controlled Vneshtorgbank owns 70% of the Armenian - Armenia Sberbank. Russia also bought the Armenian national rail network with an investment in mining operations in Armenia and invaded its telecommunications sector.[423] Many of these enterprises in Russia were not needed because the interests of Russia in the South Caucasus are not economic but geopolitical. Therefore, the acquisition of these companies also had geopolitical implications. Given that Armenia in the South Caucasus is the only state, which is an ally of Russia, Russia thus ensures the loyalty of Armenia in this way. In addition to the write-off of debt in return for assets, Russia began to supply natural gas to Armenia at discounted prices. At that time, the price for Georgia in 2006 was increased to 110 US dollars per thousand cubic meters, while Armenia paid only 56 US dollars.[424] In 2022, this price is only 165 US dollars per thousand cubic meters.

At the same time, considering that Georgia and Azerbaijan have tried to minimize this kind of relationship with Russia, which could lead to a dependence on these countries, the same concern and desire might arise in Armenia. Armenia originally wanted to balance the policy with external actors, but acquiring strategic state assets from Russia strengthened this country's dependence.

After September 11 in the US, along with the fact that the role of the South Caucasus for *NATO* increased in ensuring the logistics of military operations in Afghanistan, Russia's influence grew even more in Armenia. Therefore, although Azerbaijan and Georgia have become actively involved in forming a transport corridor for *NATO* troops and allies, Armenia has remained aloof. At the same time, Armenia has sent its peacekeeping troops to Afghanistan. By the way, Armenia has been very active in this kind of peacekeeping activity. Apart from Afghanistan, Armenia sent its troops to Kosovo, Iraq, Lebanon, and Mali.[425]

As mentioned before, along with the change in the geopolitical importance of the South Caucasus, in connection with the fight against terrorism in Afghanistan, it began to change the attitude of *NATO* and the *EU* in this region. After the last expansion of both organizations, the question arose regarding developing relationships with the *NIS*. None of these structures did want further enlargement but knew that these countries needed to develop relations in the framework of the new proposals. As a result, *NATO* has developed *IPAP*, *EU-ENP*, and then the *EP*.

Armenia enthusiastically adopted the new proposals of these structures that meet its foreign policy - *complementarianism*. Immediately after Georgia and Azerbaijan, on December 16, 2005, it agreed with *NATO IPAP* and continued to develop relations with this structure. At the same time, Armenia is developing relations with the *EU*. Together with the other South Caucasus countries, Armenia in 2004 became a member of the *ENP*. Both programs allow Armenia to gain access to additional financial flows, which in contrast to the Russian loan, have not need to be returned.

In addition, Armenia is looking for ways to balance relations with Russia. Transfer of Russia's strategic enterprises on account of debt, as well as a further deepening of political dependence, led to the fact that the chairman of the Russian parliament, Boris Gryzlov, at a meeting with the chairman of the Armenian parliament Artur Baghdasaryan, called Armenia "Russia's *outpost in the South Caucasus*".[426]

This development could not satisfy Armenia. Therefore, proposed by the *EU* and *NATO* programs were perceived by Armenia as an opportunity to achieve this balance. Besides, Armenia believed that her desire to develop relations with the *West* would not meet misunderstanding and dissatisfaction in Russia as before.

In 2008, the second presidential term of Robert Kocharyan came to an end. In this way, he was not eligible to run for the post again. As a result, the candidate has been identified, which would have continued his line of domestic and foreign policy. This candidate became Serzh Sargsyan, who, at that time, was the Prime Minister of Armenia. Serzh Sargsyan and Robert Kocharyan represented the "*Karabakh clan*" and participated actively in hostilities in the Karabakh war. Thus, this was expected to transfer power to a successor to maintain the current rate.

Interestingly, in these elections, the first president of Armenia, Levon Ter-Petrosyan, was also nominated as a candidate. He became a leading opponent of Sargsyan. Both candidates' meetings gathered tens of thousands of people. Ter-Petrosyan criticized the primary policy line promoted by "*the Karabakh party*."

The elections took place on February 19, 2008. According to voting results, Serzh Sargsyan scored 52.8%, while Levon Ter-Petrosyan, who became the second, had 21.5% of the vote. The other day in Yerevan, Ter-Petrosyan held a rally to protest the results, demanding new elections. Protesters pitched tents in Liberty Square. However, on March 1, the protesters were dispersed by troops. It was applied to a firearm. As a result, ten people died.[427] A state of emergency was declared in the city. Curiously, the US and several European countries have refrained from congratulations Sargsyan on his election victory.[428]

Foreign Policy of Serzh Sargsyan

Since the beginning of the reign of the third Armenian President, Serzh Sargsyan, Armenia's foreign policy has been marked by many events, it should be noted that Armenia's actions were more reflective, responding to events taking place both in the region and in the international arena as a whole. In short, immediately after the election of President Sargsyan, relations with Türkiye intensified. At that time, Türkiye began to develop a new strategy in foreign policy that was different from its traditional course. The main aim of this policy was to improve relations with its geographic neighbors, including Armenia. In connection with this, a new formula for relations with its neighbors has been derived: "*zero problems*." This formula resolved controversies and created conditions for their further development. The main objective of this strategy is to avoid the "freezing" of the existing problems and try to intensify efforts to resolve the problems with a win-win approach.[429] Regarding Armenia, the formula for improving relations with this country has been defined as "*from zero relations to zero problems*." Türkiye unilaterally began to search for ways to resolve disagreements with Armenia and take confidence-building measures.[430] However, the problems that Türkiye wanted to solve extend far beyond the borders of this *Small Power*. The improvement of relations between Türkiye and Armenia needs the opening of borders between the two countries. As mentioned before, this border was closed in April 1993 because of the Kelbajar region occupation by the Armenian forces. After the adoption of the UN Security Council Resolution 822 on April 30, 1993,[431] which demanded the immediate withdrawal of Armenia's occupying forces. Türkiye joined Azerbaijan, imposing an economic embargo on Armenia, and the borders were closed. Thus, the negotiations between Armenia and Türkiye on opening the border have caused bewilderment in Azerbaijan, which has demanded an explanation from Türkiye.[432]

As for Armenia, it was encouraged by the opportunity to improve relations with Türkiye. First, it would put an end to the consolidation between Türkiye and Azerbaijan in the issue of the Nagorno-Karabakh conflict. In addition, this would improve the economic situation in Armenia, begin trade relations with Türkiye, and reduce the cost of cargo transportation. Armenia hoped diplomatic relations with Türkiye and the border opening would be implemented without any preconditions.

In the beginning, bilateral relations turned up the opportunity. National football teams of both countries were in the same group in the European zone of qualification for the 2010 *FIFA* World Cup competition. Thus, began a process that became known as "*football diplomacy*." Armenian President Serzh Sargsyan invited his counterpart President of Türkiye Abdullah Gul, to participate in the game between the teams of these two countries, which was held on September 6, 2008, in Yerevan. He became the first Turkish president to visit this country. A year later, on October 14, 2009, Sargsyan visited Türkiye to see the response teams play in Bursa. Visits also were accompanied by talks, in which Türkiye considered the possibility of opening the border without preconditions as the best option to achieve a rapprochement.[433] Türkiye believed that establishing close political and economic relations would create favorable conditions for discussing the *"1915 events"*, described by Armenians as an act of genocide.

However, the development of relations between the two sides began to be accompanied by a deterioration in relations between Türkiye and Azerbaijan. It was followed by a series of disputes between the two countries, with no consensus. Azerbaijan calls on Türkiye to address the issue of opening the borders with Armenia in the context of resolving the Nagorno-Karabakh conflict. Do not want to spoil relations with its strategic partner, Türkiye agreed with it, believing that it could persuade Armenia to change its position about the conflict. Moreover, Türkiye believes that if she can put the beginning of the resolution of the conflict, it will only strengthen its image as a regional actor. However, Armenia has not been ready to link the development of relations with Türkiye in the context of the liberation of the occupied territories of Azerbaijan. As a result, the signing of the protocols on establishing diplomatic relations and opening of borders, on October 10, 2009, in Zurich, Switzerland, between the Foreign Ministers of Türkiye and Armenia, Ahmet Davutoglu and Edward Nalbandyan, turned into a formality. The parliaments of both countries have not ratified protocols. The border with Türkiye remains closed for Armenia.[434] Thus, once again, the interests of Armenia were considered by the interests of the Karabakhian group, resulting in the impossibility of resolving disputes with Türkiye, and rapprochement has not happened.

At least Armenia's dependence on Russia was growing, and the country was looking for ways and opportunities to balance and form of alternative to this country's relations. An opportunity for this was a little. One of the initiatives, which Armenia paid particular attention to, was the *EP* program. Based on conducted reforms, *NIS* has had the opportunity to sign the *Association Agreement* and create *a Deep and Comprehensive Free Trade Area*. Armenia, for three years, has worked hard on this project with the *EU*, hoping that the creation of *DCFTA* will allow it to enter the markets of the 28 countries members of the *EU*, as well as create a significant balance of growing Russian influence. It was expected that Armenia would put his signature to the agreement with the *EU* at the Vilnius Summit in November 2013. However, two months before the event, on 3 September 2013, the President of Armenia, Serzh Sargsyan, paid a visit to Moscow, the surprise of many, they refused to sign the *Association Agreement* with the *EU* and announced that Armenia intended to join the *EAEU*.[435] Without a doubt, President Sargsyan was forced to make such a statement because of Russian pressure on Armenia and the inability to refuse the requirements of its northern neighbor. Curiously, it was the exact opposite of this position of Armenia about the *EAEU*. Armenian Prime Minister Tigran Sargsyan said in his statement that the accession of Armenia to the Eurasian Customs Union was inappropriate since Armenia has no common border with any of the countries of its members (at that time, Russia, Kazakhstan, Belarus).[436] Thus, Armenia failed to strengthen its foreign policy as part of the complementarism strategy and became more dependent on Russia.

Changing foreign policy direction in just one day during a visit to Moscow pointed to the need for more maneuverability and the ability to independently make decisions for Armenia in the case when it needs. Armenia realized that the policy of *complementarism* depends on the Russian reaction to changes in the international agenda. If Russia had no objections to the *NIS Small Powers* relations with *NATO* and the *EU* in the early stages of their formation, and Armenia took part in them, the follow-up initiatives of these structures were perceived as a threat to Russian interests. As a result, Russia was followed by pressure on *NIS Small Powers* that have tried to develop relations in the framework of the new *NATO* and *EU* initiatives. Thus, although Armenia did not want such a development, it was forced to accept the demands of Russia.

In the process of accession to the *EAEU*, Armenia faced yet another unpleasant incident. During the discussions at the summit *EAEU*, held May 29, 2013, in Astana, the question was raised about the accession of Armenia to this organization. In a word, the president of Kazakhstan, Nursultan Nazarbayev, asked to clarify questions concerning the borders of the Customs Union. He expressed concern about the need for adequate customs control between Armenia and Nagorno Karabakh, noting that Armenia may be admitted to the *EAEU* only within its internationally recognized borders. The reaction of the Armenian authorities was to follow quickly. President Serzh Sargsyan said, *"The fact that Nazarbayev has said it was unpleasant, but it cannot harm."*[437]

This action Armenia was ambiguously perceived in the *EU*, and the country stated that Armenia could not participate simultaneously in two integration processes. As a result, Armenia also had to revise its priorities in relations with the *EU. Association Agreement* has yet to be signed. Despite this, the *EU* is considering new formats for the continuation of relations with Armenia.[438] Continuation relations also wished Armenia,[439] which, however, do so with an eye on Russia.

This development has received an adverse reaction in wide circles of Armenia. Armenia has agreed to join the *EAEU*, but it was seen as increasing dependence on Russia, which would have negative political and economic consequences. In turn, the government tried to convince it not to increase dependence and to strengthen relations with its northern neighbor, strengthening Armenia's position in the region. Russia is an essential ally of Armenia. However, these relationships are interdependent connection since Russia also depends on Armenia.

However, disappointment sweat towards Russia in Armenian society continued to grow. In January 2015, a military serviceman of the 102nd military base (by the way, the term lease of this base was extended for another 49 years (until 2044) during the visit of Russian President Dmitry Medvedev to Armenia in 2010[440]) Valery Permyakov autocratically left the base's location and became the reason for the death of the seven members of the Armenian family Avetisyan. Later Permyakov was detained by the Russian border guards and handed over to the command of the 102nd military base. Despite the demands of the Armenian side, Russia has refused to extradite Permyakov; it was decided that the trial would be held on the territory of the Russian base following the Russian legislation.[441]

The response was the mass protests demanding the withdrawal of military bases from the territory of Armenia. There was also dissatisfaction with the fact that Armenia did not conduct trial of Permyakov. It was stated that Russia violates the terms of a 1997 bilateral treaty according to which Russian military personnel who commit crimes outside the Gyumri military base fall under Armenian jurisdiction.[442] The response was mass protests demanding the withdrawal of military bases from the territory of Armenia. There was also dissatisfaction with the fact that Armenia needed to conduct the trial of Permyakov. It was stated that Russia violates the terms of a 1997 bilateral treaty according to which Russian military personnel who commit crimes outside the Gyumri military base fall under Armenian jurisdiction.[443] At the same time, Inter RAO requires more significant price increases than it has been done. It was the third increase in prices over the past three years.[444] In Armenia, mass protests began; among the demands of protestants were the abolition of increases in electricity prices and the nationalization of the company Electric Networks of Armenia. As a result, the Armenian government canceled the decision to raise prices.[445]

One of the reasons why electricity prices rose was the price of gas that Armenia pays Russia. At that time, it had grown several times and reached 189 US dollars per thousand cubic meters, while the gas price for the population was US 320 US dollars per thousand cubic meters. Thus, any preferences for an ally in the gas price were left, and Russia proceeded from purely commercial interests. After protests in Armenia, Russia agreed to reduce the price of gas to 165 US dollars per thousand cubic meters.[446] At the same time, in compensation, Russia has allocated a loan of 200 million US dollars for the purchase of Russian arms to Armenia.[447]

By the way, the question of selling Russian arms was another topic of disagreement between Armenia and Russia. Russia is the leading supplier of weapons to Azerbaijan. Thus, following the contracts signed in 2009-2014, Azerbaijan purchased weapons of different applications for four billion US dollars.[448] With these supplies, Azerbaijan has modernized and improved its armed forces. This development of the situation is very concerning for Armenia.

This topic is particularly relevant during a period of *"four-day war,"* which took place on the frontline in Nagorno Karabakh on 2-5 April 2016. On the night of April 2, there was a ceasefire violation on the contact line between Armenian and Azerbaijani armed forces. For the first time since the signing of the ceasefire agreement in 1994, the Azerbaijani army launched an offensive in several areas on the front line. As a result, it could pass the fortified line of defense of Armenian troops, freeing part of the territory, and Azerbaijani forces took several strategic heights. On April 5, 2016, under the mediation of Russia in Moscow, during the meeting, the heads of the general staffs of Armenia and Azerbaijan signed an agreement of ceasefire along the line of contact.[449] As a result of the military conflict, both sides suffered losses in manpower and military equipment.

The *"four-day war"* was a revelation for Armenia. First, Armenia lost belief in the impregnability of the fortifications along the front lines, which were built after 1994. In addition, the Azerbaijani army was better equipped and had modern weapons, which allowed it to establish superiority over the enemy, and in the short term, to change the status quo on the front line. The central part of this weaponry was supplied from Russia. In this regard, Armenia filed a protest and demanded to suspend arms supplies to Azerbaijan. Armenia's central thesis was that both countries are allies in the *CSTO*, but Russia continues to supply to Azerbaijan. On the demand of Armenia, Russian officials announced that the supply of weapons will continue because if it does not make Russia, Azerbaijan will still buy it from other sources.[450] For Russia, Azerbaijan is a profitable partner in arms exports, which, along with significant acquisitions, pay their orders on time. Russia's statements regarding selling weapons to Azerbaijan have caused a very adverse reaction in Armenia.

At the same time, Armenia realized that the *CSTO* mechanisms would not be involved in the event of a full-scale war in Karabakh with Azerbaijan. The organization of collective security provides for action by the Allies if the aggression threatens the territory of the *CSTO* member states. As Nagorno Karabakh is the Azerbaijani territory, and clashes occurred there, none of the *CSTO* member states supported Armenia. It is especially true for the Turkic states of Central Asia, which have common ethnic roots with Azerbaijan. In addition, the leaders of the *CSTO* member states: Kazakhstan and Belarus Presidents Nursultan Nazarbayev and Alexander Lukashenko, considered it necessary to contact the President of Azerbaijan, Ilham Aliyev, during the "*four days war.*".[451] Another blow for Armenia was the transfer of the summit of Prime Ministers of *EAEU* countries, on the proposal of Kazakhstan, from Yerevan to Moscow, to be held April 7-8, immediately after the signing of the armistice. The reason for the transfer was the fact that participation in such an event by the prime ministers of the *EAEU* countries could be regarded as support for one of the parties to the conflict.[452]

However, Armenia hoped that, at minimum, Russia would support its ally in the region. Armenia was represented before the fact that due to its interests Russia would not spoil relations with Azerbaijan. Thus, the relations with Azerbaijan have become neutral and seem more important to Russia than with a single ally in the South Caucasus- Armenia. It became clear that as long as Azerbaijan will not cross the "red lines" that define the interests of Russia in the South Caucasus, Russia would not complicate its relations with Azerbaijan for Armenia.

Thus, Armenia found itself in a situation where its activity depends entirely on Russia, the interests of which it adjusts its internal and external policies. At the same time, this "altruism" by Armenia is not paid to her as support from its main ally in the region. At the same time, this situation will eventually go, and a possible scenario does not permit the desired situation for Armenia.

Foreign Policy of Nikol Pashinyan

Serzh Sargsyan's second presidential term came to an end in 2018. However, Armenia changed its constitution in a referendum on December 6, 2015, and it became a parliamentary republic like Georgia. President Sargsyan pushed for the referendum so that he could continue to stay in power as a Prime Minister. He was able to achieve his goal, albeit for a short time: Although his Republican Party won parliamentary elections on April 2, 2017, and gained the majority of votes in parliament (58 seats)[453] allowing him to be elected as Prime Minister of the country on April 9, 2018; his appointment was met with massive protests. The Velvet Revolution took place in Armenia, led by journalist Nikol Pashinyan. Under pressure from mass demonstrations, Serzh Sargsyan was forced to resign, and early parliamentary elections were announced. Nikol Pashinyan's alliance "My Step" won the majority in the parliament (88 seats).[454] Pashinyan was elected the Prime Minister of Armenia, legitimizing the actual situation in the country that had formed then.

Unlike the previous two presidents, who represented the Karabakh clan and ruled Armenia for about 20 years, Pashinyan and his party attempted to pursue a pro-Western foreign policy course. They believed that integration into Euro-Atlantic institutions was possible. Pashinyan's foreign policy began to resemble

Saakashvili's. Although he made his first official visit to Russia as the head of government, his policies coursed tensions with Russia. Pashinyan also demonstrated an anti-Russian stance in 2013 when he voted against Armenian's membership in the Eurasian Economic Union as an opposition MP.

The disagreement between Russia and Armenia was the recall and then the arrest by Armenia at that time of the Secretary General of the *CSTO*, Yuri Khachaturov. Armenia wished to appoint another representative instead of Khachaturov, which led to a crisis within the organization.

In addition, the arrest of former President Kocharyan, a friend of Russian President Putin, has also caused Moscow's displeasure. Despite Putin's petition, Kocharyan was never released from custody. Additionally, several Russian companies operating in Armenia were subjected to checks and prosecutions. Among these companies is the South Caucasus Railway, operated by Russian Railways, which took over these functions for 30 years in 2008. In total, seven lawsuits were brought against the company.[455]

The culminating event in Pashinyan's foreign policy was *the 44-day war* with Azerbaijan. After the start of the counter-offensive along the entire front line from the side of the Azerbaijani troops, it became clear that Armenia could not wage war and resist. While Armenia hoped for military assistance from Russia and the *CSTO*, Russian officials[456] and the *CSTO* stated[457] all military actions occur in Azerbaijani territories, so there is no international law violation. The *CSTO* also stated that Azerbaijani territory is not included within its jurisdiction.

Armenia agreed to sign a ceasefire statement on the night of November 9-10 after suffering heavy losses and the liberation of Shusha by the Azerbaijani army at the moment when Azerbaijan was on the outskirts of Khankendi; this statement is trilateral, as it was signed with the direct mediation of Russia. As a result of the call, Armenia agreed to withdraw its troops from all regions around Karabakh, and Russia brought its peacekeeping forces into the region.

Pashinyan won early elections again with 54% of the vote on June 20, 2021.[458] After a *44-day war*, Armenia was forced to seek closer relations with Russia. Robert Kocharyan was released from arrest, and the court cases against Russian companies were dropped. Armenian leadership was forced to recognize the critical role of Russia in Armenia.

Endnotes:

[1] Tom Crowards, "Defining the Category of `Small` States," Journal of International Development, 14 (2002): 168, Accessed December 7, 2015. Doi:10.1002/jid860.

[2] Annete Baker Fox, The Power of Small States: Diplomacy in World War II (Chicago: The University of Chicago Press, 1959).

[3] David Vital, "The Inequality of the States: A study of Small Power in International Relations," in Small States in International Relations, ed. Jessica Beyer et al (Seattle: University of Washington Press, 2006), 77.

[4] Robert L. Rotshtein, Alliances and Small Powers (New York and London: Columbia University Press, 1968), 29.

[5] Robert O Keohane, "Lilliputian`s Dilemmas: Small States in International Politics," in Small States in International Relations, ed. Jessica Beyer et al, (Seattle: University of Washington Press, 2006), 60.

[6] L.G.M. Jaquet, "The Role of Small States Within Alliance Systems," in Small States in International Relations, ed. A. Schou and A.O. Brundtland, (Stokholm: Almquist and Wiksell, 1971), 58-59.

[7] Maurice A. East, "Size and Foreign Policy Behavior: A Test of Two Models," World Politics 4 (1973), 557.

[8] Jerome Blum, Rondo Cameron and Thomas G. Barnes, A History: The European World, (Boston: Little, Brown and Company, 1966), 211.

[9] Blum, Cameron, and Barnes, History, 212-213.

[10] Henry Kissinger, Diplomacy, (New York: Simon&Schuster Paperbacks, 1994), 59.

[11] Kissinger, Diplomacy, 67.

[12] Paul Kennedy, The Rise and Fall of the Great Powers (New York: Vintage Books, 1987), 73.

[13] Daniel S. Papp, Contemporary International Relations (London: Macmillan Publishing Company, 1988),20

[14] Papp, Contemporary, 20.

[15] Kissinger, Diplomacy, 67.

[16] Rotshtein, Alliances, 188.

[17] Rotshtein, Alliances, 62.

[18] Kennedy, Rise, 102.

[19] Kennedy, Rise, 103.

[20] Paul Dukes, A History of Europe 1648-1948: The Arrival, The Rise and The Fall (London: Macmillian, 1989), 73.

[21] Dukes, History, 73.

[22] Blum, Cameron, and Barnes, History, 374.

[23] Kissinger, Diplomacy, 69.

[24] Dukes, History, 131.

[25] Blum, Cameron, and Barnes, History, 289.

[26] Blum, Cameron, and Barnes, History, 456.

[27] Blum, Cameron, and Barnes, History, 465.

[28] Dukes, History, 180-181.

[29] Papp, Contemporary, 22.

[30] Agatha Ramm, Europe in the Nineteenth Century 1789-1905, (London: Longman, 1984), 49.

[31] Ramm, Europe, 67.

[32] Ramm, Europe, 94-95.

[33] Papp, Contemporary, 22.

[34] Ramm, Europe, 78.

[35] Ramm, Europe, 82.

[36] Treaty of Luneville, Accessed December 25, 2015, http://www.napoleon-series.org/research/government/diplomatic/c_luneville.html.

[37] Ramm, Europe, 103.

[38] Dukes, History, 205.

[39] Kissinger, Diplomacy, 74.

[40] Ramm, Europe, 124-125.

[41] Ramm, Europe, 128.

[42] Dukes, History, 208.

[43] Kissinger, Diplomacy, 77.

[44] "Treaty of Chaumont," Accessed December 19, 2015, http://www.napoleon-series.org/research/government/diplomatic/c_chaumont.html

[45] Erling Bjol, "The Small State in International Politics", in the Small States in International Relations, ed. A. Schou and A.O. Brundtland, (Stockholm: Almquist and Wiksell, 1971), 30.

[46] Rotshtein, Alliances, 12-13.

[47] Rothstein, Alliances, 197-198.

[48] Ernest Llewellyn Woodward, War and Peace in Europe: 1815-1870, (Hamden: Archon Books, 1963), 48.

[49] Rotshtein, Alliances, 202.

[50] Jaquet, Role, 58.

[51] Woodward, 6.

[52] Ramm, Europe, 144-145.

[53] Jaquet, Role, 58.

[54] Woodward, War, 10-11.

[55] Richard N. Rosencrance, Action and Reaction in World Politics: International System Perspective, (Connecticut: Greenwood Press, 1963), 117.

[56] Rotshtein, Alliances, 203.

[57] Dukes, History, 264-267.

[58] Papp, Contemporary, 22.

[59] Woodward, War, 19.

[60] Papp, Contemporary, 24.

[61] Kennedy, Rize, 249-250.

[62] Rotshtein, Alliances, 203-204.

[63] Rotshtein, Alliances, 209.

[64] Rotshtein, Alliances, 217-219.

[65] Robert O. Paxton, Europe in the Twentieth Century, (New York: Harcourt Brace Jovanovich, Inc, 1965), 51-52.

[66] H. Stuart Hughes, Contemporary Europe: A History, (New Jersey: Prentice-Hall, Inc., 1966), 31.

[67] Kissinger, Diplomacy, 191.

[68] Hajo Holborn, The Political Collapse of Europe, (New York: Alfred A. Knopf, 1966), 81-82.

[69] Kissinger, Diplomacy, 215-216.

[70] Blum, Cameron and Barnes, History, 801.

[71] Paxton, Europe, 85.

[72] Blum, Cameron and Barnes, History, 803.

[73] Hughes, Contemporary, 56.

[74] "Швеция во Время Первой Мировой Войны (1914–1922 гг.)", Accessed January 09, 2016, http://svspb.net/istorija-shvecii/mirovaja-vojna.php.

[75] Blum, Cameron and Barnes, History, 806.

[76] Blum, Cameron and Barnes, History, 810.

[77] Hughes, Contemporary, 109.

[78] Kissinger, 239.

[79] Blum, Cameron and Barnes, History, 824.

[80] Hughes, Contemporary, 99.

[81] Daniel S. Papp, Contemporary, 25.

[82] J. Salwyn Schapiro, Modern and Contemporary European History (1815-1928), (New York: Houghton Mifflin Company, 1929), 780.

[83] Wilson's Fourteen Points, 1918, U.S. Department of State, Office of the Historian, Accessed January 09, 2016, https://history.state.gov/milestones/1914-1920/fourteen-points.

[84] Holborn, Political, 98.

[85] Kissinger, Diplomacy, 247.

[86] Kissinger, Diplomacy 222.

[87] Paxton, Europe, 175.

[88] Jeffry A. Frieden, David A Lake, Kenneth A. Schultz, World Politics: Interests, Interactions, Institutions, (New York: W.W. Norton& Company), 21.

[89] Schapiro, Modern, 748.

[90] Rothstein, Alliances, 224.

[91] Paxton, Europe, 175.

[92] Blum, Cameron and Barnes, History, 815.

[93] Kissinger, Diplomacy, 298.

[94] Kissinger, Diplomacy, 286.

[95] Blum, Cameron and Barnes, History, 901.

[96] Holborn, Political, 153.

[97] Blum, Cameron and Barnes, History, 904-906.

[98] Frieden, Lake, Schultz, World, 23.

[99] Fox, Power, 41-42.

[100] Fox, Power, 106-107.

[101] Dukes, History, 449.

[102] Frieden, Lake, Schultz, World, 23.

[103] Dukes, History, 448.

[104] Fox, Power, 77.

[105] Frieden, Lake, Schultz, World, 23.

[106] Blum, Cameron and Barnes, History, 916.

[107] Blum, Cameron and Barnes, History, 922.

[108] Blum, Cameron and Barnes, History, 941.

[109] Blum, Cameron and Barnes, History, 923.

[110] Frieden, Lake, Schultz, World, 24.

[111] Daniel S. Papp, Contemporary, 256.

[112] Blum, Cameron and Barnes, History, 942.

[113] Blum, Cameron and Barnes, History, 941.

[114] The Situation Between Iraq and Kuweyt, Resolution 661 (1990) of the UN Security Council, 6 August, 1990, Accessed January 28, 2016, http://daccess-dds-ny.un.org/doc/RESOLUTION/GEN/NR0/575/10/IMG/NR057510.pdf?OpenElement.

[115] Blum, Cameron and Barnes, History, 939.

[116] Daniel S. Papp, Contemporary, 253.

[117] J.P.D.Dunbabin, The Cold War, The Great Powers and Their Allies, (London: Longman, 1996), 90-92.

[118] Blum, Cameron and Barnes, History, 974.

[119] Blum, Cameron and Barnes, History, 982.

[120] Frieden, Lake, Schultz, World, 24-25.

[121] Blum, Cameron and Barnes, History, 948.

[122] Daniel S. Papp, Contemporary, 257.

[123] Daniel S. Papp, Contemporary, 251.

[124] Blum, Cameron and Barnes, History, 1009.

[125] Daniel S. Papp, Contemporary, 399.

[126] Daniel S. Papp, Contemporary, 397.

[127] "The Warsaw Treaty Organization, 1955", U.S. Department of State, Office of Historian, Accessed February 07, 2016, https://history.state.gov/milestones/1953-1960/warsaw-treaty.

[128] Frieden, Lake, Schultz, World, 27.

[129] Kissinger, Diplomacy, 550.

[130] Daniel S. Papp, Contemporary, 260.

[131] Kissinger, Diplomacy, 564.

[132] Frieden, Lake, Schultz, World, 28.

[133] Frieden, Lake, Schultz, World, 30.

[134] Operations and Missions: Past and Present, June 23, 2016, Accessed February 15, 2015, http://www.nato.int/cps/en/natohq/topics_52060.htm?selectedLocale=en.

[135] The History of the European Union, Accessed February 15, 2016, http://europa.eu/about-eu/eu-history/index_en.htm#goto_6.

[136] Why Isn't Norway in the EU?, March 29, 2013, Accessed February 15, 2016, http://www.euronews.com/2013/03/29/norway-and-the-eu/.

[137] "Large and Small Member States in the European Union: Reinventing the Balance", January 29, 2010, Accessed February 16, 2016, http://www.euractiv.com/section/future-eu/opinion/large-and-small-member-states-in-the-european-union-reinventing-the-balance/.

[138] The North Atlantic Cooperation Council (NACC), October 20, 2011, Accessed February 16, 2016, http://www.nato.int/cps/en/natolive/topics_69344.htm.

[139] NATO Handbook, (Brussels: NATO Office of Information and Press, 2001), 67.

[140] Christopher Preston, Enlargement and Integration in the European Union, (London: Routledge, 1997), 196.

[141] Karen Smith, The Making of EU Foreign Policy: The Case of Eastern Europe, (London: Palgrave Macmillan, January 2004), 136.

[142] Smith, Making, 35.

[143] Smith, Making, 118.

[144] Pal Dunay, "Strategy with Fast-Moving Targets East-Central Europe." in European Union Foreign and Security Policy Towards a Neighbourhood Strategy, ed. Roland Dannreuther, (London: Routledge, 2005), 31.

[145] Marja Obradoviç, "Milliyetçilik ve Avrupacılık, Doğu Avrupa Elitlerin Durumu.", in Soğuk Savaşı Sonrası Avrupa ve Türkiye, ed. Cem Karadeli, (Ankara: Atlas Yayınevi, 2003), 56.

[146] Stuart Croft et al., The Enlargement of Europe, Manchester, Manchester University, 1999, 22-23.

[147] Marise Cremona, "Enlargement and External Policy", The Enlargement of the European Union, ed. Marise Cremona, (Oxford: Oxford Press, 2003), 197.

[148] Smith Karen, The Making of EU Foreign Policy: The Case of Eastern Europe, (Basingstoke: Palgrave, Macmillan, 2004), 77.

[149] 40 Years of EU Enlargements Who Has Joined the EU so FAR?, Accessed February 16, 2016, http://www.europarl.europa.eu/external/html/euenlargement/default_en.htm.

[150] Simon J. Nutall, European Foreign Policy, (Oxford: Oxford University, 2000), 195.

[151] Stephen George, Ian Bache, Politics in the European Union, (Oxford: Oxford University Press, 2001), 87.

[152] Tufk Burzanoviç, "Bosna Örneğinde ABD'nin Balkan Siyaseti Anlamak", In Balkan Diplomasisi, eds. Ömer E., Lütem & Çoşgun Birgül Demirtaş, (Ankara: ASAM Yayınları, 2001), 280-281.

[153] Rogel Carole, The Breakup of Yugoslavia and the War in Bosnia, (London: Greenwood Press, 1998), 60.

[154] Charlotte Bretherton, John Vogler, The European Union as a Global Actor, (London: Routledge, 2006), 164.

[155] Stephen George, Ian Bache, Politics in the European Union, (Oxford: Oxford University Press, 2001), 88.

[156] Nurşin Güney Ateşoğlu, "Bosna-Hersek Sorunu ve Barış Görüşmeleri Süreci", In Yeni Balkanlar, Eski Sorunlar, eds. Kemali Saybaşılı, Özcan Gencer, (İstanbul: Bağlam Yayınları, 1997), 269.

[157] Lester, H. Brune, The United States & the Balkan Crisis, 1990-2005: Conflict in Bosnia & Kosovo, (Claremont: Regina Books, 2005), 32.

[158] Charlotte Bretherton, John Vogler, The European Union as a Global Actor, (London: Routledge, 2006), 196.

[159] Lester H., Brune, 39-40.

[160] Mike Bowker, "European Security", Foundations, in Contemporary Europe, eds. Richard Sakwa, Anne Stevens, (New York: St. Martin Press, 2000), 213.

[161] Necmettin Alkan, "Dayton Sonrasında Bosna-Hersek'te Yapılan Seçimler ve Barış Sürecine Etkileri (1996-2006)", Avrasya Etütleri, No 29-30, (Ankara: TİKA Yayınları, 2006), 98.

[162] EU relations with the Western Balkans, Accessed February 17, 2016, http://eeas.europa.eu/western_balkans/index_en.htm.

[163] Özge Onursal, "Regional Cooperation as Political Conditionality: the Case of the Western Balkans", Turkish Review of Balkan Studies, 10, (Istanbul: Bigart Yayınları, 2005), 169- 172.

[164] Commission Communication from the Commission to the European Parliament and the Council, Commission Opinion on Montenegro's Application for Membership of the European Union, {SEC (2010) 1334}, European Commission, Brussels, 9.11. 2010, COM (2010) 670.

[165] Slovenia Unblocks Croatian EU Bid, September 11, 2009, http://www.news.bbc.co.uk/2/hi/europe/8250441.stm.

[166] Brussels Gives Green light to Albania and Macedonia, October 16, 2013, Accessed February 18, 2016, http://www.presseurop.eu/en/content/news-brief/4240351-brussels-gives-green-light-albania-and-macedonia.

[167] Chronology of Kosovo's Path to Independence, Accessed February 17, 2016, http://www.dw.com/en/chronology-of-kosovos-path-to-independence/a-3132060.

[168] Brune, 87.

[169] NATO's Role in Relation to the Conflict in Kosovo, Accessed February 18, 2016, http://www.nato.int/kosovo/history.htm.

[170] UN Mission in Kosovo, Accessed February 18, 2016, http://www.unmikonline.org/Pages/about.aspx.

[171] Kosovo Declaration of Independence, February 17, 2008, Accessed February 18, 2016, http://www.assembly-kosova.org/?cid=2,128,1635.

[172] Georgi Gotev, Serbia fears EU will Pressure Greece to Recognize Kosovo, August 17, 2015, Accessed February 18, http://www.euractiv.com/section/enlargement/news/serbia-fears-eu-will-pressure-greece-to-recognise-kosovo/.

[173] What is EULEX?, Accessed February 18, 2016, http://www.eulex-kosovo.eu/?page=2,16.

[174] Erhan Eürbedar, Balkan Ülkelerin Avrupa Birliği Yolculuğu, Stratejik Analiz, (Ankara: ASAM Yayınları, February, 2007), 76.

[175] Ian Bancroft, An Unlikely Serbian Alliance, Accessed February 18, 2016, http://www.theguardian.com/commentisfree/2008/jul/10/serbia.eu.

[176] EU relations with Serbia, Accessed February 18, 2016, http://eeas.europa.eu/serbia/index_en.htm.

[177] Erel Tellal, "Rusya Federasyonunun Dış Politikası, "Yakın Çevre" ve "Askeri Doktrin"", In Dış Politikası, Kurtuluş Savaşından Bugüne Olgular, Belgeler, Yorumlar, Volume II: 1980-2001, ed. Baskın Oran, (Istanbul: Iletişim Yayınları, 2003), 329.

[178] Frank Schimmelfennig, The EU, NATO and the Integration of Europe, (Cambridge: Cambridge University, 2003), 38.

[179] TACIS, Accessed February 19, 2016, http://europa.eu/rapid/press-release_MEMO-92-54_en.htm.

[180] Partnership and Cooperation Agreements, Accessed February 19, 2016, http://eur-lex.europa.eu/legal-content/EN/TXT/?uri=URISERV%3Ar17002.

[181] European Neighbourhood Policy, Accessed February 19, 2016, http://eeas.europa.eu/enp/.

[182] Benita Ferrero-Waldner, "The European Neighbourhood Policy: The EU's Newest Foreign Policy Instrument", European Foreign Affairs Review, Volume 11, No 2, (Holland: Kluwer Law International, Summer, 2006), 139-140.

[183] Robert Aliboni, "The Geopolitical Implications of the European Neighborhood Policy", European Foreign Affairs Review, Volume 10, No 1, (Holland: Kluwer Law International, Summer, 2006), 3.

[184] Union for the Mediterranean, Assessed March 4, 2016, http://www.enpi-info.eu/medportal/content/341/.

[185] Sevilay Kahraman, "The European Neighbourhood Policy: A Critical Assessment", Avrupa Çalışmaları, Volume 5, No 3, (Ankara: ATAUM, Spring, 2006), 14.

186 Individual Partnership Action Plans, Accessed March 4, 2016, http://www.nato.int/cps/en/natohq/topics_49290.htm.

187 Claire Bigg, NATO: What Is A Membership Action Plan?, April, 2, 2006, Accessed March 4, 2016, http://www.rferl.org/content/article/1079718.html.

188 Eastern Partnership, Accessed March 4, 2016, http://.eeas.europa.eu/eastern/index_en.htm.

189 Eastern Partnership.

190 Carl Haub, Ukraine's Demographic Reality, Accessed March 8, 2016, http://www.prb.org/Publications/Articles/2014/ukraine-population.aspx.

191 Population Pyramids of the World from 1950 to 2100, Uzbekistan, Accessed March 8, 2016, http://populationpyramid.net/uzbekistan/1990/.

192 Population Pyramids of the World from 1950 to 2100, Kazakhstan, Accessed March 8, 2016, http://populationpyramid.net/kazakhstan/1990/.

193 The Lisbon Protocol at a Glance, updated March, 2014, Accessed March 8, 2016, https://www.armscontrol.org/print/3289.

194 The Collapse of the Soviet Union, US Department of State, Office of the Historian, October 31, 2013, Accessed March 13, 2016, https://history.state.gov/milestones/1989-1992/collapse-soviet-union.

195 Соглашение о Создании Содружества Независимых Государств, December 8, 1991, Accessed March 11, 2016, http://cis.minsk.by/page.php?id=176.

196 Султыгов М. И., К Вопросу Создания Содружества Независимых Государств, Accessed March 11, 2016, http://www.law.edu.ru/doc/document.asp?docID=1126873#_ftn2.

197 Gorbachev Resigns as President of the USSR, Accessed March 11, 2016, http://www.history.com/this-day-in-history/gorbachev-resigns-as-president-of-the-ussr.

198 Operation Desert Storm, Accessed March 11, 2016, http://www.ushistory.org/us/60a.asp.

199 Svante E. Cornell, Azerbaijan Since Independence, (New York: M.E. Sharpe, 2011), 405.

200 The Collapse of the Soviet Union, US Department of State, Office of the Historian, Accessed March 13, 2016, https://history.state.gov/milestones/1989-1992/collapse-soviet-union.

201 Abram Chayes, Lara Olson & Georg Raah, "The Development of U.S. Policy Toward the Former Soviet Union", In Managing Conflict in the Former Soviet Union: Russian and American Perspectives, eds. Alexey Arbatov, Abram Chayes, Antonia Handler Chayes, Lara Olson, (Cambridge:Harvard University, 1997), 512.

202 Michael Slobodchikoff, Russia's Monroe Doctrine Just Worked in Ukraine, November 21, 2013, Accessed March 15, 2016, http://www.russia-direct.org/opinion/russia%E2%80%99s-monroe-doctrine-just-worked-ukraine.

203 Pami Aalto, "Post-Soviet Geopolitics in the North of Europe", In Post-Cold War Identity Politics: Northern and Baltic Experiences, eds. Marco Lehti, David J. Smith, (Portland: Frank Cass Publishers, 2005), 253.

204 Frank Schimmelfennig, The EU, NATO and the Integration of Europe, Rules and Rhetoric, (Cambridge: Cambridge University Press, 2003), 164.

205 Partnership for Peace (Partnership Tools), November 13, 2014, Accessed March 15, 2016, http://www.nato.int/cps/en/natohq/topics_80925.htm.

[206] Partnership and Cooperation Agreements (PCAs): Russia, Eastern Europe, the Southern Caucasus and Central Asia, Accessed March 13, 2016, http://eur-lex.europa.eu/legal-content/EN/TXT/?uri=URISERV:r17002.

[207] Bradley Axmith, Denying History, The United States` Policies Towards Russia in the Caspian Region, 1991-2001, (Hamburg: Anchor Academic Publishing, 2013), 43-44.

[208] GUAM, Accessed March 16, 2016, http://guam-organization.org/en/node.

[209] Заявление Президентов Азербайджанской Республики, Грузии, Республики Молдова, Украины и Республики Узбекистан, Official site of Organisation for Democracy and Economic Development, GUAM, Accessed March 16, 2015, http://guam-organization.org/node/305.

[210] Статус Черноморского флота РФ. Справка, 21 October 2010, Accessed March 16, 2016, http://ria.ru/spravka/20100421/225145286.html.

[211] Shanghai Cooperation Organization, Accessed March 16, 2016, https://aric.adb.org/initiative/shanghai-cooperation-organization.

[212] Что Такое ШОС?, Accessed March 16, 2016, http://infoshos.ru/ru/?id=51.

[213] Винсен де Китспоттер, Большая Игра в Центральной Азии, Accessed March 16, 2016, http://www.perspektivy.info/print.php?ID=36122.

[214] "Революция Роз" в Грузии в Ноябре 2003 года, РиА Новости, November 23, 2013, Accessed March 18, 2016, http://ria.ru/spravka/20131123/978914952.html.

[215] "Оранжевая Революция" на Украине, РиА Новости, November 22, 2014, Accessed March 18, 2016, http://ria.ru/spravka/20141122/1034455095.html.

[216] "Тюльпановая Революция" в Киргизии (2005), March 24, 2016, Accessed March 18, 2016, http://ria.ru/spravka/20150324/1053953942.html.

[217] Stephen Aris, Eurasian Regionalism: The Shanghai Cooperation Organisation, (Basingstoke: Palgrave Macmillan, 2011), 149.

[218] EurAsEC, Accessed March 16, 2016, http://www.eurasian-ec.com/index.php?option=com_content&task=view&id=2&Itemid=7.

[219] Vidya Nadkarni, Strategic Partnerships in Asia: Balancing Without Alliances, (London: Routledge, 2010), 194.

[220] Eurasian Economic Union, Accessed March 16, 2016, http://www.eaeunion.org/?lang=en#about

[221] Oleg Salimov, Tajikistan Paves the Way to Eurasian Union, January 7, 2016, Accessed March 16, 2016, http://www.cacianalyst.org/publications/field-reports/item/13113-tajikistan-paves-the-way-to-eurasian-union.html.

[222] Concept of the Foreign Policy of the Russian Federation, February 18, 2013, Accessed March 16, 2016, http://www.mid.ru/en/foreign_policy/official_documents/-/asset_publisher/CptICkB6BZ29/content/id/122186.

[223] Russia-Belarus Union State Most Advanced Post-Soviet Integration Bloc, October 17, 2014, Accessed March 16, 2016, http://tass.ru/en/russia/754950.

[224] Charles King, "The Five-Day War: Managing Moscow after the Georgia Crisis", Foreign Affairs, November, December 2008, Accessed March 18, 2016, https://www.foreignaffairs.com/articles/russia-fsu/2008-11-01/five-day-war.

[225] Ian Traynor, Luke Harding, Helen Womack, Georgia and Russia Declare Ceasefire, August 16, 2008, Accessed March 18, 2016, https://www.theguardian.com/world/2008/aug/16/georgia.russia2.

[226] To Recognize or Not to Recognize Abkhazia? That is Vanuatu's Question, July 11, 2016, Accessed March 19, 2016, http://www.rferl.org/content/abkhazia-vanuatu-georgia-russia-recognition/24688283.html.

[227] Valeriy Dzutsev, Russia to Strip Abkhazia and South Ossetia of their Limited Sovereignty, March 18, 2015, Accessed March 19, 2016, http://www.cacianalyst.org/publications/analytical-articles/item/13163-russia-to-strip-abkhazia-and-south-ossetia-of-their-limited-sovereignty.html.

[228] 2008 Georgia Russia Conflict Fast Facts, March 21, 2016, Accessed March 25, 2016, http://edition.cnn.com/2014/03/13/world/europe/2008-georgia-russia-conflict/

[229] Госдума Грозит Выйти из Договора о Дружбе с Украиной в Случае Шагов по Вступлению в НАТО, April 1, 2008, Accessed March 25, 2016, http://newsru.com/russia/01apr2008/antinato.html.

[230] Лариса Усова, "Внешняя Политика Украины: Между Внеблоковостью и Атлантической Интеграцией", Власть, Journal, No 7, 2011, 157, Accessed March 25, 2016, http://cyberleninka.ru/article/n/vneshnyaya-politika-ukrainy-mezhdu-vneblokovostyu-i-evroatlanticheskoy-integratsiey#ixzz3oHzoYcf0.

[231] Правительство Украины Одобрило Соглашение об Ассоциации с ЕС, September 18, 2013, Accessed March 23, 2016, http://www.svoboda.org/content/article/25109856.html.

[232] Ukraine crisis: Viktor Yanukovych leaves Kiev for Support Base, February 22, 2014, Accessed March 23, 2016, http://www.telegraph.co.uk/news/worldnews/europe/ukraine/10655335/Ukraine-crisis-Viktor-Yanukovych-leaves-Kiev-for-support-base.html.

[233] Ukraine Crisis: Protesters Declare Donetsk 'Republic', April 7, 2014, Accessed March 23, 2016, http://www.bbc.com/news/world-europe-26919928.

[234] Will Englung, Kremlin Says Crimea is Now Officially Part of Russia After Treaty Signing, Putin Speech, March 18, 2014, Accessed March 24, 2016, https://www.washingtonpost.com/world/russias-putin-prepares-to-annex-crimea/2014/03/18/933183b2-654e-45ce-920e-4d18c0ffec73_story.html.

[235] How far do EU-US Sanctions on Russia Go?, September 15, 2014, Accessed March 24, 2016, http://www.bbc.com/news/world-europe-28400218.

[236] Andrey Devyatkov, Transnistria: Support not Abandonment, May 20, 2016, Accessed June 25, 2016, http://intersectionproject.eu/article/russia-europe/transnistria-support-not-abandonment.

[237] Приднестровье Попросило Путина о Признании, April 16, 2016, Accessed March 25 2016, http://lenta.ru/news/2014/04/16/ask/.

[238] EU Relations with Moldova, Accessed March 25, 2016, http://eeas.europa.eu/moldova/.

[239] Вступление в Таможенный союз на референдуме в Гагаузии поддержали 98,4% избирателей, 3 February, Accessed 26 March 2016, http://tass.ru/mezhdunarodnaya-panorama/934052

[240] Judy Dempsey, Moldova is Next Battleground for Russia and EU, December 4, 2014, Accessed March 25, 2016, http://www.themoscowtimes.com/opinion/article/moldova-is-next-battleground-for-russia-and-eu/512583.html.

²⁴¹ Россия Ограничивает Ввоз Молдавской Продукции Через Белоруссию, April 4, 2016, Accessed 26 April, 2016, http://ria.ru/economy/20160304/1384383595.html.

²⁴² Артем Кречетников, Почему Армения просится в Таможенный союз?, October 24, 2013, Accessed April 5, 2016, http://www.bbc.com/russian/international/2013/10/131024_armenia_custom_union_analysis.

²⁴³ Thomas De Waal, "A Broken Region: The Persistent Failure of Integration Projects in the South Caucasus", Europe-Asia Studies, Vol. 64, No 9 (Routledge, Taylor& Francis Group, November, 2012), 1710-1711.

²⁴⁴ Azerbaijan: Economy, Accessed April 10, 2016, http://www.adb.org/countries/azerbaijan/economy.

²⁴⁵ Azerbaijan: Economy.

²⁴⁶ ВВП Азербайджана в 2015 году Вырос Более Чем на 1% - Президент Алиев, January 10, 2016, Accessed April 10, 2016, http://www.cbc.az/ru/news/economics/vvp-azerbaydjana-v-2015-godu-viros-bolee-chem-na-1-prezident-aliev.page.

²⁴⁷ Azerbaijan GDP - Gross Domestic Product, Accessed June 19, 2022, Accessed April 10 2016, https://countryeconomy.com/gdp/azerbaijan.

²⁴⁸ Расим Бабаев, На долю Азербайджана Приходится 75% Экономики Южного Кавказа – Министр, July 29 2010, Accessed April 10, 2016, http://1news.az/economy/20100729105903671.html.

²⁴⁹Georgia's GDP growth rate reaches 10.4% in 2021, March 21, 2022, Accessed June 19, 2022, https://agenda.ge/en/news/2022/824#:~:text=The%20nominal%20gross%20domestic%20product,of%20Georgia%20(Geostat)%20show.

²⁵⁰ Georgia: Economy, Accessed April 10, 2016, http://www.adb.org/countries/georgia/economy.

²⁵¹ Armenia GDP - Gross Domestic Product, Accessed June 19, 2022, https://countryeconomy.com/gdp/armenia.

²⁵² Azerbaijan: A Country of Unusual Shia-Sunni Harmony, May 23, 2016, Accessed July 12, 2016, http://www.1news.az/hub/20160523014450256.html.

²⁵³ Natalia Antelava, Georgia: Orthodoxy in the Classroom, May 7, 2015, Accessed July 12, 2016, http://www.bbc.com/news/world-europe-32595514.

²⁵⁴ The Armenian Church, Accessed July 12, 2016, http://www.armenianchurch-ed.net/our-church/history-of-the-church/history/.

²⁵⁵ Nakhchivan Autonomous Republic, Accessed July 12, 2016, http://www.nakhchivan.az/portal-en/index-22.htm.

²⁵⁶ Geogia and Armenia Joined to UEFA in 1992, while Azerbaijan in 1994.

²⁵⁷ Kulevi Oil Terminal, Accessed April 14 2016, http://www.kulevioilterminal.com/.

²⁵⁸ Thomas De Waal, The Caucasus, an Introduction, Oxford University Press, 2010, 121.

²⁵⁹ Товарооборот Армении и России за 9 месяцев 2015 года Уменьшился на 14,1%, November 1, 2015, Accessed April 14, 2016, http://www.finmarket.ru/news/4148537.

²⁶⁰ Ashley Corinne Killough, Armenia in Need of an Alternative Export-Import Route, Eurasia Daily Monitor Volume: 5 Issue: 195, October 2008, 2008, Accessed April 14, 2016, http://www.jamestown.org/regions/thecaucasus/single/?tx_ttnews%5Bpointer%5D=5&tx_ttnews%5Btt_news%5D=34015&tx_ttnews%5BbackPid%5D=643&cHash=04c48a2be2e402e8c6f2ec1237348364#.V4TJJPmLTDc.

[261] Giorgi Menabde, Russia and Georgia Expand Their Only Border Crossing Point, Eurasia Daily Monitor Volume 10, Issue 163, September 16, 2013, Accessed April 14, 2016, http://www.jamestown.org/single/?tx_ttnews%5Btt_news%5D=41364&no_cache=1#.V4TLg_m LTDc.

[262] Stephen F. Jones, Minorities in the Georgian Republic, in the Politics of Nationality and the Erosion of the USSR, Zvi Y. Gitelman, (Great Britain: St. Martin Press, 1992), 88-89.

[263] Rebecca Ratliff, South Ossetian Separatism in Georgia, ICE Case Studies, No 180, May, 2006, Accessed April 14, 2016, http://www1.american.edu/ted/ice/ossetia.htm.

[264] George Fridman, The Russo-Georgian War and the Balance of Power, Geopolitical Weekly, August 12, 2008, Accessed April 15, 2016, https://www.stratfor.com/weekly/russo_georgian_war_and_balance_power.

[265] Gareth Evans, Russia and the 'Responsibility to Protect', in Los Angeles Times, August 31, 2008, Accessed April 15, 2008, http://www.latimes.com/la-oe-evans31-2008aug31-story.html.

[266] South Ossetia Profile, April 21, 2016, Accessed July 12, 2016, http://www.bbc.com/news/world-europe-18269210.

[267] B. George Hewitt, Abhazia, "A Problem of Identity and Ownership", in Transcaucasian Boundaries, ed. John F. R. Wright et al., (London: UCL Press, 1996), 216.

[268] Всесоюзная Перепись Населения 1989 года. Распределение Городского и Сельского Населения Областей Республик СССР по Полу и Национальности, Абхазская ССР, Accessed April 17, 2016, http://demoscope.ru/weekly/ssp/resp_nac_89.php?reg=65.

[269] Paul B. Henze, "Russia and the Caucasus", Perceptions: Journal of International Affairs, Volume 1, No 2, (Ankara: Stratejik Araştırmalar Merkezi, June-August, 1996), 62-63.

[270] Соглашения о Прекращении Огня и Разъединении Сил, May 14, 1994, Accessed April 17, 2016, http://www.un.org/ru/peacekeeping/missions/past/unomig/94-583.pdf.

[271] Грузия Объявила Южную Осетию и Абхазию Оккупированными Территориями, August 28, 2008, Accessed April 17, 2016, http://ria.ru/osetia_news/20080828/150770017.html.

[272] Aras Aslanlı, "Tarihten Günümüze Karabağ Sorunu", Avrasya Dosyası, Volume 7, No 1, Ankara, Spring, 2001, 45.

[273] Emin Şihaliyev, Türkiye ve Azerbaycan Açısından Ermeni Sorunu, Ankara, Türk Kültür ve Eğitim Norm Geliştirme Vakfı Yayınları, 2002, 150.

[274] Chronology of Key Events February 1988-June 2003, http://www.nkrusa.org/nk_confict/nkr_position.shtml.

[275] Declaration on State Independence of the Nagorno-Karabakh Republic, Accessed April 10 2016, http://www.nkrusa.org/nk_confict/declaration_independence.shtml.

[276]История Конфликта и Процесс Урегулирования, Accessed April 10 2016, http://www.azerbembassy.org.cn/rus/background.html.

[277] Commission Staff Working Paper, Annex to "European Neighbourhood Policy", Country Report, Azerbaijan, (COM (2005) 72 Final), Brussels, EU Comission, March 02, 2005.

[278] Svante E. Cornell, 85-86.

[279] Fatma Aslı Kelkitli, Russian Foreign Policy in South Caucasus Under Putin, (Ankara: Perception, Winter, 2008), 74.

[280] James Nixey, The Long Goodbye: Waning Russian Influence in the South Caucasus and Central Asia, (London: Chatham House, June 2012), 2.

[281] Richard Pipes, The Formation of the Soviet Union: Communism and Nationalism 1917-1923, (London: Harvard University Press, 1997), 224.

[282] The Constitutional Act on the State Independence of the Republic of Azerbaijan, October 10, 1991, Accessed May 16, 2016, http://azerbaijan.az/portal/History/HistDocs/Documents/en/09.pdf.

[283] People Cluster: Azerbaijani, Accessed May 16, 2016, http://joshuaproject.net/clusters/126; Brenda Shaffer, Borders and Brethren: Iran and the Challenge of Azerbaijani Identity, (Cambridge: MIT Press, 2003), 221–225.

[284] Speech of the President of the Republic of Azerbaijan Heydar Aliyev at the Reception in Honor of the President of the Republic of Azerbaijan in «Chankaya» Palace, February 8, 1994, Ankara, Accessed May 16, 2016, http://lib.aliyevheritage.org/en/2565380.html.

[285] The Names of the Occupied Regions: Kelbajar, Lachin, Kubatly, Jebrail, Zangelan, Aghdam, Fizuli.

[286] Karabakh, Official Site of President of Azerbaijan Republic, Accessed May 16, 2016, http://en.president.az/azerbaijan/karabakh.

[287] Karabakh, Official Site of President of Azerbaijan Republic.

[288] Anakhanum Khidayatova, Russia Wants "No War, No Peace" Situation with Karabakh Conflict, Bryza Says, October 19, 2015, Accessed May 16, 2016, http://en.trend.az/azerbaijan/karabakh/2445451.html.

[289] Svante E. Cornell, Azerbaijan Since Independence, (New York: M.E. Sharpe, 2011), 63.

[290] Emmanuel Karagiannis, Energy and Security in the Caucasus, (London: Routledge Curzon, 2002), 112-113.

[291] Thomas De Waal, The Caucasus: An Introduction, (Oxford: Oxford University Press, 2010), 117-118.

[292] Svante E. Cornell, 63.

[293] Elchibey Gets Vote of No-confidence in Azeri Referendum, August 30, 1993, Accessed May 17, 2016, http://www.upi.com/Archives/1993/08/30/Elchibey-gets-vote-of-no-confidence-in-Azeri-referendum/8499746683200/.

[294] Karabakh, Official Site of the President of the Republic of Azerbaijan, Accessed May 17, 2016, http://en.president.az/azerbaijan/karabakh/.

[295] Rovshan Ibrahimov, Azerbaijan`s Energy History and Policy: From Past till Our Days, In Energy and Azerbaijan: History, Strategy and Cooperation, ed. Rovshan Ibrahimov, (Baku: SAM, 2013), 18.

[296] Rovshan Ibrahimov, Azerbaijan`s Energy, 23.

[297] Михаил Ростовский, Искушение Нефтью. Как Россия Теряет Азербайджан, Кавказ и Каспий, Accessed May 17, 2016, http://www.iicas.org/page.php?id=204.

[298] Contract of Century, Official Site of the President of Azerbaijan Republic, Accessed May 17, 2016, http://en.president.az/azerbaijan/contract.

[299] Rovshan Ibrahimov, Azerbaijan`s Energy, 23.

[300] Emmanuel Karamanlis, Energy and Security in the Caucasus, (London: Routledge Curson, 2002), 116.

[301] Svante E. Cornell, 85-86.

[302] Заур Расулзаде, Аяз Муталлибов: Мне Было Сложнее, чем Ильхаму Алиеву Сейчас, November 18, 2013, Accessed May 18, 2016, http://www.haqqin.az/news/11483.

[303] Rovshan Ibrahimov, U.S.-Azerbaijan Relations: A View from Baku, Rething Paper 17, (Washington DC: Rething Institution, , October 2014), 4-5.

[304] Svante. E. Cornell, 406.

[305] Rovshan Ibrahimov, U.S.-Azerbaijan Relations, 10.

[306] Общая Историческая Справка о 907-й Поправке к «Акту в Поддержку Свободы» Конгресса США и о деятельности Президента Азербайджанской Республики Гейдара Алиева в Связи с ее Ликвидацией, URL, Accessed May 18, 2016, http://lib.aliyevheritage.org/ru/3711428.html.

[307] Rovshan Ibrahimov, Azerbaijan`s Energy, 32.

[308] Rovshan Ibrahimov, U.S. – Azerbaijan Relations, 8.

[309] Rovshan Ibrahimov, Azerbaijan Energy Strategy and the Importance of the Diversification of Exported Transport Routes, No 29, (Baku: Journal of Qafqaz University, 2010), 26.

[310] Rovshan Ibrahimov, U.S. – Azerbaijan Relations, 9.

[311] Ровшан Ибрагимов, Реквием по «Набукко»: Исполнение в Трех Актах, February 10, 2012, Accessed May 19, 2016, http://www.1news.az/authors/ribrahimov/20120210042404884.html.

[312] Ровшан Ибрагимов, Евросоюз, Экзамен на Зрелость: Быть или не Быть ЕС Региональным Актором, November 11, 2011, Accessed May 19, 2016, http://www.1news.az/authors/ribrahimov/20120210042404884.html.

[313] Bucharest Summit Declaration Issued by the Heads of State and Government Participating in the Meeting of the North Atlantic Council in Bucharest on 3 April 2008, April 3, 2008, Accessed May 19, 2016, http://www.nato.int/cps/en/natolive/official_texts_8443.htm.

[314] Rovshan Ibrahimov, EU External Policy Towards the South Caucasus: How Far is it From Realization?, (Baku: SAM, 2014), 30.

[315] Rovshan Ibrahimov, EU External Policy, 87.

[316] Partnership and Cooperation Agreements (PCAs): Russia, Eastern Europe, the Southern Caucasus and Central Asia, Accessed May 19, 2016, http://europa.eu/legislation_summaries/external_relations/relations_with_third_countries/eastern_europe_and_central_asia/r17002_en.htm.

[317] Rovshan Ibrahimov, After the 2013 Azerbaijani Presidential Elections: Challenges and Expectations, Caucasus International, Vol. 3, No 4, Winter 2013-2014, 108.

[318] For More Information See: Partnership and Cooperation Agreements (PCAs): Russia, Eastern Europe, the Southern Caucasus and Central Asia, Accessed May 20, 2016, http://eur-lex.europa.eu/legal-content/EN/TXT/?uri=URISERV:r17002

[319] Conditions for Membership, Accessed May 20, 2016, http://ec.europa.eu/enlargement/policy/conditions-membership/index_en.htm.

[320] EU Relations with Eastern Partnership, Accessed May 20, 2016, http://eeas.europa.eu/eastern/index_en.htm.

[321] Ilham Aliyev: 'We Will Become a Member of WTO but Only we Know When it will Happen', February 7, 2014, Accessed May 20, 2016, http://news.az/articles/official/86381.

[322] Azerbaijani President: "Southern Gas Corridor is a project of energy security", February 14, 2015, Accessed May 20, 2016, http://en.apa.az/xeber_azerbaijani_president___southern_gas_cor_223095.html.

[323] Виктория Дементьева, Азербайджан Стал Членом Движения Неприсоединения, May 25, 2011, Accessed May 20, 2016, http://ru.apa.az/news/193912.

[324] Ровшан Ибрагимов, Движение Неприсоединения Как Инструмент Реализации Национальных Интересов Азербайджана, May 11, 2012, Accessed May 20, 2016, http://www.1news.az/authors/ribrahimov/20120511104117876.html

[325] Эльмар Мамедьяров: "Председательство Азербайджана в СБ ООН Запомнилось Рядом Важных Резолюций и Обращений", January 10, 2014, Accessed May 21, 2016, http://news.day.az/politics/457625.html.

[326] Ильхам Шабан: "Южный Газовый Коридор Будет Служить Процветанию не Одной-Двух Стран, а Целого Региона", February 13, 2015, Accessed May 21, 2016, http://caspianbarrel.org/?p=27182.

[327] На Линии Баку-Тбилиси-Карс Запущен Первый Тестовый Поезд, January 4, 2015, Accessed May 21, 2016, http://www.vestikavkaza.ru/news/Na-linii-Baku-Tbilisi-Kars-zapushchen-pervyy-testovyy-poezd.html.

[328] Francis X. Clines, Secession Decreed by Soviet Georgia, The New York Times, April 10, 2016, Accessed June 15, 2016, http://www.nytimes.com/1991/04/10/world/secession-decreed-by-soviet-georgia.html.

[329] Zaur Shiriyev, Korneli Kakachia, Azerbaijan-Georgian Relations, The Foundation and Challenges of the Strategic Alliance, SAM Review, Special Double Issue, Volume 7-8, July, 2013, 18.

[330] Kornely Kakachia, Salome Minesashvili, Identity politics, Exploring Georgian Foreign Policy Behavior, Journal of Eurasian Studies, Volume 6, Issue 2, July, 2015, doi:10.1016/j.euras.2015.04.002, 174, Accessed April 10, 2016, 2016http://www.sciencedirect.com/science/article/pii/S1879366515000111.

[331] Recognition of Georgia, Office of History, Accessed April 10, 2016, https://history.state.gov/countries/georgia.

[332] Stephen Jones, Georgia: Nationalism from under the Rubble, After Independence: Making and Protecting the Nation in Postcolonial and Postcommunist States, Ed. Lowell W. Barrington, (Michigan: The University of Michigan Press, 2009), 264.

[333] Kornely Kakachia, Salome Minesashvili, Identity politics, Exploring Georgian Foreign Policy Behavior, Journal of Eurasian Studies, Volume 6, Issue 2, July 2015, doi:10.1016/j.euras.2015.04.002, 175, Accessed April 10, 2016, http://www.sciencedirect.com/science/article/pii/S1879366515000111.

[334] Грузия Покинула СНГ, August 18, 2016, Accessed September 10, 2016, http:^||rg/ru|sujet|3895|

[335] Rovshan Ibrahimov, EU External Policy Towards the South Caucasus: How Far is it From Realizations?, SAM, Baku, 2013, 84.

[336] Kornely Kakachia, Salome Minesashvili, Identity politics, Exploring Georgian Foreign Policy Behavior, Journal of Eurasian Studies, Volume 6, Issue 2, July 2015, doi:10.1016/j.euras.2015.04.002, 175, Accessed April 10, 2016, http://www.sciencedirect.com/science/article/pii/S1879366515000111.

[337] Charles King, The Ghost of Freedom, A History of Caucasus, Oxford Univercity Press, 2010, 230.

[338] Rovshan Ibrahimov, 79.

[339] EU Cooperation with Georgia, Accessed April 10, 2016,

http://www.delgeo.ec.Europa.eu/en/eu_and_georgia/cooperation.html.

[340] Annotated Summary of Agreements Linking with Non-member Countries, European Commission, Brussels, June, 2000.

[341] Zaur Shiriyev, Korneli Kakachia, Azerbaijan-Georgian Relations, The Foundation and Challenges of the Strategic Alliance, SAM Review, Special Double Issue, Volume7-8, July 2013, 18.

[342] Stephen Jones, Georgia: A Political History since Independence, (London: I.B. Taurus, 2015), 154.

[343] Rovshan Ibrahimov, "Link in the Chain: South Caucasus as a transport and logistics hub between Regions", Interregional Cooperation in Eurasia: Transport and Logistics Projects as an Accelerator of Integration Within and Between the Black Sea Region, the South Caucasus and the Central Asia", SAM, Baku, 2013, 64.

[344] Rovshan Ibrahimov, 96.

[345] GUAM, Ministry of Foreign Affairs and European Integration of the Republic of Moldova, Accessed June 17, 2016, http://www.mfa.gov.md/about-guam-en/.

[346] Kornely Kakachia, Salome Minesashvili.

[347] Georgia's Knock at NATO's Door: Quieter but More Persistent, 7 January 2000, The Jamestown Foundation, Fortnight in Review Volume 6 Issue: 1, Accessed April 10, 2016, http://www.jamestown.org/single/?tx_ttnews%5Btt_news%5D=24354&tx_ttnews%5BbackPid%5D=207&no_cache=1#.V2OL27uLTDc.

[348] Kornely Kakachia, The End of Russian Military Bases in Georgia, In Military Bases: Historical Perspectives, Contemporary Challenges, eds. Luis Rodrigues, Sergiy Glebov, (Amsterdam: IOC Press, 2009), 198.

[349] Alexander Rondelli, The Choice of Independent Georgia, The Security of Caspian Sea Region, ed. Gennady Chufrin, (Oxford: Oxford University Press, 2001), 199.

[350] Andrey Illarionov, The Russian Leadership`s Preparation for War, 1999-2008, In The Guns of August 2008: Russia`s War in Georgia, eds. Svante E. Cornell, S. Frederick Starr, (London: Routledge, 2009), 51.

[351] Georgia Joins the WTO, WTO News: 2000 Press Releases, 14 June 2000, Accessed April 10, 2016, https://www.wto.org/english/news_e/pres00_e/pr182_e.htm.

[352] Shireen Hunter, Jefrey L. Thomas, Alexander Melikishvili, Islam in Russia: The Politics of Identity and Security, (New York: M.E. Sharpe, 2004), 353.

[353] Irakly G. Areshidze, Helping Georgia?, Perspective, Volume XII, Number 4, March-April 2002, Accessed June 18, 2016, http://www.bu.edu/iscip/vol12/areshidze.html.

[354] Georgia "Train and Equip" Program Begins, News Release of the U.S. Department of Defense, April 29, 2002, Accessed June 18, 2016, http://www.bits.de/NRANEU/Russia-Caucasus/georgia%20train%20and%20equip%20program.htm.

[355] Georgia Sustainment and Stability Operations Program (GSSOP), Accessed June 18, 2016, http://www.globalsecurity.org/military/ops/gssop.htm.

[356] Stephen Jones, 154.

[357] Ahto Lobjakas, NATO Lacks the Stomach for South Caucasus Fight, NATO and The South Caucasus, Caucasus Analitical Digest, No 15, April, 16 2009, 2, Accessed June 18, 2006, http://www.laender-analysen.de/cad/pdf/CaucasusAnalyticalDigest05.pdf.

[358] Official Site of the Office of the State Minister of Georgia on European& Euro-Atlantic Integration, http://www.eu-nato.gov.ge/en/node.

[359] EU Flags to Fly over Georgian Governmental Offices, April 19, 2016, Accessed June 19, 2016, http://www.civil.ge/eng/article.php?id=6716.

[360] Molli Corso, Bush Visit to Georgia is a Great Political Victory- Saakashvili, May 10, 2005, Accessed June 19, 2016, http://www.eurasianet.org/departments/insight/articles/eav051105.shtml.

[361] NATO Grants 'Intensified Dialogue' to Georgia, September 212006, Accessed June 19, 2016, http://civil.ge/eng/article.php?id=13613.

[362] Корнелий Какачия, Конец Российских Военных Баз в Грузии: Социальные, Политические и Стратегические Последствия их Вывода, Центральная Азия и Кавказ, No 2, 2008, 68.

[363] Steve Gutterman, Russia Set to Resume Imports of Georgian Wine and Water, February 4, 2013, Accessed June 18, 2016, http://www.reuters.com/article/us-russia-georgia-idUSBRE91402R20130205.

[364] Грузия, Нефть, Газ, Уголь, Accessed June 18, 2016, http://polpred.com/?ns=1&ns_id=48589.

[365] Oleg Kusov, Газпром Сделал Скидку Армении, January 2, 2006, Accessed June 18, 2016, http://www.svoboda.mobi/a/129161.html.

[366] Vladimir Novikov, Энергокризис в Грузии Заканчивается Вместе с Продажами "Газпрома", January 30, 2006, Accessed June 18, 2016, http://www.kommersant.ru/doc/644882.

[367] Газпром: Цена на Газ для Грузии в 2008г. Может Остаться Примерно на Уровне 2007г. - 235 долл. за 1 тыс. куб. м., August 4, 2007, Accessed June 18, 2016, http://www.trend.az/business/economy/967778.html.

[368] Condoleezza Rice, Remarks with the President of Georgia Mikheil Saakashvili on the Signing of the Millennium Challenge Compact, September 12, 2005, Accessed June 19, 2016, http://2001-2009.state.gov/secretary/rm/2005/53034.htm.

[369] Тбилиси: США в 2005 году Запретили Саакашвили Продавать Грузинский Газопровод Газпрому, October, 20, 2015, Accessed June 19, 2016,

http://vz.ru/news/2015/10/20/773332.html.

[370] Газпром: Цена на Газ для Грузии в 2008г. Может Остаться Примерно на Уровне 2007г. - 235 долл. за 1 тыс. куб. м., August 4, 2007, Accessed June 19, 2016, http://www.trend.az/business/economy/967778.html.

[371] Россия и Грузино-Абхазский Конфликт, Accessed June 19, 2016, http://www.abkhaziya.org/books/prav_konflict/russia.html.

[372] Bucharest Summit Declaration Issued by the Heads of State and Government Participating in the Meeting of the North Atlantic Council in Bucharest on 3 April 2008, Press Release (2008) 049, April 8, 2008, Accessed June 19, 2016, http://www.nato.int/cps/ru/natohq/official_texts_8443.htm?selectedLocale=en.

[373] Nicolai N. Petro, The Russia-Georgia War: Causes and Consequences, Global Dialoque, Volume 11, Winter/Spring 2009, Accessed June 19, 2016, http://www.worlddialogue.org/content.php?id=439.

[374] Nicolai N. Petro.

[375] Новая Концепция Национальной Безопасности Грузии, Civil Georgia, December 23, 2011, Accessed June 20, 2016, http://www.civil.ge/rus/article.php?id=22911.

[376] Жене Миллиардера Иванишвили Вернули Гражданство Грузии, December 27, 2011, Accessed June 20, 2016, https://lenta.ru/news/2011/12/27/lost/.

[377] Ivanishvili Expects GDDG to Win About 95 Seats in Parliament, June 8, 2016, Accessed June 20, 2016, http://www.civil.ge/eng/article.php?id=29207.

[378] Georgia's Constitutional Changes, Accessed June 20, 2016, http://www.crisisgroup.org/en/multimedia/podcasts/2012/georgia-turashvili-georgias-constitutional-changes.aspx.

[379] Giorgi Margvelashvili, Biography, Accessed June 21, 2016, https://www.president.gov.ge/en/President/Biography.

[380] European Commission Proposes to Lift Visa Obligations for Citizens of Georgia, European Commission - Press release, Brussels, March 9, 2016, Accessed June 21, 2016, http://europa.eu/rapid/press-release_IP-16-702_en.htm.

[381] РИА Новости, Литва и еще Четыре Страны ЕС требуют Предоставить Грузии Безвизовый Режим, June 11, 2016, Accessed June 21, 2016, http://ria.ru/world/20160611/1445842555.html#ixzz4BobdTqrA.

[382] Президент Грузии Выразил Уверенность во Вступлении Страны в ЕС, March 8, 2016, Accessed June 22, 2016, http://www.rbc.ru/politics/08/05/2016/572fa06d9a79478a567515be

[383] Luke Coffey, NATO Summit 2016: Keeping Georgia on the Membership Track, Accessed June 22, 2016, http://www.heritage.org/research/reports/2016/06/nato-summit-2016-keeping-georgia-on-the-membership-track#.V2GEhlct8Rk.twitter.

[384] Judy Dempsey, NATO and the E.U. Desert Georgia, June 16, 2016, Accessed June 22, 2016, https://www.washingtonpost.com/opinions/nato-and-the-eu-desert-georgia/2016/06/16/20f2c7dc-33be-11e6-8758-d58e76e11b12_story.html.

[385] Luke Coffey.

[386] Judy Dempsey.

[387] NATO Opens Training Center in Georgia Amid Russia Tensions, August 31, 2015, Accessed June 23, 2016, http://www.defensenews.com/story/defense/2015/08/27/nato-opens-training-center-georgia-amid-russia-tensions/32476321/.

[388] Maciej Falkowscki, Georgian Drift, the Crisis of Georgian`s Way Westwards, No 57, (Warsaw: Centre for Eastern Studies, February, 2016), 19.

[389] Гулбаат Рцхиладзе, Новая Внешняя Политика Грузии, October 12, 2012, Accessed June 23, 2016, http://politforumi.com/rus/1328/saqartvelos-axali-sagareo-politika.html.

[390] Ivanishvili Suggests Georgia Must 'Patiently Wait' For Russian Approval On NATO, June 03, 2016, Accessed June 23, 2016, http://www.rferl.org/content/georgia-ivanishvili-nato-russia-approval/27778208.html.

[391] Judy Dempsey.

[392] Maciej Falkowscki, 33.

[393] Sedat Laçiner, Ermenistan Dış Politikası ve Belirleyici Temel Faktörler 1991-2002, Ermeni Araştırmaları, No 5, (Ankara: Eraren, Spring, 2002), Accessed June 26, 2016, http://www.eraren.org/index.php?Page=DergiIcerik&IcerikNo=303.

[394] Armenian Declaration of Independence, Accessed June 26, 2016, http://www.gov.am/en/independence/.

[395] Сергей Минасян, Внешняя Политика Постсоветской Армении:20 Лет Одновременно на Нескольких Стульях, Мировая Политика и Международные Отношения, 2013, No 1, 85.

[396] Сергей Минасян, 86.

[397] Минасян: Основа Внешней Политики Армении – Комплементаризм, July 8, 2008, Accessed June 26, 2016, http://www.kavkaz-uzel.ru/articles/138885/.

[398] The Russian Base in Gyumri. Facts and Figures, February 4, 2015, Accessed June 26, 2016, http://www.horizonweekly.ca/news/details/60972.

[399] Charles King, The Ghost of Freedom, A History of Caucasus, (Oxford: Oxford University Press, 2010), 244.

[400] Сергей Минасян, Внешняя Политика, 89.

[401] Kamer Kasım, Armenia's Foreign Policy: Basic Parameters of Ter-Petrosyan and Kocharyan Era, (Ankara: Turkish Weekly, October 13, 2013), Accessed June 26, 2016, http://www.turkishweekly.net/2004/10/13/article/armenia-039-s-foreign-policy-basic-parameters-of-ter-petrosyan-and-kocharyan-era/.

[402] Sedat Laçiner.

[403] Alla Mirzoyan, Armenia, The Regional Powers, and the West Between History and Geopolitics, (New York:Palgrave Macmillan, 2010), 38.

[404] Alla Mirzoyan, 39.

[405] ANCA Welcomes Appointment of Robert Kocharyan as Prime Minister, 21 March, 1997, Accessed June 26, 2016, http://asbarez.com/33269/anca-welcomes-appointment-of-robert-kocharyan-as-prime-minister/.

[406] Томас Де Ваал, Черный сад, Accessed June 26, 2016, http://news.bbc.co.uk/hi/russian/in_depth/newsid_4685000/4685141.stm.

[407] Левон Тер-Петросян: «Война, или мир? Пора Стать Серьезнее», Armenian Research Center, May 27, 2015, Accessed June 26, 2016, http://www.aniarc.am/2015/05/27/war-or-peace-ter-petrosyan-1997/.

[408] Инициативы Минской Группы ОБСЕ по Урегулированию Армяно - Азербайджанского Нагорно - Карабахского конфликта, Accessed June 26, 2016, http://articlekz.com/article/7338.

[409] Alla Mirzoyan, 40.

[410] Armenia, Presidential Election, 16 and 30 March 1998: Final Report, April 9, 1998, Accessed June 26, 2016, http://www.osce.org/odihr/elections/armenia/14192.

[411] Alexander Markarov, Semi-Presidentalism in Armenia, Semi-Presidentalism in the Caucasus and Central Asia, eds., Robert Elgie, Sophia Moestrup, (London: Palgrave Macmillan, 2016), 84.

[412] Kamer Kasım, Armenia's Foreign Policy: Basic Parameters of Ter-Petrosyan and Kocharyan Era, Turkish Weekly, October 13, 2013, Accessed June 27, 2016, http://www.turkishweekly.net/2004/10/13/article/armenia-039-s-foreign-policy-basic-parameters-of-ter-petrosyan-and-kocharyan-era/.

[413] Kamer Kasım, Armenia's Foreign.

[414] Rovshan Ibrahimov, EU External Policy, 141.

[415] Sevil Erkuş, Turkey Could Reopen Railway in Parallel with Karabakh Progress, November 8, 2013, Accessed June 27, 2016, http://www.hurriyetdailynews.com/turkey-could-reopen-railway-in-parallel-with-karabakh-progress-.aspx?pageID=238&nID=57565.

[416] Russia, Iran and Azerbaijan Start Working on North-South Transport Corridor, Russia & India Report, April 7, Accessed June 27, 2016, https://in.rbth.com/news/2016/04/07/russia-iran-and-azerbaijan-start-working-on-north-south-transport-corridor_582773.

[417] Сергей Минасян, Внешняя Политика, 86.

[418] Игорь Мурадян, Отношение США к Политическому Руководству Армении, July 9, 2015, Accessed June 27, 2016, http://www.lragir.am/index/rus/0/comments/51810/43179.

[419] Armenian-American Bilateral Relations, Accessed June 27, 2016, http://www.mfa.am/en/country-by-country/us/.

[420] Joint Declaration of the European Union and the Republics of Armenia, Azerbaijan and Georgia, Luxembourg, C/99/202 22, June 1999, 9405/99 (Presse 202).

[421] Армянские Предприятия, Переданные России по Схеме «Имущество в Счет Долга», Будут Слиты в Единый Научно-Производственный Комплекс, February 6, 2008, Accessed June 27, 2016, https://regnum.ru/news/economy/952992.html.

[422] А теперь – АЭС…, Accessed June 27, 2016, http://www.etpress.ru/?content=article&id=5660

[423] Джеймс Никси, Долгое Прощание: Уменьшение Русского Влияния на Южном Кавказе и в Центральной Азии, Accessed June 27, 2016, http://www.geopolitica.ru/article/dolgoe-proshchanie-umenshenie-russkogo-vliyaniya-na-yuzhnom-kavkaze-i-v-centralnoy-azii#.V3ATdvmLTDc.

[424] Oleg Kusov, Газпром сделал скидку Армении, January 2, 2006, Accessed June 27, 2016, http://www.svoboda.mobi/a/129161.html.

[425] Армения Продолжит Содействие в Установлении Мира в Афганистане, December 2, 2015, Accessed June 27, 2016, http://newsarmenia.am/news/politics/armeniya-prodolzhit-sodeystvie-v-ustanovlenii-mira-v-afganistane-nalbandyan/.

[426] Борис Грызлов: Армения является форпостом России на Южном Кавказе, December 15, 2015, Accessed June 27, 2016, https://regnum.ru/news/polit/376296.html.

[427] Armenia: Skewed Prosecution Over 2008 Clashes, Ensure Impartial Investigation and Justice in Use of Force Against Protesters, February 25, 2009, Accessed June 28, 2016, https://www.hrw.org/news/2009/02/25/armenia-skewed-prosecution-over-2008-clashes.

[428] Serzh Sargsyan Thinks George Bush Did Not Congrtulate Him Because of Country's Post Election Conditions, March 14, 2008, Accessed June 28, 2016,http://www.armeniandiaspora.com/showthread.php?125950-Serzh-Sargsyan-Thinks-George-Bush-Did-Not-Congratulate-Him-Because-O.

[429] For More Information See: Policy of Zero Problems with our Neighbors, Official site of the Ministry of Foreign Affairs Republic of Turkey, Accessed June 28, 2016, http://www.mfa.gov.tr/policy-of-zero-problems-with-our-neighbors.en.mfa.

[430] Relations between Turkey and Armenia, Official site of the Ministry of Foreign Affairs Republic of Turkey, Accessed June 28, 2016, Accessed June 28, 2016, http://www.mfa.gov.tr/relations-between-turkey-and-armenia.en.mfa

[431] Resolution 822 (1993) Adopted by the Security Council at its 3205th meeting, April 30, 1993, Accessed June 28, 2016, http://www.refworld.org/cgi-bin/texis/vtx/rwmain?docid=3b00f15764.

[432] Rovshan Ibrahimov, Turkish Foreign Policy Towards Armenia in 2008-2009: Impact on Azerbaijani-Turkish Relations, Bilge Strateji, Vol 7, No 12, (Istanbul: Bilgesam, Spring, 2015), 52.

[433] Ahmet Davudoğlu, Turkish-Armenian Relations in the Process of De-Ottomanisation or Dehistorisation: is a "Just Memory" Possible?, Journal of Policy Quartely, Vol 13, No 1, (Istanbul: Spring, 2014), 28.

[434] Rovshan Ibrahimov, Turkish Foreign, 51.

[435] Serzh Sargsyan Announced about Armenia`s Decision to Join Custom Union, September 3, 2013, Accessed June 28, 2016, https://armenpress.am/eng/news/731583/.

[436] «Таможенный Союз не Имеет для нас Смысла», Премьер Армении о Взаимоотношениях с РФ, Accessed June 28, 2016, http://www.kommersant.ru/doc-y/1908052.

[437] Асем Токаева, Две Цитаты Назарбаева Вызвали Долгие Споры в Армении, November 5, 2014, Accessed June 28, 2016, http://rus.azattyq.org/a/armenia-eaes-karabakh-nursultan-nazarbayev/26673820.html.

[438] Final Statement and Recommendations Adopted at the 16th Meeting of EU-Armenia Parliamentary Cooperation Committee (21/01/2016), Accessed June 28, 2016, http://eeas.europa.eu/delegations/armenia/press_corner/all_news/news/2016/2016_01_21_en.htm.

[439] Statement by Edward Nalbandian, Minister of Foreign Affairs of Armenia at the Eastern Partnership Informal Dialogue Meeting of the Foreign Ministers, July 11, 2016, Accessed July 20, 2016, http://www.mfa.am/en/speeches/item/2016/07/11/min_eap_kyiv/.

[440] Армения Выслушала Российскую Оценку Карабахского Вопроса, August 20, 2010, Accessed June 28, 2016, http://www.vesti.ru/doc.html?id=387102.

[441] Marianna Grigoryan, Armenia's Russian Murder Scandal: Can Justice Be Served?, February 3, 2016, Accessed June 28, 2016, http://www.eurasianet.org/node/77146.

[442] Serouj Aprahamian, Mass Protests in Armenia as Killings Test Loyalty to Moscow, June 20, 2015, Accessed June 28, 2016, http://armenianweekly.com/2015/06/20/electricity-protest/.

[443] Serouj Aprahamian, Demonstrators Vow to Remain in Liberty Square Until June 22.

[444] Thousands Protest in Yerevan Against Electricity Prices, July 3, 2015, Accessed June 28, 2016, http://www.rferl.org/content/armenia-protest-electricity-prices/27086605.html.

[445] В Армении Отложили Рост Тарифов на Электричество, Протестующие Празднуют Победу, June 27, 2015, Accessed June 29, 2016, http://www.newsru.com/world/27jun2015/erevan.html.

[446] Russia Reduces Gas Price for Armenia, March 29, 2016, Accessed June 29, 2016, http://news.az/articles/armenia/106039.

[447] Hasmik Mkrtchyan, Russia Grants $200 million Loan to Armenia to Help Modernise Army, July 2, 2016, Accessed July 20, 2016, http://uk.reuters.com/article/uk-armenia-russia-loan-idUKKCN0PC1PY20150702.

[448] Медведев: Поставки Оружия Еревану и Баку Неизбежны, April 9, 2016, Accessed June 29, 2016, http://www.bbc.com/russian/news/2016/04/160409_medvedev_karabakh_arms.

[449] Laurence Broers, The Nagorno Karabakh Conflict: Defaulting War, (London: Chatham House, 2016), 12.

[450] Медведев: Поставки Оружия Еревану и Баку Неизбежны, April 9, 2016, Accessed August 22, 2021, http://www.bbc.com/russian/news/2016/04/160409_medvedev_karabakh_arms.

[451] Алиев Рассказал Лукашенко о Деталях Обострившегося Конфликта в Карабахе, April 2, 2016, Accessed 29 July, 2016, http://news.tut.by/politics/490948.html; Назарбаев Позвонил Алиеву и Саргсяну, April 6, 2016, Accessed 29 July, 2016, http://haqqin.az/news/67489.

[452] Саммит ЕАЭС Перенесли из Еревана в Москву, но Медведев в Армению все же Приедет, April 5, 2016, Accessed 29 July, 2016, http://www.panarmenian.net/rus/news/209672/.

[453] Татевик Лазарян, Национальное Собрание 6-го Созыва Завтра Начнет Свою Работу, May 17, 2017, Accessed 29 August, 2021, https://rus.azatutyun.am/a/28493702.html.

[454] Блок Пашиняна по Итогам Выборов в Армении Получил 88 мест в 132-местном парламенте, December 18, 2018, Accessed 29 August, 2021, https://tass.ru/mezhdunarodnaya-panorama/5918851.

[455] МИД РФ Надеется на Урегулирование Судебных Процессов В Отношении Проектов с Арменией, April 21, 2021, Accessed August 22, 2021, https://tass.ru/politika/8294575.

[456] Путин: Карабах Является Частью Азербайджана, December 12, 2021, Accessed August 22, 2021, https://www.kommersant.ru/doc/4617117.

[457] В ОДКБ Назвали Условие Вмешательства в Конфликт в Карабахе, October 8, 2020, Accessed August 22, 2021, https://ria.ru/20201008/karabakh-1578859528.html.

[458] На выборах в парламент Армении победила партия Пашиняна, June 20, 2021, Accessed August 22, 2021, https://www.svoboda.org/a/v-armenii-zavershilosj-golosovanie-na-dosrochnyh-vyborah-v-parlament/31317469.html.

References

1. Aalto Pami, "Post-Soviet Geopolitics in the North of Europe", In Post-Cold War Identity Politics: Northern and Baltic Experiences, eds. Marco Lehti, David J. Smith, (Portland: Frank Cass Publishers, 2005).

2. Aliboni Robert, "The Geopolitical Implications of the European Neighborhood Policy", European Foreign Affairs Review, Volume 10, No 1, (Holland: Kluwer Law International, Summer, 2006).

3. Aliyev Ilham: "We Will Become a Member of WTO but Only we Know When it will Happen", February 7, 2014, Accessed May 20, 2016, http://news.az/articles/official/86381.

4. Alkan Necmettin, "Dayton Sonrasında Bosna-Hersek'te Yapılan Seçimler ve Barış Sürecine Etkileri (1996-2006)", Avrasya Etütleri, No 29-30, (Ankara: TİKA Yayınları, 2006).

Annotated Summary of Agreements Linking with Non-member Countries, European Commission, Brussels, June, 2000.

5. ANCA Welcomes Appointment of Robert Kocharyan as Prime Minister, 21 March, 1997, Accessed June 26, 2016, http://asbarez.com/33269/anca-welcomes-appointment-of-robert-kocharyan-as-prime-minister/.

6. Antelava Natalia, Georgia: Orthodoxy in the Classroom, May 7, 2015, Accessed July 12, 2016, http://www.bbc.com/news/world-europe-32595514.

7. Aprahamian Serouj, Demonstrators Vow to Remain in Liberty Square Until June 22.

8. Aprahamian Serouj, Mass Protests in Armenia as Killings Test Loyalty to Moscow, June 20, 2015, Accessed June 28, 2016, http://armenianweekly.com/2015/06/20/electricity-protest/.

9. Areshidze Irakly G., Helping Georgia?, Perspective, Volume XII, Number 4, March-April 2002, Accessed June 18, 2016, http://www.bu.edu/iscip/vol12/areshidze.html.

10. Aris Stephen, Eurasian Regionalism: The Shanghai Cooperation Organisation, (Basingstoke: Palgrave Macmillan, 2011).

11. Armenian-American Bilateral Relations, Accessed June 27, 2016, http://www.mfa.am/en/country-by-country/us/.

12. Armenia as Killings Test Loyalty to Moscow, June 20, 2015, Accessed June 28, 2016, http://armenianweekly.com/2015/06/20/electricity-protest/.

13. Armenia: Economy, Accessed April 10, 2016, http://www.adb.org/countries/armenia/economy.

14. Armenia, Economic Indicators, Accessed April 10, 2016, http://www.tradingeconomics.com/armenia/indicators.

15. Armenian Declaration of Independence, Accessed June 26, 2016, http://www.gov.am/en/independence/.

16. Armenia, Presidential Election, 16 and 30 March 1998: Final Report, April 9, 1998, Accessed June 26, 2016, http://www.osce.org/odihr/elections/armenia/14192.

17. Armenia: Skewed Prosecution Over 2008 Clashes, Ensure Impartial Investigation and Justice in Use of Force Against Protesters, February 25, 2009, Accessed June 28, 2016, https://www.hrw.org/news/2009/02/25/armenia-skewed-prosecution-over-2008-clashes.

18. Aslanlı Aras, "Tarihten Günümüze Karabağ Sorunu", Avrasya Dosyası, Volume 7, No 1, Ankara, Spring, 2001.

19. Ateşoğlu Nurşin Güney, "Bosna-Hersek Sorunu ve Barış Görüşmeleri Süreci", In Yeni Balkanlar, Eski Sorunlar, eds. Kemali Saybaşılı, Özcan Gencer, (Istanbul: Bağlam Yayınları, 1997).

20. Axmith Bradley, Denying History, The United States` Policies Towards Russia in the Caspian Region, 1991-2001, (Hamburg: Anchor Academic Publishing, 2013).

21. Azerbaijan: A Country of Unusual Shia-Sunni Harmony, May 23, 2016, Accessed July 12, 2016, http://www.1news.az/hub/20160523014450256.html.

22. Azerbaijan, Economic Indicators, Economy, Accessed April 10, 2016, http://www.tradingeconomics.com/azerbaijan/indicators.

23. Azerbaijani President: "Southern Gas Corridor is a project of energy security", February 14, 2015, Accessed May 20, 2016, http://en.apa.az/xeber_azerbaijani_president___southern_gas_cor_223095.html.

24. Bancroft Ian, An Unlikely Serbian Alliance, Accessed February 18, 2016, http://www.theguardian.com/commentisfree/2008/jul/10/serbia.eu.

25. Bjol Erling, "The Small State in International Politics", in the Small States in International Relations, ed. A. Schou and A.O. Brundtland, (Stockholm: Almquist and Wiksell, 1971).

26. Bigg Claire, NATO: What is A Membership Action Plan?, April, 2, 2006, Accessed March 4, 2016, http://www.rferl.org/content/article/1079718.html.

27. Blum Jerome, Rondo Cameron and Thomas G. Barnes, A History: The European World, (Boston: Little, Brown and Company, 1966).

28. Bowker Mike, "European Security", Foundations, In Contemporary Europe, eds. Richard Sakwa, Anne Stevens, (New York: St. Martin Press, 2000).

29. Bretherton Charlotte, Vogler John, The European Union as a Global Actor, (London: Routledge, 2006).

30. Broers Laurence, The Nagorno Karabakh Conflict: Defaulting War, (London: Chatham House, 2016).

31. Brune Lester, H., The United States & the Balkan Crisis, 1990-2005: Conflict in Bosnia & Kosovo, (Claremont: Regina Books, 2005).

32. Brussels Gives Green light to Albania and Macedonia, October 16, 2013, Accessed February 18, 2016, http://www.presseurop.eu/en/content/news-brief/4240351-brussels-gives-green-light-albania-and-macedonia.

33. Bucharest Summit Declaration Issued by the Heads of State and Government Participating in the Meeting of the North Atlantic Council in Bucharest on 3 April 2008, April 3, 2008, Accessed May 19, 2016, http://www.nato.int/cps/en/natolive/official_texts_8443.htm.

34. Burzanoviç Tufk, "Bosna Örneğinde ABD'nin Balkan Siyaseti Anlamak", In Balkan Diplomasisi, eds. Ömer E., Lütem & Çoşgun Birgül Demirtaş, (Ankara: ASAM Yayınları, 2001).

35. Chayes Abram, Olson Lara & Raah Georg, "The Development of U.S. Policy Toward the Former Soviet Union", In Managing Conflict in the Former Soviet Union: Russian and American Perspectives, eds. Alexey Arbatov, Abram Chayes, Antonia Handler Chayes, Lara Olson, (Cambridge:Harvard University, 1997).

36. Chronology of Key Events February 1988-June 2003, http://www.nkrusa.org/nk_confict/nkr_position.shtml.

37. Chronology of Kosovo's Path to Independence, Accessed February 17, 2016, http://www.dw.com/en/chronology-of-kosovos-path-to-independence/a-3132060.

38. Clines Francis X., Secession Decreed by Soviet Georgia, The New York Times, April 10, 2016, Accessed June 15, 2016, http://www.nytimes.com/1991/04/10/world/secession-decreed-by-soviet-georgia.html.

39. Cluster People: Azerbaijani, Accessed May 16, 2016, http://joshuaproject.net/clusters/126; Brenda Shaffer, Borders and Brethren: Iran and the Challenge of Azerbaijani Identity, (Cambridge: MIT Press, 2003).

40. Coffey Luke, NATO Summit 2016: Keeping Georgia on the Membership Track, Accessed June 22, 2016, http://www.heritage.org/research/reports/2016/06/nato-summit-2016-keeping-georgia-on-the-membership-track#.V2GEhlct8Rk.twitter.

41. Concept of the Foreign Policy of the Russian Federation, February 18, 2013, Accessed March 16, 2016, http://www.mid.ru/en/foreign_policy/official_documents/-/asset_publisher/CptICkB6BZ29/content/id/122186.

42. Conditions for Membership, Accessed May 20, 2016,

http://ec.europa.eu/enlargement/policy/conditions-membership/index_en.htm.

43. Contract of Century, Official Site of the President of Azerbaijan Republic, Accessed May 17, 2016, http://en.president.az/azerbaijan/contract.

44. Commission Communication from the Commission to the European Parliament and the Council, Commission Opinion on Montenegro's application for membership of the European Union, {SEC (20□0) 1334}, European Commission, Brussels, 9.11. 2010, COM (2010) 670.

45. Commission Staff Working Paper, Annex to "European Neighbourhood Policy", Country Report, Azerbaijan, (COM (2005)72 Final), Brussels, EU Commission, 02.03.2005.

46. Cornell Svante E., Azerbaijan Since Independence, (New York: M.E. Sharpe, 2011).

47. Corso Molli, Bush Visit to Georgia is a Great Political Victory- Saakashvili, May 10, 2005, Accessed June 19, 2016, http://www.eurasianet.org/departments/insight/articles/eav051105.shtml.

48. Crowards Tom, "Defining the Category of `Small` States," Journal of International Development, 14 (2002): 168, accessed December 7, 2015. Doi:10.1002/jid860.

49. Cremona Marise, "Enlargement and External Policy", The Enlargement of the European Union, ed. Marise Cremona, (Oxford: Oxford Press, 2003).

50. Croft Stuart et al., The Enlargement of Europe, Manchester, Manchester University, 1999.Dukes Paul, A History of Europe 1648-1948: The Arrival, The Rise and The Fall (London: Macmillian, 1989).

51. Davudoğlu Ahmet, Turkish-Armenian Relations in the Process of De-Ottomanisation or Dehistorisation: is a "Just Memory" Possible?, Journal of Policy Quartely, Vol 13, No 1, (Istanbul: Spring, 2014).

52. Declaration on State Independence of the Nagorno-Karabakh Republic, http://www.nkrusa.org/nk_confict/declaration_independence.shtml.

53. Dempsey Judy, Moldova is Next Battleground for Russia and EU, 04.12.2014, http://www.themoscowtimes.com/opinion/article/moldova-is-next-battleground-for-russia-and-eu/512583.html.

54. Dempsey Judy, NATO and the E.U. Desert Georgia, June 16, 2016, Accessed June 22, 2016, https://www.washingtonpost.com/opinions/nato-and-the-eu-desert-georgia/2016/06/16/20f2c7dc-33be-11e6-8758-d58e76e11b12_story.html.

55. Devyatkov, Andrey Transnistria: Support not Abandonment, May 20, 2016, Accessed June 25, 2016, http://intersectionproject.eu/article/russia-europe/transnistria-support-not-abandonment.

Dunay Pal, "Strategy with Fast-Moving Targets East-Cental Europe." In European Union Foreign and Security Policy Towards a Neighbourhood Strategy, ed. Roland Dannreuther, (London: Routledge, 2005).

56. Dunbabin J.P.D., The Cold War, The Great Powers and Their Allies, (London: Longman, 1996).

57. Dzutsev Valeriy, Russia to Strip Abkhazia and South Ossetia of their Limited Sovereignty, March 18, 2015, Accessed 19, 2016, http://www.cacianalyst.org/publications/analytical-articles/item/13163-russia-to-strip-abkhazia-and-south-ossetia-of-their-limited-sovereignty.html.

58. East Maurice A., "Size and Foreign Policy Behavior: A Test of Two Models," World Politics 4 (1973).

59. Eastern Partnership, Accessed March 4, 2016, http://.eeas.europa.eu/eastern/index_en.htm.

60. Elchibey Gets Vote of No-confidence in Azeri Referendum, August 30, 1993, Accessed May 17, 2016, http://www.upi.com/Archives/1993/08/30/Elchibey-gets-vote-of-no-confidence-in-Azeri-referendum/8499746683200/.

61. Englung Will, Kremlin Says Crimea is Now Officially Part of Russia After Treaty Signing, Putin Speech, March 18, 2014, Accessed March 24, 2016, https://www.washingtonpost.com/world/russias-putin-prepares-to-annex-crimea/2014/03/18/933183b2-654e-45ce-920e-4d18c0ffec73_story.html.

62. Erkuş Sevil, Turkey Could Reopen Railway in Parallel with Karabakh Progress, November 8, 2013, Accessed June 27, 2016, http://www.hurriyetdailynews.com/turkey-could-reopen-railway-in-parallel-with-karabakh-progress-.aspx?pageID=238&nID=57565.

63. EurAsEC, Accessed March 16, 2016, http://www.eurasian-ec.com/index.php?option=com_content&task=view&id=2&Itemid=7.

64. Eurasian Economic Union, Accessed March 16, 2016, http://www.eaeunion.org/?lang=en#about.

European Neighbourhood Policy, Accessed February 19, 2016, http://eeas.europa.eu/enp/.

65. European Commission hProposes to Lift Visa Obligations for Citizens of Georgia, European Commission - Press release, Brussels, March 9, 2016, Accessed June 21, 2016, http://europa.eu/rapid/press-release_IP-16-702_en.htm.

66. EU Cooperation with Georgia,

http://www.delgeo.ec.Europa.eu/en/eu_and_georgia/cooperation.html.

67. EU Flags to Fly over Georgian Governmental Offices, April 19, 2016, Accessed June 19, 2016, http://www.civil.ge/eng/article.php?id=6716.

68. EU Relations with Eastern Partnership, Accessed May 20, 2016, http://eeas.europa.eu/eastern/index_en.htm.

69. EU Relations with the Western Balkans, Accessed February 17, 2016, http://eeas.europa.eu/western_balkans/index_en.htm.

70. EU Relations with Moldova, Accessed March 25, 2016, http://eeas.europa.eu/moldova/.

71. EU Relations with Serbia, Accessed February 18, 2016, http://eeas.europa.eu/serbia/index_en.htm.

72. Eürbedar Erhan, Balkan Ülkelerin Avrupa Birliği Yolculuğu, Stratejik Analiz, (Ankara: ASAM Yayınları, February, 2007).

73. Evans Gareth, Russia and the 'responsibility to protect', In Los Angeles Times, August 31, 2008, Accessed April 15, 2008, http://www.latimes.com/la-oe-evans31-2008aug31-story.html.

74. Falkowscki Maciej, Georgian Drift, the Crisis of Georgian`s Way Westwards, No 57, (Warsaw: Centre for Eastern Studies, February, 2016).

75. Ferrero-Waldner Benita, "The European Neighbourhood Policy: The EU's Newest Foreign Policy Instrument", European Foreign Affairs Review, Volume 11, No 2, (Holland: Kluwer Law International, Summer, 2006).

76. Final Statement and Recommendations Adopted at the 16th Meeting of EU-Armenia Parliamentary Cooperation Committee (21/01/2016), Accessed June 28, 2016, http://eeas.europa.eu/delegations/armenia/press_corner/all_news/news/2016/2016_01_21_en.ht.

77. Fridman George, The Russo-Georgian War and the Balance of Power, Geopolitical Weekly, August 12, 2008, Accessed April 15, 2016, https://worldview.stratfor.com/article/russo-georgian-war-and-balance-power.

78. Frieden Jeffry A., David A Lake, Kenneth A. Schultz, World Politics: Interests, Interactions, Institutions, (New York: W.W. Norton& Company).

79. Georgia's Constitutional Changes, Accessed June 20, 2016, http://www.crisisgroup.org/en/multimedia/podcasts/2012/georgia-turashvili-georgias-constitutional-changes.aspx.

80. Georgia: Economy, Accessed April 10, 2016, http://www.adb.org/countries/georgia/economy.

81. Georgia GDP Annual Growth Rate, Accessed April 10, 2016, http://www.tradingeconomics.com/georgia/gdp-growth-annual.

82. Georgia Joins the WTO, WTO News: 2000 Press Releases, 14 June 2000, https://www.wto.org/english/news_e/pres00_e/pr182_e.htm.

83. Georgia's Knock at NATO's Door: Quieter But More Persistent, 7 January 2000, The Jamestown Foundation, Fortnight in Review Volume: 6 Issue: 1, http://www.jamestown.org/single/?tx_ttnews%5Btt_news%5D=24354&tx_ttnews%5BbackPid%5D=207&no_cache=1#.V2OL27uLTDc.

84. Georgia Sustainment and Stability Operations Program (GSSOP), Accessed June 18, 2016, http://www.globalsecurity.org/military/ops/gssop.htm.

85. Georgia "Train and Equip" Program Begins, News Release of the U.S. Department of Defense, April 29, 2002, Accessed June 18, 2016, http://www.bits.de/NRANEU/Russia-Caucasus/georgia%20train%20and%20equip%20program.htm.

86. George Stephen, Ian Bache, Politics in the European Union, (Oxford: Oxford University Press, 2001). https://www.stratfor.com/weekly/russo_georgian_war_and_balance_power.

87. Giorgi Margvelashvili, Biography, Accessed June 21, 2016, https://www.president.gov.ge/en/President/Biography.

88. Gorbachev Resigns as President of the USSR, Accessed March 11, 2016, http://www.history.com/this-day-in-history/gorbachev-resigns-as-president-of-the-ussr.

89. Gotev Georgi, Serbia fears EU will Pressure Greece to Recognize Kosovo, August 17, 2015, Accessed February 18, http://www.euractiv.com/section/enlargement/news/serbia-fears-eu-will-pressure-greece-to-recognise-kosovo/.

90. Grigoryan Marianna, Armenia's Russian Murder Scandal: Can Justice Be Served?, February 3, 2016, Accessed June 28, 2016, http://www.eurasianet.org/node/77146.

91. GUAM, Accessed March 16, 2016, http://guam-organization.org/en/node.

Haub Carl, Ukraine's Demographic Reality, Accessed March 8, 2016, http://www.prb.org/Publications/Articles/2014/ukraine-population.aspx.

92. GUAM, Ministry of Foreign Affairs and European Integration of the Republic of Moldova, Accessed June 17, 2016, http://www.mfa.gov.md/about-guam-en/.

93. Gutterman Steve, Russia Set to Resume Imports of Georgian Wine and Water, February 4, 2013, Accessed June 18, 2016, http://www.reuters.com/article/us-russia-georgia-idUSBRE91402R20130205.

94. Henze Paul B., "Russia and the Caucasus", Perceptions: Journal of International Affairs, Volume 1, No 2, (Ankara: Stratejik Araştırmalar Merkezi, June-August, 1996).

95. Hewitt B. George, Abhazia, "A Problem of Identity and Ownership", In Transcaucasian Boundaries, ed. John F. R. Wright et al., (London: UCL Press, 1996).

96. Holborn Hajo, The Political Collapse of Europe, (New York: Alfred A. Knopf, 1966).

97. How far do EU-US Sanctions on Russia Go?, September 15, 2014, Accessed 24, 2016, http://www.bbc.com/news/world-europe-28400218.

98. Hughes Stuart H., Contemporary Europe: A History, (New Jersey: Prentice-Hall, Inc., 1966).

Fox Annete Baker, The Power of Small States: Diplomacy in World War II (Chicago: The University of Chicago Press, 1959).

99. Hunter Shireen, Thomas Jefrey L., Melikishvili Alexander, Islam in Russia: The Politics of Identity and Security, (New York: M.E. Sharpe, 2004).

100. Jaquet L.G.M., "The Role of Small States Within Alliance Systems," in Small States in International Relations, ed. A. Schou and A.O. Brundtland, (Stokholm: Almquist and Wiksell, 1971).

101. Joint Declaration of the European Union and the Republics of Armenia, Azerbaijan and Georgia, Luxembourg, C/99/202 22, June 1999, 9405/99 (Presse 202).

102. Jones Stephen, Georgia: A Political History since Independence, (London: I.B. Taurus, 2015).

103. Jones Stephen, Georgia: Nationalism from under the Rubble, After Independence: Making and Protecting the Nation in Postcolonial and Postcommunist States, Ed. Lowell W. Barrington, (Michigan: The University of Michigan Press, 2009).

104. Jones Stephen, Minorities in the Georgian Republic, In the Politics of Nationality and the Erosion of the USSR, Zvi Y. Gitelman, (Great Britain: St. Martin Press, 1992).

105. Individual Partnership Action Plans, Accessed March 4, 2016, http://www.nato.int/cps/en/natohq/topics_49290.htm.

106. Ibrahimov Rovshan, After the 2013 Azerbaijani Presidential Elections: Challenges and Expectations, Caucasus International, Vol. 3, No 4, Winter 2013-2014.

107. Ibrahimov Rovshan, Azerbaijan`s Energy History and Policy: From Past till Our Days, In Energy and Azerbaijan: History, Strategy and Cooperation, ed. Rovshan Ibrahimov, (Baku: SAM, 2013).

108. Ibrahimov Rovshan, Azerbaijan Energy Strategy and the Importance of the Diversification of Exported Transport Routes, No 29, (Baku: Journal of Qafqaz University, 2010).

109. Ibrahimov Rovshan, EU External Policy Towards the South Caucasus: How Far is it From Realizations?, SAM, Baku, 2013.

109. Ibrahimov Rovshan, "Link in the Chain: South Caucasus as a transport and logistics hub between Regions", Interregional Cooperation in Eurasia: Transport and Logistics Projects as an Accelerator of Integration Within and Between the Black Sea Region, the South Caucasus and the Central Asia", SAM, Baku, 2013.

110. Ibrahimov Rovshan, Turkish Foreign Policy Towards Armenia in 2008-2009: Impact on Azerbaijani-Turkish Relations, Bilge Strateji, Vol 7, No 12, (Istanbul: Bilgesam, Spring, 2015).

111. Ibrahimov Rovshan, U.S.-Azerbaijan Relations: A View from Baku, Rething Paper 17, (Washington DC: Rething Institution, October 2014).

112. Illarionov Andrey, The Russian Leadership`s Preparation for War, 1999-2008, in The Guns of August 2008: Russia`s War in Georgia, eds. Svante E. Cornell, S. Frederick Starr, (London: Routledge, 2009).

113. Ivanishvili Expects GDDG to Win About 95 Seats in Parliament, June 8, 2016, Accessed June 20, 2016, http://www.civil.ge/eng/article.php?id=29207.

114. vanishvili Suggests Georgia Must 'Patiently Wait' For Russian Approval On NATO, June 03, 2016, Accessed June 23, 2016, http://www.rferl.org/content/georgia-ivanishvili-nato-russia-approval/27778208.html.

115. Kahraman Sevilay, "The European Neighbourhood Policy: A Critical Assessment", Avrupa Çalışmaları, Volume 5, No 3, (Ankara: ATAUM, Spring, 2006).

116. Kakachia Kornely, Salome Minesashvili, Identity politics, Exploring Georgian Foreign Policy Behavior, Journal of Eurasian Studies, Volume 6, Issue 2, July, 2015, doi:10.1016/j.euras.2015.04.002, http://www.sciencedirect.com/science/article/pii/S1879366515000111.

117. Kakachia Kornely, The End of Russian Military Bases in Georgia, In Military Bases: Historical Perspectives, Contemporary Challenges, eds. Luis Rodrigues, Sergiy Glebov, (Amsterdam: IOC Press, 2009).

118. Karabakh, Official Site of President of Azerbaijan Republic, Accessed May 16, 2016, http://en.president.az/azerbaijan/karabakh.

119. Karamanlis Emmanuel, Energy and Security in the Caucasus, (London: Routledge Curson, 2002).

120. Karen Smith, The Making of EU Foreign Policy: The Case of Eastern Europe, (Basingstoke: Palgrave, Macmillan, 2004).

121. Kasım Kamer, Armenia's Foreign Policy: Basic Parameters of Ter-Petrosyan and Kocharyan Era, (Ankara: Turkish Weekly, October 13, 2013), Accessed June 26, 2016, http://www.turkishweekly.net/2004/10/13/article/armenia-039-s-foreign-policy-basic-parameters-of-ter-petrosyan-and-kocharyan-era/.

122. Kelkitli Fatma Aslı, Russian Foreign Policy in South Caucasus Under Putin, (Ankara: Perception, Winter, 2008).

123. Kennedy Paul, The Rise and Fall of the Great Powers (New York: Vintage Books, 1987).

124. Keohane Robert O, "Lilliputian`s Dilemmas: Small States in İnternational Politics," in Small States in International Relations, ed. Jessica Beyer et al, (Seattle: University of Washington Press, 2006).

125. Khidayatova Anakhanum, Russia Wants "No War, No Peace" Situation with Karabakh Conflict, Bryza Says, October 19, 2015, Accessed May 16, 2016, http://en.trend.az/azerbaijan/karabakh/2445451.html.

126. Killough Ashley Corinne, Armenia IN Need of an Alternative Export-Import Route, Eurasia Daily Monitor Volume: 5 Issue: 195, October 2008, 2008, Accessed April 14, 2016, http://www.jamestown.org/regions/thecaucasus/single/?tx_ttnews%5Bpointer%5D=5&tx_ttnews%5Btt_news%5D=34015&tx_ttnews%5BbackPid%5D=643&cHash=04c48a2be2e402e8c6f2ec1237348364#.V4TJJPmLTDc.

127. King Charles, "The Five-Day War: Managing Moscow after the Georgia Crisis", Foreign Affairs, November, December 2008, Accessed March 18, 2016, https://www.foreignaffairs.com/articles/russia-fsu/2008-11-01/five-day-war.

128. King Charles, The Ghost of Freedom, A History of Caucasus, Oxford Univercity Press, 2010.

129. Kissinger Henry, Diplomacy, (New York: Simon&Schuster Paperbacks, 1994).

130. Kosovo Declaration of Independence, February 17, 2008, Accessed February 18, 2016, http://www.assembly-kosova.org/?cid=2,128,1635.

131. Kulevi Oil Terminal, Accessed April 14 2016, http://www.kulevioilterminal.com/.

Papp Daniel S., Contemporary International Relations (London: Macmillan Publishing Company, 1988).

132. Kusov Oleg, Газпром сделал скидку Армении, January 2, 2006, Accessed June 27, 2016, http://www.svoboda.mobi/a/129161.html.

133. "Large and Small Member States in the European Union: Reinventing the Balance", January 29, 2010, Accessed February 16, 2016, http://www.euractiv.com/section/future-eu/opinion/large-and-small-member-states-in-the-european-union-reinventing-the-balance/.

134. Laçiner Sedat, Ermenistan Dış Politikası ve Belirleyici Temel Faktörler 1991-2002, Ermeni Araştırmaları, No 5, (Ankara: Eraren, Spring, 2002), Accessed June 26, 2016, http://www.eraren.org/index.php?Page=DergiIcerik&IcerikNo=303.

135. Lobjakas Ahto, NATO Lacks the Stomach for South Caucasus Fight, Nato and The South Caucasus, Caucasus Analitical Digest, No 15, 16 April, 2009, 2, Accessed June 18, 2006, http://www.laender-analysen.de/cad/pdf/CaucasusAnalyticalDigest05.pdf.

136. Markarov Alexander, Semi-Presidentalism in Armenia, Semi-Presidentalism in the Caucasus and Central Asia, eds., Robert Elgie, Sophia Moestrup, (London: Palgrave Macmillan, 2016).

137. Menabde Giorgi, Russia and Georgia Expand Their Only Border Crossing Point, Eurasia Daily Monitor Volume: 10 Issue: 163, September 16, 2013, Accessed April 14, 2016, http://www.jamestown.org/single/?tx_ttnews%5Btt_news%5D=41364&no_cache=1#.V4TLg_mLTDc.

138. Mirzoyan Alla, Armenia, The Regional Powers, and the West Between History and Geopolitics, (New York:Palgrave Macmillan, 2010).

139. Mkrtchyan Hasmik, Russia Grants $200 million Loan to Armenia to Help Modernise Army, July 2, 2016, Accessed July 20, 2016, http://uk.reuters.com/article/uk-armenia-russia-loan-idUKKCN0PC1PY20150702.

140. Nadkarni Vidya, Strategic Partnerships in Asia: Balancing Without Alliances, (London: Routledge, 2010).

141. NATO Grants "Intensified Dialogue" to Georgia, September 212006, Accessed June 19, 2006, http://civil.ge/eng/article.php?id=13613.

142. NATO Handbook, (Brussels: NATO Office of Information and Press, 2001).

143. NATO Opens Training Center in Georgia Amid Russia Tensions, August 31, 2015, Accessed June 23, 2016, http://www.defensenews.com/story/defense/2015/08/27/nato-opens-training-center-georgia-amid-russia-tensions/32476321/.

144. NATO's Role in Relation to the Conflict in Kosovo, Accessed February 18, 2016, http://www.nato.int/kosovo/history.htm.

145. Nakhichevan Autonomous Republic, Accessed July 12, 2016, http://www.nakhchivan.az/portal-en/index-22.htm.

146. Nixey James, The Long Goodbye: Waning Russian Influence in the South Caucasus and Central Asia, (London: Chatham House, June 2012).

147. Novikov Vladimir, Энергокризис в Грузии Заканчивается Вместе с Продажами "Газпрома", January 30, 2006, Accessed June 18, 2016, http://www.kommersant.ru/doc/644882.

148. Nutall Simon J., European Foreign Policy, (Oxford: Oxford University, 2000).

149. Obradoviç Marja, "Milliyetçilik ve Avrupacılık, Doğu Avrupa Elitlerin Durumu.", in Soğuk Savaşı Sonrası Avrupa ve Türkiye, ed. Cem Karadeli, (Ankara: Atlas Yayınevi, 2003).

150. Official Site of the Office of the State Minister of Georgia on European& Euro-Atlantic Integration, http://www.eu-nato.gov.ge/en/node.

151. Oleg Kusov, Газпром Сделал Скидку Армении, January 2, 2006, Accessed June 18, 2016, http://www.svoboda.mobi/a/129161.html.

152. Onursal Özge, "Regional Cooperation as Political Conditionality: The Case of the Western Balkans", Turkish Review of Balkan Studies, 10, (Istanbul: Bigart Yayınları, 2005).

153. Operation Desert Storm, Accessed March 11, 2016, http://www.ushistory.org/us/60a.asp.

154. Operations and Missions: Past and Present, June 23, 2016, Accessed February 15, 2015, http://www.nato.int/cps/en/natohq/topics_52060.htm?selectedLocale=en.

155. Partnership and Cooperation Agreements (PCAs): Russia, Eastern Europe, the Southern Caucasus and Central Asia, Accessed March 13, 2015, http://eur-lex.europa.eu/legal-content/EN/TXT/?uri=URISERV:r17002.

156. Partnership for Peace (Partnership Tools), November 13, 2014, Accessed March 15, 2016, http://www.nato.int/cps/en/natohq/topics_80925.htm.

157. Petro Nicolai N., The Russia-Georgia War: Causes and Consequences, Global Dialoque, Volume 11, Winter/Spring 2009, Accessed June 19, 2016, http://www.worlddialogue.org/content.php?id=439.

158. Policy of Zero Problems with our Neighbors, Official site of the Ministry of Foreign Affairs Republic of Turkey, Accessed June 28, 2016, http://www.mfa.gov.tr/policy-of-zero-problems-with-our-neighbors.en.mfa.

159. Ramm Agatha, Europe in the Nineteenth Century 1789-1905, (London: Longman, 1984).

Partnership and Cooperation Agreements, Accessed February 19, 2016, http://eur-lex.europa.eu/legal-content/EN/TXT/?uri=URISERV%3Ar17002.

160. Ratliff Rebecca, South Ossetian Separatism in Georgia, ICE Case Studies, No 180, May, 2006, Accessed April 14, 2016, http://www1.american.edu/ted/ice/ossetia.htm.

161. Rogel Carole, The Breakup of Yugoslavia and the War in Bosnia, (London: Greenwood Press, 1998).

162. Rice Condoleezza, Remarks with the President of Georgia Mikheil Saakashvili on the Signing of the Millennium Challenge Compact, September 12, 2005, Accessed June 19, 2016, http://2001-2009.state.gov/secretary/rm/2005/53034.htm.

163. Paxton Robert O., Europe in the Twentieth Century, (New York: Harcourt Brace Jovanovich, Inc, 1965).

164. Population Pyramids of the World from 1950 to 2100, Kazakhstan, Accessed March 8, 2016, http://populationpyramid.net/kazakhstan/1990/.

165. Population Pyramids of the World from 1950 to 2100, Uzbekistan, Accessed March 8, 2016, http://populationpyramid.net/uzbekistan/1990/.

166. Recognition of Georgia, Office of History, https://history.state.gov/countries/georgia.

167. Rondelli Alexander, The Choice of Independent Georgia, The Security of Caspian Sea Region, ed. Gennady Chufrin, (Oxford: Oxford University Press, 2001).

168. Resolution 822 (1993) Adopted by the Security Council at its 3205th meeting, April 30, 1993, Accessed June 28, 2016, http://www.refworld.org/cgi-bin/texis/vtx/rwmain?docid=3b00f15764.

169. Rotshtein Robert L., Alliances and Small Powers (New York and London: Columbia University Press, 1968).

170. Rosencrance Richard N., Action and Reaction in World Politics: International System Perspective, (Connecticut: Greenwood Press, 1963).

171. Russia-Belarus Union State Most Advanced Post-Soviet Integration Bloc, October 17, 2014, Accessed March 16, 2016, http://tass.ru/en/russia/754950.

172. Russia, Iran and Azerbaijan Start Working on North-South Transport Corridor, Russia & India Report, April 7, Accessed June 27, 2016, https://in.rbth.com/news/2016/04/07/russia-iran-and-azerbaijan-start-working-on-north-south-transport-corridor_582773.

173. Russia Reduces Gas Price for Armenia, March 29, 2016, Accessed June 29, 2016, http://news.az/articles/armenia/106039.

174. Pipes Richard, The Formation of the Soviet Union: Communism and Nationalism 1917-1923, (London: Harvard University Press, 1997).

175. Preston Christopher, Enlargement, and Integration in the European Union, (London: Routledge, 1997).

176. Salimov Oleg, Tajikistan Paves the Way to Eurasian Union, January 7, 2016, Accessed March 16, 2016, http://www.cacianalyst.org/publications/field-reports/item/13113-tajikistan-paves-the-way-to-eurasian-union.html.

177. Schapiro Salwyn J., Modern and Contemporary European History (1815-1928), (New York: Houghton Mifflin Company, 1929).

178. Schimmelfennig Frank, The EU, NATO and the Integration of Europe, (Cambridge: Cambridge University, 2003).

179. Serzh Sargsyan Announced about Armenia`s Decision to Join Custom Union, September 3, 2013, Accessed June 28, 2016, https://armenpress.am/eng/news/731583/.

180. Serzh Sargsyan Thinks George Bush Did Not Congrtulate Him Because of Country's Post Election Conditions, March 14, 2008, Accessed June 28, 2016, http://www.armeniandiaspora.com/showthread.php?125950-Serzh-Sargsyan-Thinks-George-Bush-Did-Not-Congratulate-Him-Because-O.

181. Shanghai Cooperation Organization, Accessed March 16, 2016, https://aric.adb.org/initiative/shanghai-cooperation-organization.

182. Shiriyev Zaur, Korneli Kakachia, Azerbaijan-Georgian Relations, The Foundation and Challenges of the Strategic Alliance, SAM Review, Special Double Issue, Volume7-8, July, 2013.

183. Slobodchikoff Michael, Russia's Monroe Doctrine Just Worked in Ukraine, November 21, 2013, Accessed March 15, 2016, http://www.russia-direct.org/opinion/russia%E2%80%99s-monroe-doctrine-just-worked-ukraine.

184. Slovenia Unblocks Croatian EU Bid, September, 11, 2009, http://www.news.bbc.co.uk/2/hi/europe/8250441.stm.

185. Smith Karen, The Making of EU Foreign Policy: The Case of Eastern Europe, (London: Palgrave).

186. South Ossetia Profile, April 21, 2016, Accessed July 12, 2016, http://www.bbc.com/news/world-europe-18269210.

187. Speech of the President of the Republic of Azerbaijan Heydar Aliyev at the Reception in Honor of the President of the Republic of Azerbaijan in «Chankaya» Palace, February 8, 1994, Ankara, Accessed May 16, 2016, http://lib.aliyevheritage.org/en/2565380.html.

188. Statement by Edward Nalbandian, Minister of Foreign Affairs of Armenia at the Eastern Partnership Informal Dialogue Meeting of the Foreign Ministers, July 11, 2016, Accessed July 20, 2016, http://www.mfa.am/en/speeches/item/2016/07/11/min_eap_kyiv/.

189. Şihaliyev Emin, Türkiye ve Azerbaycan Açısından Ermeni Sorunu, Ankara, Türk Kültür ve Eğitim Norm Geliştirme Vakfı Yayınları, 2002.

190. TACIS, Accessed February 19, 2016, http://europa.eu/rapid/press-release_MEMO-92-54_en.htm.

191. Tellal Erel, "Rusya Federasyonunun Dış Politikası, "Yakın Çevre" ve "Askeri Doktrin"", In Dış Politikası, Kurtuluş Savaşından Bugüne Olgular, Belgeler, Yorumlar, Volume II: 1980-2001, ed. Baskın Oran, (Istanbul: Iletişim Yayınları, 2003).

192. The Armenian Church, Accessed July 12, 2016, http://www.armenianchurch-ed.net/our-church/history-of-the-church/history/.

193. The Collapse of the Soviet Union, US Department of State, Office of the Historian, October 31, 2013, Accessed 13 March, 2016, https://history.state.gov/milestones/1989-1992/collapse-soviet-union.

194. The Constitutional Act on the State Independence of the Republic of Azerbaijan, October 10, 1991, Accessed May 16, 2016,

http://azerbaijan.az/portal/History/HistDocs/Documents/en/09.pdf.

195. The History of the European Union, Accessed February 15, 2016, http://europa.eu/about-eu/eu-history/index_en.htm#goto_6.

196. The Lisbon Protocol at a Glance, updated March, 2014, Accessed 8 March 2016, https://www.armscontrol.org/print/3289.

197. The North Atlantic Cooperation Council (NACC), October 20, 2011, Accessed February 16, 2016, http://www.nato.int/cps/en/natolive/topics_69344.htm.

198. The Russian Base in Gyumri. Facts and Figures, February 4, 2015, Accessed June 26, 2016, http://www.horizonweekly.ca/news/details/60972.

199. The Situation Between Iraq and Kuweyt, Resolution 661 (1990) of the UN Security Council, 6 August, 1990, Acceessed January 28, 2016, http://daccess-dds-ny.un.org/doc/RESOLUTION/GEN/NR0/575/10/IMG/NR057510.pdf?OpenElement.

200. "The Warsaw Treaty Organization, 1955", U.S. Department of State, Office of Historian, accessed February 07, 2016, https://history.state.gov/milestones/1953-1960/warsaw-treaty.

201. Thousands Protest in Yerevan Against Electricity Prices, July 3, 2015, Accessed June 28, 2016, http://www.rferl.org/content/armenia-protest-electricity-prices/27086605.html.

202. To Recognize or Not to Recognize Abkhazia? That is Vanuatu's Question, July 11, 2016, Accessed March 19, 2016, http://www.rferl.org/content/abkhazia-vanuatu-georgia-russia-recognition/24688283.html.

203. Treaty of Luneville, Accessed December 25, 2015, http://www.napoleon-series.org/research/government/diplomatic/c_luneville.html.

204. "Treaty of Chaumont," Accessed December 19, 2015, http://www.napoleon-series.org/research/government/diplomatic/c_chaumont.html.

205. Ukraine crisis: Viktor Yanukovych leaves Kiev for Support Base, February 22, 2014, Accessed March 23, 2016,

http://www.telegraph.co.uk/news/worldnews/europe/ukraine/10655335/Ukraine-crisis-Viktor-Yanukovych-leaves-Kiev-for-support-base.html.

206. Union for the Mediterranean, Assessed March 4, 2016, http://www.enpi-info.eu/medportal/content/341/.

207. UN Mission in Kosovo, Accessed February 18, 2016, http://www.unmikonline.org/Pages/about.aspx.

208. Vital David, "The Inequality of the States: A study of Small Power in International Relations," in Small States in International Relations, ed. Jessica Beyer et al (Seattle: University of Washington Press, 2006).

209. Waal Thomas De, "A Broken Region: The Persistent Failure of Integration Projects in the South Caucasus", Europe-Asia Studies, Volume 64, No 9 (Routledge, Taylor& Francis Group, November, 2012).

210. Waal Thomas De, The Caucasus, An Introduction, Oxford University Press, 2010.

211. What is EULEX?, Accessed February 18, 2016, http://www.eulex-kosovo.eu/?page=2,16.

212. Why isn`t Norway in the EU?, March 29, 2013, Accessed February 15, 2016, http://www.euronews.com/2013/03/29/norway-and-the-eu/.

213. Wilson's Fourteen Points, 1918, U.S. Department of State, Office of the Historian, Accessed January 09, 2016, https://history.state.gov/milestones/1914-1920/fourteen-points.

214. Woodward Ernest Llewellyn, War and Peace in Europe: 1815-1870, (Hamden: Archon Books, 1963).

215. Алиев Рассказал Лукашенко о Деталях Обострившегося Конфликта в Карабахе, April 2, 2016, Accessed 29 July, 2016, http://news.tut.by/politics/490948.html;

216. Армения Выслушала Российскую Оценку Карабахского Вопроса, August 20, 2010, Accessed June 28, 2016, http://www.vesti.ru/doc.html?id=387102.

217. Армения Продолжит Содействие в Установлении Мира в Афганистане, December 2, 2015, Accessed June 27, 2016, http://newsarmenia.am/news/politics/armeniya-prodolzhit-sodeystvie-v-ustanovlenii-mira-v-afganistane-nalbandyan/.

218. Армянские Предприятия, Переданные России по Схеме «Имущество в Счет Долга», Будут Слиты в Единый Научно-Производственный Комплекс, February 6, 2008, Accessed June 27, 2016, https://regnum.ru/news/economy/952992.html.

219. А теперь – АЭС…, Accessed June 27, 2016, http://www.etpress.ru/?content=article&id=5660.

220. Бабаев Расим, На Долю Азербайджана Приходится 75% Экономики Южного Кавказа – Министр, July 29 2010, Accessed April 10, 2016, http://1news.az/economy/20100729105903671.html.

221. Блок Пашиняна по Итогам Выборов в Армении Получил 88 Мест в 132-местном Парламенте, December 18, 2018, Accessed 29 August, 2021, https://tass.ru/mezhdunarodnaya-panorama/5918851.

222. Борис Грызлов: Армения Является Форпостом России на Южном Кавказе, December 15, 2015, Accessed June 27, 2016, https://regnum.ru/news/polit/376296.html.

223. В Армении Отложили Рост Тарифов на Электричество, Протестующие Празднуют Победу, June 27, 2015, Accessed June 29, 2016, http://www.newsru.com/world/27jun2015/erevan.html.

224. ВВП Азербайджана в 2015 году Вырос Более Чем на 1% - Президент Алиев, January 10, 2016, Accessed April 10, 2016, http://www.cbc.az/ru/news/economics/vvp-azerbaydjana-v-2015-godu-viros-bolee-chem-na-1-prezident-aliev.page.

225. В ОДКБ Назвали Условие Вмешательства в Конфликт в Карабахе, October 8, 2020, Accessed August 22, 2021, https://ria.ru/20201008/karabakh-1578859528.html.

226. Всесоюзная Перепись Населения 1989 года. Распределение Городского и Сельского Населения Областей Республик СССР по Полу и Национальности, Абхазская ССР, Accessed April 17, 2016, http://demoscope.ru/weekly/ssp/resp_nac_89.php?reg=65.

227. Вступление в Таможенный Союз на Референдуме в Гагаузии Поддержали 98,4% избирателей, 3 February, Last Accessed 26 March 2016, http://tass.ru/mezhdunarodnaya-panorama/934052.

228. Газпром: Цена на Газ для Грузии в 2008г. Может Остаться Примерно на Уровне 2007г. - 235 долл. за 1 тыс. куб. м., August 4, 2007, Accessed June 18, 2016, http://www.trend.az/business/economy/967778.html.

229. Госдума Грозит Выйти из Договора о Дружбе с Украиной в Случае Шагов по Вступлению в НАТО, April 1, 2008, Accessed March 23, 2016, http://newsru.com/russia/01apr2008/antinato.html.

230. Грузия Вышла из СНГ, 19.08.2016, http://rg.ru/sujet/3895/.Грузия Объявила Южную Осетию и Абхазию Оккупированными Территориями, August 28, 2008, Accessed April 17, 2016, http://ria.ru/osetia_news/20080828/150770017.html.

231. Де Китспоттер Винсен, Большая Игра в Центральной Азии, Accessed March 16 2016, http://www.perspektivy.info/print.php?ID=36122.

232. Де Ваал Томас, Черный Сад, Accessed June 26, 2016, http://news.bbc.co.uk/hi/russian/in_depth/newsid_4685000/4685141.stm.

233. Дементьева Виктория, Азербайджан Стал Членом Движения Неприсоединения, May 25, 2011, Accessed May 20, 2016, http://ru.apa.az/news/193912.

234. Жене Миллиардера Иванишвили Вернули Гражданство Грузии, December 27, 2011, Accessed June 20, 2016, https://lenta.ru/news/2011/12/27/lost/.

235. Заявление Президентов Азербайджанской Республики, Грузии, Республики Молдова, Украины и Республики Узбекистан, Official site of Organisation for Democracy and Economic Development, GUAM, Accessed 16.03.2015, http://guam-organization.org/node/305.

236. Ибрагимов Ровшан, Движение Неприсоединения Как Инструмент Реализации Национальных Интересов Азербайджана, May 11, 2012, Accessed May 20, 2016, http://www.1news.az/authors/ribrahimov/20120511104117876.html

237. Ибрагимов Ровшан, Евросоюз, Экзамен на Зрелость: Быть или не Быть ЕС Региональным Актором, Accessed May 19, 2016, 25.11.2011, https://1news.az/authors/ribrahimov/20110125043113449.html.

238. Ибрагимов Ровшан, Реквием по «Набукко»: Исполнение в Трех Актах, February 10, 2012, Accessed May 19, 2016, https://1news.az/authors/ribrahimov/20120210042404884.html.

239. Инициативы Минской Группы ОБСЕ по Урегулированию Армяно - Азербайджанского Нагорно - Карабахского конфликта, Accessed June 26, 2016, http://articlekz.com/article/7338.

240. История Конфликта и Процесс Урегулирования, http://www.azerbembassy.org.cn/rus/background.html.

241. Назарбаев Позвонил Алиеву и Саргсяну, April 6, 2016, Accessed 29 July, 2016, http://haqqin.az/news/67489.

242. Кречетников Артем, Почему Армения Просится в Таможенный Союз?, October 24, 2013, Last accessed 5 April 2016,

http://www.bbc.com/russian/international/2013/10/131024_armenia_custom_union_analysis.

243. Какачия Корнелий, Конец Российских Военных Баз в Грузии: Социальные, Политические и Стратегические Последствия их Вывода, Центральная Азия и Кавказ, No 2, 2008.

244. Левон Тер-Петросян: «Война, или Мир? Пора Стать Серьезнее», Armenian Research Center, May 27, 2015, Accessed June 26, 2016, http://www.aniarc.am/2015/05/27/war-or-peace-ter-petrosyan-1997/.

245. Мамедьяров Эльмар: "Председательство Азербайджана в СБ ООН Запомнилось Рядом Важных Резолюций и Обращений", January 10, 2014, Accessed May 21, 2016, http://news.day.az/politics/457625.html.

246. Медведев: Поставки Оружия Еревану и Баку Неизбежны, April 9, 2016, Accessed June 29, 2016, http://www.bbc.com/russian/news/2016/04/160409_medvedev_karabakh_arms.

247. МИД РФ Надеется на Урегулирование Судебных Процессов в Отношении Проектов с Арменией, April 21, 2021, Accessed August 22, 2021, https://tass.ru/politika/8294575.

248. Минасян Сергей, Внешняя Политика Постсоветской Армении:20 Лет Одновременно на Нескольких Стульях, Мировая Политика и Международные Отношения, 2013, No 1.

249. Минасян: Основа Внешней Политики Армении – Комплементаризм, July 8, 2008, Accessed June 26, 2016, http://www.kavkaz-uzel.ru/articles/138885/.

250. Мурадян Игорь, Отношение США к Политическому Руководству Армении, July 9, 2015, Accessed June 27, 2016, http://www.lragir.am/index/rus/0/comments/51810/43179.

251. На Выборах в Парламент Армении Победила Партия Пашиняна, June 20, 2021, Accessed August 22, 2021, https://www.svoboda.org/a/v-armenii-zavershilosj-golosovanie-na-dosrochnyh-vyborah-v-parlament/31317469.html.

252. На Линии Баку-Тбилиси-Карс Запущен Первый Тестовый Поезд, January 4, 2015, Accessed May 21, 2016, http://www.vestikavkaza.ru/news/Na-linii-Baku-Tbilisi-Kars-zapushchen-pervyy-testovyy-poezd.html.

253. Никси Джеймс, Долгое Прощание: Уменьшение Русского Влияния на Южном Кавказе и в Центральной Азии, Accessed June 27, 2016, http://www.geopolitica.ru/article/dolgoe-proshchanie-umenshenie-russkogo-vliyaniya-na-yuzhnom-kavkaze-i-v-centralnoy-azii#.V3ATdvmLTDc.

254. Новая Концепция Национальной Безопасности Грузии, Civil Georgia, December 23, 2011, Accessed June 20, 2016, http://www.civil.ge/rus/article.php?id=22911.

255. Общая Историческая Справка о 907-й Поправке к «Акту в Поддержку Свободы» Конгресса США и о деятельности Президента Азербайджанской Республики Гейдара Алиева в Связи с ее Ликвидацией, URL, Accessed May 18, 2016, http://lib.aliyevheritage.org/ru/3711428.html.

256. "Оранжевая Революция" на Украине, РиА Новости, November 22, 2014, Accessed March 18, 2016, http://ria.ru/spravka/20141122/1034455095.html.

257. Путин: Карабах Является Частью Азербайджана, December 12, 2021, Accessed August 22, 2021, https://www.kommersant.ru/doc/4617117.

258. Правительство Украины Одобрило Соглашение об Ассоциации с ЕС, September 18, 2013, Accessed March 23, 2016, http://www.svoboda.org/content/article/25109856.html.

259. Президент Грузии Выразил Уверенность во Вступлении Страны в ЕС, March 8, 2016, Accessed June 22, 2016, http://www.rbc.ru/politics/08/05/2016/572fa06d9a79478a567515be.

260. Приднестровье Попросило Путина о Признании, April 16 2016, Accessed March 25 2016, http://lenta.ru/news/2014/04/16/ask/.

261. Расулзаде Заур, Аяз Муталлибов: Мне Было Сложнее, чем Ильхаму Алиеву Сейчас, November 18, 2013, Accessed May 18, 2016, http://www.haqqin.az/news/11483.

262. "Революция Роз" в Грузии в Ноябре 2003 года, РиА Новости, November 23, 2013, Accessed March 18, 2016, http://ria.ru/spravka/20131123/978914952.html.

263. РИА Новости, Литва и еще Четыре Страны ЕС требуют Предоставить Грузии Безвизовый Режим, June 11, 2016, Accessed June 21, 2016, http://ria.ru/world/20160611/1445842555.html#ixzz4BobdTqrA.

264. Россия и Грузино-Абхазский Конфликт, Accessed June 19, 2016, http://www.abkhaziya.org/books/prav_konflict/russia.html.

265. Россия Ограничивает Ввоз Молдавской Продукции Через Белоруссию, 4 April 2016, Last Accessed 26 March 2016, http://ria.ru/economy/20160304/1384383595.html.

266. Ростовский Михаил, Искушение Нефтью. Как Россия Теряет Азербайджан, Кавказ и Каспий, Accessed May 17, 2016, http://www.iicas.org/page.php?id=204.

267. Рцхиладзе Гулбаат, Новая Внешняя Политика Грузии, October 12, 2012, Accessed June 23, 2016, http://politforumi.com/rus/1328/saqartvelos-axali-sagareo-politika.html.

268. Саммит ЕАЭС Перенесли из Еревана в Москву, но Медведев в Армению Все Же Приедет, April 5, 2016, Accessed 29 July, 2016, http://www.panarmenian.net/rus/news/209672/.

269. Соглашения о Прекращении Огня и Разъединении Сил, May 14, 1994, Accessed April 17, 2016, http://www.un.org/ru/peacekeeping/missions/past/unomig/94-583.pdf.

270. Соглашение о Создании Содружества Независимых Государств, December 8, 1991, Accessed March 11, 2016, http://cis.minsk.by/page.php?id=176.

271. Статус Черноморского Флота РФ. Справка, 21 October 2010, Accessed 16 March 2016, http://ria.ru/spravka/20100421/225145286.html.

272. Султыгов М. И., К Вопросу Создания Содружества Независимых Государств, Accessed March 11, 2016, http://www.law.edu.ru/doc/document.asp?docID=1126873#_ftn2.

273. «Таможенный Союз не Имеет для нас Смысла», Премьер Армении о Взаимоотношениях с РФ, Accessed June 28, 2016, http://www.kommersant.ru/doc-y/1908052.

274. Татевик Лазарян, Национальное Собрание 6-го Созыва Завтра Начнет Свою Работу, May 17,2017, Accessed 29 August, 2021, https://rus.azatutyun.am/a/28493702.html.

275. Тбилиси: США в 2005 году Запретили Саакашвили Продавать Грузинский Газопровод Газпрому, October, 20, 2015, Accessed June 19, 2016, http://vz.ru/news/2015/10/20/773332.html.

276. Товарооборот Армении и России за 9 месяцев 2015 года Уменьшился на 14,1%, November 1, 2015, Accessed April 14 2016, http://www.finmarket.ru/news/4148537.

277. Токаева Асем, Две Цитаты Назарбаева Вызвали Долгие Споры в Армении, November 5, 2014, Accessed June 28, 2016, http://rus.azattyq.org/a/armenia-eaes-karabakh-nursultan-nazarbayev/26673820.html.

278. "Тюльпановая Революция" в Киргизии (2005), March 24, 2015, Accessed March 18, 2016, http://ria.ru/spravka/20150324/1053953942.html.

279. Усова Лариса, "Внешняя Политика Украины: Между Внеблоковостью и Атлантической Интеграцией", Власть, Journal, No 7, 2011, 157, http://cyberleninka.ru/article/n/vneshnyaya-politika-ukrainy-mezhdu-vneblokovostyu-i-evroatlanticheskoy-integratsiey#ixzz3oHzoYcf0.

280. Что Такое ШОС?, Accessed March 16, 2016, http://infoshos.ru/ru/?id=51.

281. Шабан Ильхам: "Южный Газовый Коридор Будет Служить Процветанию не Одной-Двух Стран, а Целого Региона", February 13, 2015, Accessed May 21, 2016, http://caspianbarrel.org/?p=27182.

282. "Швеция во Время Первой Мировой Войны (1914–1922 гг.)", Accessed January 09, 2016, http://svspb.net/istorija-shvecii/mirovaja-vojna.php.

283. 2008 Georgia Russia Conflict Fast Facts, March 21, 2016, Accessed March 18, 2016, http://edition.cnn.com/2014/03/13/world/europe/2008-georgia-russia-conflict/.

284. 40 Years of EU Enlargements Who Has Joined the EU so Far?, Accessed February 16, 2016, http://www.europarl.europa.eu/external/html/euenlargement/default_en.htm.

Politikwissenschaft

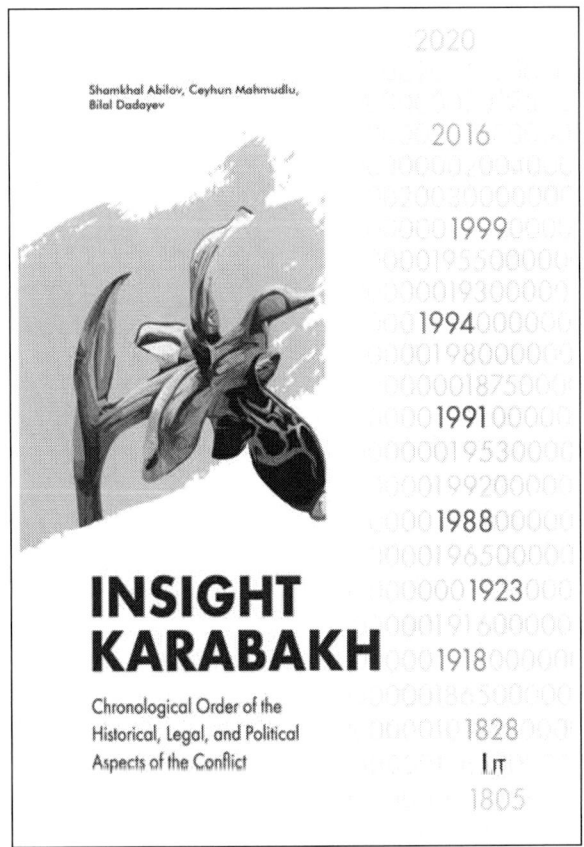

Shamkhal Abilov; Ceyhun Mahmudlu; Bilal Dadayev
Insight Karabakh
Chronological Order of the Historical, Legal, and Political Aspects of the Conflict
This Book introduces the main historical, political, and legal facts and arguments regarding the Karabakh region in general and the former Nagorno-Karabakh conflict in particular as a collection of 99 questions. Each chapter is academically substantiated and developed in detail according to local and international sources, documents, and treaties. The contributions are presented with appropriate academic references. Thus, the Book develops questions and answers regarding the Karabakh region and the Nagorno-Karabakh conflict and contains the main documents and treaties mentioned.
vol. 230, 2023, 400 pp., 39,90 €, pb., ISBN-CH 978-3-643-91574-0

LIT Verlag Berlin – Münster – Wien – Zürich – London
Auslieferung Deutschland / Österreich / Schweiz: siehe Impressumsseite

Forum Politische Geographie
hrsg. von Prof. Dr. Paul Reuber (Universität Münster, Federführung),
Prof. Dr. Georg Glasze (Universität Erlangen-Nürnberg), Prof. Dr. Olivier Graefe (Université de Fribourg), Prof. Dr. Benedikt Korf (Universität Zürich),
Prof. Dr. Julia Lossau (Universität Bremen), Prof. Dr. Annika Mattissek (Universität Freiburg), Prof. Dr. Martin Müller (Universität Lausanne), Prof. Dr. Anke Strüver (Universität Graz)
Schriftleitung: Dipl.-Ing. Claudia Schroer

Elisabeth Militz
Affective Nationalism
Bodies, Materials and Encounters with the Nation in Azerbaijan
This book develops the concept of affective nationalism – the banal affirmation of the national emerging in moments of encounter between different bodies and objects. Based on eight months of ethnographic field work, conducted between 2012 and 2014 in Azerbaijan, the book examines the ways in which moments of bodily encounter perpetuate banal enactments and experiences of national belonging and alienation.
The book advances scholarship on nationalism and affect by suggesting to study nationalisms not as given, but as potential and emergent experiences of differently positioned bodies in a world divided into nations.
vol. 15, 2019, 178 pp., 24,90 €, pb., ISBN-CH 978-3-643-80278-1

Asien: Forschung und Wissenschaft / L IT Studies on Asia

Markus Porsche-Ludwig; Ying-Yu Chen (Eds.)
Handbook Near and Middle East States
Geography – History – Culture – Politics – Economy
This handbook presents precise yet accessible up-to-date information about the geography, history, culture, politics, and economy of 26 Near and Middle East states, ranging from Morocco to Pakistan, from Turkey to South Sudan. The targeted readership consists primarily of scholars, students, teachers, journalists, and other mediators of political education as well as anyone interested in politics. It is a basic work that contributes to comparative assessments of this hugely important and diverse region.
vol. 9, 2022, 476 pp., 64,90 €, pb., ISBN-CH 978-3-643-91136-0

Markus Porsche-Ludwig; Ying-Yu Chen (Eds.)
Handbook of Asian States
Geography – History – Culture – Politics – Economy
This handbook presents precise yet accessible up-to-date information about the geography, history, culture, politics, and economy of 49 Asian states, ranging from Afghanistan, Bangladesh, and China to India, Russia, and Yemen. The targeted readership consists primarily of scholars, students, teachers, journalists, and other mediators of political education as well as anyone interested in politics. It is a basic work that contributes to comparative assessments of this hugely important and diverse region.
vol. 8, 2021, 858 pp., 99,90 €, pb., ISBN-CH 978-3-643-91100-1

L IT Verlag Berlin – Münster – Wien – Zürich – London
Auslieferung Deutschland / Österreich / Schweiz: siehe Impressumsseite

Halle Studies in the Anthropology of Eurasia
General Editors: Christoph Brumann, Kirsten Endres, Chris Hann, Burkhard Schnepel, Lale Yalçın-Heckmann

Florian Mühlfried; Sergey Sokolovskiy (Eds.)
Exploring the Edge of Empire
Soviet Era Anthropology in the Caucasus and Central Asia
This collection explores theoretical and empirical developments in the anthropology of the Caucasus and Central Asia, originating in or shaped by the Soviet era. Special attention is paid to the creation of local and national schools as well as to the role of institutional and biographical dis/continuities. Within the academic field of anthropology in the Soviet republics, Russia-based research institutes and regional branches of the former Soviet Academy of Sciences played a special role. Explorations of this role and of the impact of ideology are pertinent to the controversial question as to whether the Soviet Union was essentially a colonial enterprise. The authors include leading anthropologists from the Caucasus and Central Asia, as well as regional specialists from the Russian Federation and western countries. Florian Mühlfried is an anthropologist working for the Caucasus Studies Program at the Friedrich Schiller University of Jena, Germany. Sergey Sokolovskiy is a Senior Researcher at the Institute of Ethnology and Anthropology of the Russian Academy of Sciences and editor-in-chief of the journal Etnograficheskoe obozrenie.
vol. 25, 2011, 344 pp., 29,90 €, pb., ISBN 978-3-643-90177-4

Lale Yalçın-Heckmann
The Return of Private Property
Rural Life after Agrarian Reform in the Republic of Azerbaijan
What makes private property valuable, desirable, or workable? In this book, Lale Yalçın-Heckmann focuses on social and economic dimensions of private property after the agrarian reforms of 1996 in Azerbaijan. She looks at the kinds of land and cultivation strategies emerging in the decades after the fall of the Soviet Union and asks why rural households are often unwilling to cultivate the privatised land shares they have received for free, despite the threat and existence of rural poverty. Consideration is given to households that engage in cultivation and households that do not – including households of internally displaced persons who were formally excluded from privatisation but were nevertheless successful and eager cultivators. The author asks, how far does private property thrive on its own, without the support of lucrative markets or the implementation of state-sponsored economic policies? Through the lens of economic anthropology she chronicles the historical legacy of authoritarian state structures and the contemporary micro- and macro-economic struggles that mark a politics of property after socialism.
vol. 24, 2011, 240 pp., 29,90 €, pb., ISBN 978-3-643-10629-2

Bruce Grant; Lale Yalçın-Heckmann (Eds.)
Caucasus Paradigms
Anthropologies, Histories and the Making of a World Area
vol. 13, 2007, 328 pp., 29,90 €, pb., ISBN 978-3-8258-9906-6

LIT Verlag Berlin – Münster – Wien – Zürich – London
Auslieferung Deutschland / Österreich / Schweiz: siehe Impressumsseite